Gift of Gratitude:

Lessons from the

Classroom

Claire E. Hallinan

ISBN: 978-1-7330356-06

For J.S.H. You are my gift.

TABLE OF CONTENTS

Introduction

It started out of the blue. "A Small Moment" was a learning topic in the writing lesson of the day in my third-grade class. I was supposed to teach how to brainstorm ideas in narrative writing. Of course, I had a well-organized lesson plan to follow. I opened the discussion with a question: "What event that really happened in your life do you remember the most?" My students looked hesitant.

Immediately, I switched gears. "Here are some moments I remember when I was in third grade." On a sheet of chart paper, I put a bullet point and wrote, "I was the boss of my class." Kids laughed. One blurted, "Boss? How?" I blurted back, "Well, I dismissed the class because our teacher didn't come back to us at the last bell. After 15 minutes, I declared, 'The class is dismissed.'" As the kids asked more questions, this lesson trailed deeply into a Q&A about my story. I quickly sensed it must be one of those "teachable moments." Unlike I had initially planned, it became an "Ask Good Questions" lesson. As a result, kids asked great questions like, "Why did you boss around?"

"How did the other kids respond?" "Did you get in trouble?" "How did your teacher find out?" And on and on... Eventually, layers of elaboration transformed this one small moment into one special moment from when I was in third grade. This whole process sparked something significant beyond a successful alternative lesson. Crafting a story empowered my inner-self.

Telling a story became an unexpectedly amusing experience for me. It triggered my memory bank. One by one, each small moment began to spill out from my memory bank. Then, I wondered, what if I can tell more stories to my students? To my friends? Are they interested in learning about me? Can I make more important connections with them when I share my stories? Sharing stories is a powerful tool that can build a bridge between one person and another. Perhaps my job at school is to teach young stars how to live a meaningful life with meaningful relationships in different contexts. What if my stories encourage someone to tell their own stories that could enrich their lives? My life can impact someone else's life when my stories are told.

1

Searching

4:49 am – Between Consciousness and Unconsciousness

How many teachers in the whole world sleep without "school dreams" during the school days? I am one of the typical sleep-deprived creatures beyond the school-themed dreams, but also a series of unexpected agonized scenes that have been created by my restless mind. It all means I don't sleep well with the constant interrupting of dreams, uplifting ones and desperate ones.

Unlike Colombia River dividing between two states, Oregon and Washington, there is no such distinguished line between my unconsciousness and consciousness. Especially getting close to the time the alarm rings, these stages are mixed like marble colors. During the foggy in-between conscious and unconscious time, I experience physical responses in both worlds.

In one instance, my body becomes rigid when I cannot find my classroom for the finals. Sometimes I may even bite my teeth really hard. I even don't know if I can finally find it or get away from it. I even see my classmate, Kaoru, walking by me. "Which classroom are we going to?" I ask. She says plainly, no expression on her face, "Over there," and starts walking very fast. I thought she was my friend, but she doesn't act friendly at all. Did I do something to her? I wonder. Soon her head disappears into the crowd of student waves coming in and out on campus. I am supposed to be desperate, and in fact, I am, but randomly my mission changes.

Now I have to find the admission office because I have to pay my tuition. The school will not accept me if I fail. "Where is the admission building?" I ask every single person passing by. Suddenly, a very kind female student stops and instructs me, "You are going to turn on this main street, then, turn slightly right around the brick building. There will be a narrow path between buildings when you walk up on the hill about 10 yards. After that, you can see the admission office sign on the left side. Be alert, because it is kind of hiding under the tree branches." Okay, I remember to stay on the main street, but I cannot remember the rest of the complicated directions. Who is the next person to help me? I look around. I can't even grab one person to save my day. My heart is beating very quickly. I have to call the district office. What is their number? I am in the ache of desperation.

Right at that moment, another randomness slips into my unconsciousness. A couple of familiar second graders' faces look up to me. "You are okay." Then they give me the wisest wisdom, "Mrs. Hallinan, you have to breathe...." Those blue-eyed, blonde-haired, hazel-eyed, curly-haired young folks surround me, all smiling. I stop. I take a deep breath in.

As if a magic wand was swung over my head, my thoughts are now drifted to my childhood memories. I ask myself, "Am I finally in France?" This next moment brought another challenge, again, randomly. I have to fly home immediately. "Was I in Japan in all those times?" I ask myself. Is my passport still valid? Are there even jobs available for me? Can I survive with my family? Nobody would ever hire because I am too old. Then a strange and annoying noise interrupts my thoughts. Zzz, zzz, zzz, zzz... "What is going on?" Of course, that is my alarm. I reach my hand and start my day. So exciting... no, exhausting...

* * *

5 Years Old – French Style Muse

I used to have a secret plan to reside in France. I could be a dream ballerina over there. But when? I had already failed once when I sneaked out from the window with my favorite cream colored knit dress with frills. My mother got rid of my favorite dress after the incident. It would have been a perfect outfit in France! The dilemma came and went frequently in my little brain. It was certain, in my immature brain, that France was my ultimate destination.

I was just five years old.

Dreaming about becoming French as I ate my sandwich at school, I poured sweetened black tea into my cup and took a sip with my pinky pointed up. French people speak French. I didn't speak French yet, but I would as soon as I became a real one. Even now, I had confidence that I could communicate with any French person because I had creativity, which was shown in the arm waving dance that I created in kindergarten music class. French people eat French bread. I could imagine it should be similar to the white bread I ate every morning. No problem. I was quite certain that they drink sweetened black tea. I have no doubt that I could easily get over any other hurdles, if there were any.

I continued the self-taught private lessons on "French" lifestyle at home, which were far from authentic, of course. I played an LP record disc on the turntable. This was *Swan Lake* by the Russian composer Tchaikovsky. Of course, Russia was quite close to France, in my opinion. My arm-flapping-act was like nothing that someone else had done in my school. My choreography expressed the elegance of a swan that was contemplating which way this beautiful swan was going to swim to and fly to. I became closer to being French with each graceful movement of my arms and tiptoes. Maybe, one day, I even might be on the stage in France.

When my mother announced that she was going to take me to the Yamaha Music Academy for the first time Tuesday after school, my heart was about to jump out of my mouth. I was even flapping my arms in a different way than the swan would. "Yamaha" sounded French to me. (I learned later that "*Yama*" means mountain, while "*Ha*" means leaf in Chinese characters.) "I'm sorry, but I can't play with you today because I have to go to Yamaha," I apologetically bragged to my friends in the school bus. As soon as I stepped down from the school bus, I rushed home and change my uniform to home-dress for my new endeavor, the Yamaha Music Academy! Yamaha offered local youngsters the quality of music classes in part of a Lutheran church building in the town where my Grandma Fumi still resided then.

The Lutheran church sounded French to me, too. I was so ecstatic to be back in this church where I used to play every day, and even went to Sunday school. We pushed open the heavy glass door, stickers stated, "The Lutheran Church." The floor had hard and shiny tiles that were gray and black. I proudly led my mother to the left and stepped up the red carpeted stairs as if walking on a cloud.

Entering into a large room, we could see more than ten majestic electric organs with double-layered keyboards. These amazing looking instruments had a bright oak brown color and were shining. A right hand was supposed to be on the top keyboard and a left hand on the bottom keyboard. I was in shock when I noticed that this already-too-amazing-organ had another set of keyboards just for feet! Ms. Nagaya told me that it was called an Electone. She guided me to the Electone that was closest to her piano. I inhaled a strong cosmetic scent from her which made me think of a clean restroom. She must be from France.

I looked over the back of the room. There were another ten regular, terribly poor looking organs. They seemed very pathetic without the luxurious functions that the Electone contains. They had air pumps for a foot, and didn't obtain double keyboards. You simply need to pump with your foot to make these instruments sound. It was totally unfair for these tedious organs to be compared to the fancy Electone. The organs' height was way shorter than the Electone, too. Their color was grayish, and it brought me back unpleasant memories of rainy days.

I was so relieved that I was not on that ugly, low-functioning, single keyboard. I determined that I would never ever be late for Yamaha so I would not miss the Electone. I had to claim the Electone before all of them were taken by the fellow Yamaha kids because a rule here seemed like "first come, first served." Everybody must have been thinking the same thing that I'd been thinking. I didn't think I could control myself if I had to sit with the regular organ. I already had had enough bad experiences in my life. Seriously.

Ms. Nagaya looked a little bit like a French woman. I had never seen a face that had such an impact. Her eyes were as huge as walnuts and underlined with black ink and painted with blue powder on the top. Her mouth was the biggest and reddest I had ever seen in my life. Snow White might have the same color lips; however, I doubt they are the same size as Ms. Nagaya's. Her hair was short and a reddish brown that was a bit too strongly permed. It almost looked like a bike helmet. Maybe French ladies looked like her. As I concluded my generalization of French on the first day, its idea also almost frightened me. With my scarcely pounding heart, I kept talking out to myself, "I am very lucky that I'm with a teacher who might be from France," with a little suspicion.

A little bird is listening to my music by the window and shaking his booty. Mama is listening to my pretty beautiful sounds. We learn at Yamaha Music Academy.

It is easy enough for me to sing the opening song the first time. I see Ms. Nagaya's large mouth and nostrils very well from my seat. As soon as she sucked up some air, she announced, "Let's stand up! We will march around the room." A big circle of little musicians started walking around the high-tech Electones and the old-fashioned organs. I stepped forward, my legs going one by one proudly. Right, left, right, left, I marched in synchronization with the marching song that Ms. Nagaya played on her piano. Nothing sounded better than the piano playing of Ms. Nagaya, besides *Fur Elise* from the school speaker that plays after lunch. And how lucky I was to be able to march with the rhythm of the beautiful sound! I acted like a soldier stepping consistently with the beat, right, left, right, left.

As the consistent rhythm gradually faded out, a soldier spotted an obstacle. There were a bunch of kid soldiers stuck up in one area. "Are you nuts? You shouldn't be. You should be a Yamaha music soldier! You are supposed to be appreciating Ms. Nagaya's sophisticated music. You must keep walking with it!" I told myself. I was too new to blurt out such rude comments. Right behind me, more people start piling up. But the line didn't go any further. It completely stopped. I was sandwiched! All of a sudden, I snapped, and becoming the General of Yamaha Army, I shouted, "Move!"

At the next second, both of my hands pushed against the girl's back. I just wanted her to move. If you didn't respond to my verbal communication, I had to use some physical force. That was what happened. As she fell, a boy before her fell. The Yamaha soldiers' domino glissandos to another person, up until one-third of the circle of soldiers totally collapsed. A girl pointed her index finger at me, and wailed, "This girl pushed me! Waaaa..."

I quickly apologized without any remorse nor eye contact. "I am sorry, but you have to move when you are supposed to." The fellow Yamaha kids looked at each other, including Ms. Nagaya. I then realized that this first terrible impression of me had just been etched into the Yamaha kids' innocent minds. I optimistically hoped that everybody would forget about this incident by next Tuesday. This place could get me connected to France. I must survive. I bit my tongue.

Sayonara, goodbye. This is all for today. Goodbye

The ending song's tune sounded pretty mellow. Ms. Nagaya whispered to my ear, "You will get along with your friends next time." "Yes ma'am," I sighed. Was I still lucky? Yes, of course. I had not been kicked out yet. I was ready for the same routine plus a different adventure next Tuesday.

Every week seemed like there was a totally different atmosphere. No one talked about their previous friends or events at the Academy. Only our routine songs were sacredly preserved; the Little Bird opening song and the Mellow-You-Down closing song. Each Tuesday, learning new tunes and songs was fascinating to me. The only thing that I was disappointed about was that there had been no more marching around the room with music since Day One. I refused to think why.

* * *

5:00 am – The Role of My Alarm

I used to be superstitious when I was six. I needed to pat my pillow and say, "Ms. Pillow, Ms. Pillow, I will wake up at 6 am and it will be sunny," three times and then go to bed. And I did. I woke up at 6 am and the weather was mostly sunny. I even didn't use the alarm. When I opened my eyes, they caught the short hand right at the 6 with the long hand right at the 12. This super power faded out gradually during my teenage years. I became always sleepy. I couldn't help it. That's when I started using the alarm. My new alarm clock looked very stylish. In fact, I adored it! It was shiny silver with traditional analog style. I fell in love with my new alarm clock as soon as I got it on my birthday, not knowing its fatal function. It rang! So loud! It was as shocking as when I heard my friend's dad's big fart right in front of me at her house. Since then, my heart never felt completely open to my supposed-to-be-befriended alarm. To this day, any kind of alarm clock sounds annoying to me and tries to destroy all of my comforts from the warm bed. That is why I take a couple of deep breaths to calm myself after I viciously turn it off with half-opened eyes. I mumble, "Nobody can ruin my day.

My day will be sound and smooth, just like classical music." Eventually and reluctantly, I get out of my bed to start a day. (Imagine Eeyore crawling out of bed!) I splash cold water on my face a couple of times, just because I have to physically wake up for the day. Then I glare at my reflection in the mirror. "Ready or not, I will start my day." My ninja feet bring me through the hallway to the kitchen. The coffee machine's starting button is waiting for a nice friendly touch from my fingertip. I shove a couple of saran-wrapped plain rice balls, a string cheese, an orange, and crackers into each of my kids' lunch bags. My brain doesn't yet have room to be creative or fancying up my kids' lunch in the morning. Am I getting an "F" on the Mama's report card?

* * *

9 Years Old – Mother's Morning

My mother's eyelids gradually lifted up like the rising sun. With her favorite classical music tune coming from the FM radio, the chilly early morning air was welcomed through her nostrils. Quickly but quietly, she folded her futon cover and mattresses lying into thirds. She swiftly hoisted the futon pile up to put it away in the closet with sliding doors. The space on the tatami mat (the straw woven floor) where her futon used to occupy by her husband's upheld the warmth that she left.

Everybody else in the family was still sound asleep. Her footsteps in the hallway didn't seem to bother anybody.

In the quiet downstairs kitchen, even before she washed her face, her daily routine began. She never wondered why she was the only one to stay busy starting from the early morning until the end of the day. Her fingertips were always looking for something to do for her family.

Napoleon didn't have the word "impossible" in his dictionary; my mother didn't have the word "sacrifice" in hers. None of her duties burdened her. All chores were done one by one with a tempo that she had established over the years.

By the time the kettle lid started dancing with boiling water, the washing machine was getting even louder in the laundry room. When the sizzling sounds from the little rectangular skillet pan on the stove joined the morning symphony, it meant my mother was diligently preparing my lunch. Every day, except for Wednesdays, my mother fixed my lunch as a part of the melody in the morning symphony.

My lunch box is a colorful, mini full-course dinner condensed into one little box. Plain white rice or mother's fist sized rice balls with a seaweed sheet sit on one side of the rectangle box. Sometimes a sour plum proudly places itself in the middle of the plain white rice. It looks just like a Japanese flag. The sour plums are known to protect food from spoiling. Because of this reason, I would find a red sour plum inside all of my rice balls when I munched. I didn't like the flag lunch box or the rice balls with sour plum inside because I felt old fashioned.

My classmates had cute tiny rice balls with colorfully sprinkled sweetened sesame seeds on them. I asked my mother, "Can you make smaller rice balls?" She replied, "Only if my hands were as tiny as yours." More than half of my lunch box is filled with three (jumbo!) mother's fist sized rice balls. I never had four rice balls because "four" in Japanese language sounded the same as "death." Holding four items would give you bad luck. In fact, there is no room number four in any Japanese hospital. No patient wants to stay in room number four.

My mother picked up a couple of little octopus-shaped wiener sausages to give the box some color along with the yellow, brick-like

12

omelet and Teriyaki sautéed green beans. Dessert was a slice of apple with its skin carved like bunny ears. My mother imagined every color as a music note. She looked satisfied in front of her creative culinary art that created a complete symphony. Steam still raised from the tin lunch box, just like music coming from a music box. My lunch box was my mother's proudest musical and visual art creation of the day, except for Wednesdays.

* * *

5:30 am – Yoga, What is Your Intention?

5:15 am is very dark after daylight savings time is over. The air coming into my nostrils is keenly cold. Until I touch my car door, I feel like I am completely lost in the stillness of this world. I hunch my back and set my bottom on the seat, then bring each leg carefully into my Honda. As soon as the ignition rambles, FM radio tries to wake me up with the beautiful sound of classical music just like it did to my mother. My mind draws into the soothing melody of the violin solo of some famous composer's concerto. And boom! At the next second, I am in the parking lot of the gym. "How did I get here?" Every movement of this routine is auto-piloted in my brain. Somehow, I am alert enough to drive from home to the gym, but do not necessarily remember the exact trip I just made. I talk to myself, "It's kind of scary that I am here already." The eastern sky begins to fill pinkish color. The inhaled chilly air coming in through my nose reaches to the back of my eyeballs. I scan my membership card and walk in the hallway to the yoga studio. On the yoga mat, my legs are crisscrossed, and I am still contemplating how I got here without noticing anything. Breaking the silence is the yoga instructor's soft voice, "What is your intention to be here today?"

* * *

16 Years Old – Practical Goal

Ms. Bamboo is a Classic Japanese Language Arts expert in the community and a teacher in our high school. She talked about one of her former students who entered a private girls' college in Kyoto. According to Ms. Bamboo, this student chose a school in Kyoto because she was obsessed in matching with a student in prestigious National Kyoto University. She was not smart enough to pass entrance into National Kyoto University herself, so she made a plan. Entering the neighbor school was the first phase. Phase two was to keep standing at the Kyoto University's gate at the same time every day. Someone must notice her sometime. That was her simplest strategy and it worked.

Ms. Bamboo recalled, "In a way, she was quite goal-oriented, though it was not academically. Her dream of marrying to the Kyoto University grad came true. She had such a strong determination. An intensive focus like hers would bring you a victory. Study hard to enter in the great college. As you know, there could be so many handsome and smart guys out there in college, too, unlike our school." Ms. Bamboo in the girls' high school lectured quite seriously, "Instead of looking for boys right now, wait until your dream college life comes to you." Someone joked, "I will wait for my future husband at Tokyo University's red gate for a few weeks instead of going to college." I wondered why we had to depend on boys who had higher degrees. I asked myself, "Why do we study so hard to get into college? To meet our future husbands? It would not be a bad idea, but I would like to have my own degree, too." I kept questioning myself for explainable reasons on why we push ourselves so hard, day and night.

Escape Plan

It seems like "going to college" was everyone's main intention throughout their entire school career, especially during the high school years. Perhaps there was no other intention. Passing straight to college was the only option that was expected of us. No one was allowed to think about finding a job or taking a break, like a "gap year," before going to college. If you failed to get into your target colleges, you had to study another whole school year until the next exam season came by. Most people who didn't pass college exams studied at college prep schools. There were no official credits in the prep schools whatsoever, but students just crammed everything until they could pass the prestigious college exams. Someone would stay in the prep schools until the best college of the country would accept them. It was not too odd. In some cases, it would take two or three years to be accepted. Regardless of the society's norm, failing a college exam was not an option in my life. In addition, whatever college I would go to must be financially affordable for my family's financial situation. How could I get over these hurdles and free from all these burdens behind me?

I was secretly searching a prospective college on my needs, far away from home. My hometown was, unfortunately, sadly, pathetically, yet obviously, not a place I belonged to. I deserved to live and study where I could be myself. My dream destination addressed to the country's capital, Tokyo.

My hometown was considered to be rural to suburb. Although Japan is a very small country, traveling through a country can be challenging because the country consists of four main islands. Surrounded by the water and mountains sounds great, however, traveling from one island to another island takes time and money. Last time I visited Tokyo was when I was four with grandma Fumi, we visited her daughter, and the first giant pandas came from China in the Ueno Zoo. Through massive amounts of people passing by on the street, I looked up to make sure I was holding my grandma's hand, not someone else I didn't know. My grandma put a bright orange dress on me for a good purpose. After over a decade, the names of big cities like Tokyo and Osaka had been still intimidating to me, like foreign countries where I had never visited. Until one day, my mother revealed that her relative lived in Tokyo.

The key person in Tokyo is Grandma Masu's cousin, Kumi. Kumi's husband Makoto was a retired forensic medical doctor. My mother bragged about them as if they were her only proud family. Their unbeatable features were 1) the doctor, 2) used to live in Germany, and 3) being fluent in German and English. In addition, two of three sons were respected medical doctors. Their names sounded German. Their first grandchild was named after the internationally recognized medical journal, *Natural.*

The special words "doctor" and "Tokyo" were the most uncommon/unfit vocabulary in my family. Father always told us that we were not smart enough to be doctors or lawyers. It was very encouraging to learn that we had relatives who were doctors. How am I going to feel if I inhale the same air with people who are "doctors" and living in "Tokyo"? They lived in the country's capital, Tokyo! After my mother's phone call and a letter which I wrote to Kumi and Makoto, they willingly invited my sister and me during our spring break for the purpose of a college tour. It was perfect timing for my sister just passed her prestigious public high school entering exam with an amazing last spurt. Mr. Rice Field, the middle school English teacher, kept warning my sister that she couldn't pass because the school level was way higher than her level. But she was way more resilient and tougher than what

16

he estimated on her ability. My sister triumphantly grabbed the victory, and her determination beautifully beat his curse.

My sister and I took a train, a boat, and a bullet train to get to the country's capital. Auntie Kumi picked us up at the busy Tokyo station platform in midday. We took a train and a bus to her house in a pretty quiet suburb away from busy downtown. Makoto was waiting for our visit quietly in the living room with baroque music on the FM classic station.

"Hello," we greeted him. He said hello back to us. We were not sure if he was friendly or not. Makoto was just a husband of Kumi who was related to Grandma Masu. My sister and I have totally no blood connection with him or her. Technically, Masu and Kumi were not blood related, either, although they were called "cousins."

Their cousin relationship had happened when Grandma Masu was adopted in their family. According to Masu and Kumi, they grew up like sisters in their grandmother's house. Since Masu and Kumi had no blood relation, my sister and I were staying in the house of total strangers. Who could've imagined a little girl's, Masu's, adoption arrangement would benefit her descendants 70 years later?

Magnificent baroque music and a sizzling steak aroma woke us up the next morning. We already knew they were rich, but eating a steak in the morning was outrageous. We had never eaten meals with classical music from the FM station, only with TV quiz shows or news shows. The former forensic MD lectured, "You are supposed to eat large [amounts] in the morning and small [amounts] at dinner. Classical music will help your digestive system." Whether it was true or not, a morning steak and classical music were good on your tummy as long as Uncle Makoto said they were. Our stomachs were not accustomed to huge meals in the morning though.

Auntie Kumi was feeding same-sized steaks to their dog. I genuinely asked, "Do you feed your dog a steak every day?" She replied without any hesitation, "We do when the meat is a little bit old." I glanced at the dog's bowl. It may be that one-fifth of the meat looked blackish, but it didn't seem much different than mine. Wow, if you are rich, you can afford to feed your dog steaks every morning.

We had 16 dogs in our house at that time besides six of us humans, including Grandma Fumi. If we had steaks for dinner one day, we would survive for the next couple of months on only a bowl of rice and some pieces of pickled yellow daikon radish.

Shockingly, Makoto added, "Bring a sketchbook with you today. You draw pictures of everything you see."

"Well, yes, my sister is an artist who draws any kind of pictures quickly, precisely, and humorously, but not me. I just sing as loud as an elephant's trumpet," I respectfully declined.

"No excuse! You must draw no matter what. That's how you improve your artistic ability," he scolded at me.

"Okay, old man, I don't need to improve my artistic ability. I am not interested in drawing pictures. Heck, no, I ain't doing what you say!" I clearly expressed my feelings in my mind. I wished I could have told him.

My sister and I were almost nauseous from the morning steaks. We held our sketchbooks provided by Uncle Makoto and stood with an aimless glance by the automatic door of the train. We were ready to explore Central Tokyo. At the Tokyo University's red gate, I reluctantly opened my sketchbook. Maybe this was going to be the first and last time to see this college in my life. Some girls, about whom Ms. Bamboo told us, might be religiously coming to this gate every day dreaming to meet up with their future husband. Otherwise, Tokyo University was impossible for ordinary people (like me) to desire to attend or even consider to pass into.

When we came back to Auntie Kumi's house, I noticed a lady with long, black, curly hair sitting in the living room chatting with Uncle Makoto. He was in an extremely good mood with her. Auntie Kumi introduced her to me, "This is Ms. Matsui, a good friend of ours. She graduated from a famous private music university and now teaches voice lessons." Ms. Matsui was willing to give me an instant voice lesson. That was a big part of the plan for this trip. I have been taking piano lessons since Yamaha, and now I am learning of joy of singing. I had to make my decision soon for my future college. I like music, but can it be my career as a professional? To connect with a professional music expert was most needed to process at that point of my life.

I had prepared my favorite song, *Lasciatemi Morire!* in the Italian song book for this instant lesson. It was a short song, but I had a hard time hitting the high F note. Ms. Matsui suggested, "Why don't you grab the piano and lift it up?" Then, she started her piano accompaniment again without waiting for my answer. I had no choice, but stood by Ms. Matsui and grabbed the piano. As the notes went up to D, E flat, E natural, I gradually tightened my fingers. As soon as I hit the high F, I used all of my physical power to lift up the piano.

Although I didn't lift the piano successfully, I hit the note! I was so excited that her trick worked for me.

"You might want to consider the vocal department in the music university," Ms. Matsui mentioned. "I would love to," I smiled at her.

But the private music university's tuition cost a fortune. My parents' budget for my education was way lower than the private university's tuition, especially the music department. I doubted if they had such an educational fund for me. Studying music at the college in Tokyo might not be a good option for me. The music college Ms. Matsui described was beyond fantastic and attractive, glamorous in many ways. Do I deserve it? Just because I didn't pass the public high school exam, my parents ended up paying my private high school tuition. Do I still want to be the family burden by going to the school where only rich people deserve attending? My teenage heart and brain were about to explode, but I never discussed my frustration with anyone. I couldn't.

After we bowed to Uncle Makoto and Auntie Kumi, my sister and I went the backward way of how we arrived here. We traveled by bus to the train, and transferred to a bullet train, to a local slow one, and finally a ferry boat. I was exhausted and excited at the same time. Being rich and living in Tokyo sounded good after all if I didn't have to eat steaks for breakfast and carry a sketchbook everywhere I went. Even the unfamiliar sound of baroque music began seeping into my body system during this trip.

Tokyo was far away from my home and more excitements would await. If I knew I wouldn't get rich soon enough, I still could "feel" rich by using my creativity. I felt uniquely confident to move myself forward to Tokyo in twelve months. It could be my new intention.

Unforgivable Music Teachers

I couldn't wait to share my experience with my music teachers who might give me some advice about my college choices. After school, I biked to the piano lesson. I knocked on the door. No one answered. I opened the sliding door, "Hello, teacher." No one answered. I had no idea what to do.

This was my piano teacher's house. Did he forget about my lesson? Should I go in? Should I go home? Sitting on the entrance porch, I contemplated for a full fifteen minutes.

As I decided to go home, the piano teacher appeared and said, "When you come here, you get up and start practicing piano until I show up. You don't wait for me in the entrance hall." His eyeballs looked down at me through his black framed eyeglasses.

As a professional pianist and piano teacher, he owned two grand pianos side by side in his lesson room. One was for him and the other for a student. When the piano teacher left again, I practiced uncomfortably for another fifteen minutes. Hearing the next student greeting and coming through the entrance door, the piano teacher finally walked into the lesson room.

After I played my assigned etude for a few minutes, he interrupted me to stop, then he turned to another student who just sat on the waiting chair and said, "Did you hear her piano piece? Although she is a voice major candidate, her piano technique is beyond your level." His bizarre compliment of my performance didn't make me feel great, but awkward. It made another student feel so uncomfortable, too. I was forced to continue playing Bach, then Beethoven in this strange atmosphere until my time was finally up.

The following week, no one answered at the door again. As I was instructed in the previous week, I went into the room and started practicing on his grand piano. After fifteen minutes, I started wondering if he was listening to me somewhere. Did he have a hidden camera to monitor me? I couldn't stay any longer in these creepy surroundings. I no longer could stand it. So, I left his house without anybody having seen or heard me unless they had a secret camera or recording system.

The next two lesson days were also creepy situations. I didn't see anyone. With the slightest hope, I decided to leave a note after another fifteen minutes of piano by myself in the next lesson. In the fifth week, surprisingly, he was there. At the end of the lesson, I declared, "Teacher, I am not coming back to your piano lesson."

"What about the p-p-p-payment...," stuttered the teacher.

I sneered (respectfully!) at his eyes behind his glasses. "I don't owe you anything for last month. You missed four lessons, which equals one whole month's payment." Wow, I said it!

He was about to argue with me, but he didn't. I stood up and bowed my head, "Sayonara (goodbye)." After I shut the sliding entrance door, I grabbed the handles and kicked a kickstand. I swung my right leg over the bike and began to pedal. Madly. My bike and I were together in full speed to head home into the orange sunset.

Neither of my voice teachers were like Ms. Matsui who was positive and inspired my energy.

My first voice teacher was too easy. She served me a cup of lemon tea in the special china and kindly offered me a chocolate piece in each lesson. She had no outside life besides her newborn baby, so she expected me to be her voice student and a gossip partner. It was fun spending time with her, but I was not sure if I was improving my singing.

The second voice teacher was too mean. Why don't adults treat and expect a teenager to be a teenager? Being a physically matured woman herself didn't mean she could expect me to do everything she would do on her scale. I was not my teachers' convenient friend, child, servant, nor mini-me. I was not a perfect student, but at least I had a desire to learn. I admitted that I might have been a little rebellious, but wasn't it a typical teenager's attitude anyway? I simply needed proper guidance at my age.

I brought my new Italian song book that she asked to me to purchase to the lesson. I was somewhat excited to learn new songs I could explore. As if she didn't detect my excitement, she did not like my brand-new book. This book was spunky new, nothing was written. That was a problem. I did not preview any pages prior to the lesson. She coldly said, "If I were you, I would have looked at all the songs and chosen my favorite." She added, "You even haven't purchased the Japanese-Italian dictionary yet. How do you know what you are singing without knowing the words' definitions?" I simply thought what she was complaining about was her job to teach me in the lesson. How am I supposed to know what the song was about by just learning each word's definition? I was wrong. She thought I was arrogant and had a terrible attitude.

Let me tell you this. I thought about her exactly the same way she saw me. She was arrogant and had a terrible attitude. I bought the exact book that she requested. Be happy about it! Teaching me a new song was her job. I came here to learn how to sing. And my parents were paying for that process of learning.

I didn't think I deserved her cranky attitude just because I didn't act as she expected me to. She hadn't explained to me clearly enough what she was looking for. Evidently, I could not read her mind. It was quite clear that I didn't want to go back to her anymore. I didn't even want to see her again. I skipped a lesson or two, in which I didn't tell my parents.

Finally, I was caught by Mother. Reluctantly, I explained what was going on in the voice lessons. She sighed, "At least you have to tell her by yourself." I picked up the phone and dialed her number. It went directly to the message machine. On the message machine, I took a breath and began to talk. "I am sorry I missed the lessons. But I don't think I will come back to you again. Thank you for having me for a while anyway." After I hang up the phone, I went up to announce to Mother, "I quit the voice lessons."

On the other hand, I wanted to continue seeing Mr. Clarinet who started teaching me piano in third grade and was now teaching the music theory for preparing for the college exam. He was a nurturing and accepting teacher. But one day he announced, "I have taught you everything you had to learn. Now you don't have to come back to me. Good luck on your college exam!" My college endeavor became a lonely journey without a northern star.

* * *

7:32 am – Stuck Behind

Timing is everything, including leaving home for work. If I am late for just one minute, I will get stuck right behind the school bus. By law, we cannot pass the school bus. While the amber light is flashing, I have to make myself a nice smiley face to watch kids going into the bus and their parents waving to them forever. At times, it is very pleasant, but other times, it is a little frustrating, especially when I can clearly visualize stacks of paper piles on my desktop at work and blank box spaces in my weekly planning notebook. And on those days is often scheduled the morning staff meeting that would occupy more than half of my morning prep time before school starts. I tell myself, "It is not going to be forever. It's going to be okay." Then, instead of tapping my fingers on the wheel as I wait for the school bus right front of me, I grab the wheel and feel its leather. Breathe in. Breathe out. Soon my memories of the Elephant School Bus drift into my early morning daydreaming mind. I would be riding on the bus with a jumbo elephant picture on its body. I would wave at her until she became a little dot in the sight.

* * *

5 Years Old – Boots Curse

This particular Wednesday morning sky made my heart gloomy. The sky was about to cry with its heavy and dark clouds. A cream sandwich and a typhoon roll would not be available today at the school bakery. Although it's still dry outside, my heart sank deeply because the moist, yet dry air equaled wearing my ugly and tight boots. My breakfast toast was repeatedly dunked into my sweetened tea, then mindlessly sucked in my mouth on that morning.

"Your bus is here. Hurry up!" The private preschool bus with a large elephant sticker on it was patiently waiting for me outside, making a rumbling noise. My body didn't want to move as my mother wanted me to because of my tight rain boots. Should I slip on my regular shoes, run onto the bus, and ignore the consequence? More than enough embarrassment would wait for me if my mother followed me into to the bus with my rain boots in her hands. She would yell at me, "Don't you dare to do that again!"

There was a particular flashback memory in my mind. When my mother didn't allow me to wear my favorite creamy white cotton dress, I wore it anyway and escaped from the second-floor window. Going

25

through the veranda, I was free and did not see anybody in my family. But someone had seen me. It turned the situation into double trouble. First, I wore something I wasn't supposed to. Second, I crawled out like a thief. Had I been grounded for disobedience? My blood would freeze instantly by just imagine what might happen again. If I sneaked out again, just like last time. Or worse. It might involve a heat pain or the darkness of the closet or both. Any potentially miserable scenarios should be avoided. So reluctantly sitting on the edge of the entrance, I stared at my boots. My toes were pointy like a ballet dancer so that they could fit into my boot. My left foot wiggled into the depth of the boot, trying to reach to the end. Then I grabbed both edges of the left boot and tightly pulled with incredible force. It reached at my maximum effort. Thud! My body flipped and rolled backward on the hallway floor. "Do I have to wear my rain boots?" I whined. My mother's voice coldly fell on my head. "Stop goofing around! Your bus is waiting just for you!"

Four minutes later, a grumpy little girl with tight boots finally stepped into the Elephant Bus. "Good morning," Mr. Principal, the driver, brightly greeted. The bus guide (a.k.a., teacher) of the week was Ms. Asada. As soon as Ms. Asada's smiled appeared on her face, my bluest thought magically blew away. A very important morning school bus routine began. I almost forgot about my intention of riding the school bus, not for going to school, but because I was a fearless story teller in the Elephant Bus.

I told all the jokes from the monthly kids' magazine beautifully. They have been stored in my brain from the night before. Telling these excellently selected jokes was an urgent task because they should be shared before I forgot. These jokes were all approved of by my sharp sense of humor. A preschooler's stand-up comedy stage was on my very own school bus. Joke after joke was spilled out from my mouth as if they were my original.

At age four, I was so proud of being able to read and select a few sensational jokes from a couple dozen selections. Since no one acknowledged my talent, an overly assertive approach was necessary in order to get the spotlight right on me. Quite simply, recognition was what I deserved and evidently lacked in my young heart. The "show" was mine. Ms. Asada seemed to enjoy my jokes that were made by somebody else! Imagine, an innocent and attention craving four-year-old had been talking non-stop until the bus rolled into the school gate— that was what happened every morning.

A few seconds before my last joke ended, the bus arrived at school.

The rest of the joke was up in the air until I would go home. Fortunately, my devastation would not last long. A series of busy activities could distract me easily. Chances were, some of the same jokes might be repeated on the way home. The merciful bus guide teacher, who was also my best audience, would never mention how many times I had repeated my jokes throughout the week. She was kind enough not to tell other teachers about my jokes, because she knew that I was looking for the next engaged audience.

All fellow kids changed from their outside shoes to their inside shoes in the entrance foyer. Every single voice and noise echoed in here. Who was talking about what? The volume of the cheerful noise from students was a bit chaotic, but it reminded everyone in the school, "It's time to begin a school day." Checking the shoe shelf nervously, I wondered how many other kids wore rain boots today. One pair almost made me hopeful, though I pathetically admitted that the pair was mine. I looked down and dragged my feet through a hallway to get to my classroom. I mumbled, "It is not even raining today anyways. Why do I have to wear my rain boots?" Even though I knew my parents' reasons and I obeyed their rules, my stomach felt sick.

* * *

7:52 am – Getting out of the Car

My Honda smoothly curves into the space between the two parking lines. From here, with a little over 50 steps, I can get into the school building. I lift my left leg to the door and notice my black slip-on shoe. I have loved the comfort of slip-on shoes for many years. In fact, a couple days ago, a little first-grade student with a bathroom pass hung over his neck stopped by me while I was posting art projects on the wall. He stared at my slip-on shoes. Then, he looked up with his index finger pointing with an astonishment at my shoes, "You wear slip-on shoes, don't you?" I lowered myself to his eye level and smilingly replied, "I do. Aren't they cool?" His face glowed, "They are!" And poof! He turned around left. Suddenly I was filled with gratitude, for being able to choose my style of footwear and being able to commute without an aggressive physical human contact in the Japanese subway. In fact, I couldn't wear my slip-on shoes when I was working in Tokyo. Let me say, I probably could, but I couldn't think about it. My feet were covered by the pointy, low-heeled pumps, in which I thought a majority of young working women in Tokyo were supposed to wear. With this style of ladylike footwear, I was proudly walking out from my apartment to the subway station, from the platform to the train, from the train to the stairs, and from another transferring train to another train, more stairs, a mile long of paved sidewalk, and eventually to the school where I worked back then. Now, my practical slip-on footwear proudly carries me towards the school building where I am going to teach all day today.

21 Years Old – Teaching Exams

The subway train was keenly air conditioned during the months of summer in Japan. Although still the same large number of business men and women were pushed into the cart by the conductor (who was called a "Pusher"), it was easily ten degrees lower temperature than my college dorm room. So let's not focus on a bunch of exhausted young and old men and women with no facial expression squished in next to each other in a box car. My sweaty body finally found joy from the limited moments in the underground train of a humid Japanese summer. There was no need to wipe the sweat on my neck or my forehead with a handkerchief anymore. I wondered if there is a "heaven" somewhere, it must be this subway train where the dry, cool air consistently blows on my forehead. Its comfort made me forget all about my steamed, sauna-like dorm room where the term papers were blown away mercilessly by the pathetic lukewarm wind from the noisy electric fan.

In this heavenly comfortable subway train, Hiroko was nervously sitting by my side, rolling her eyeballs up and down. "Hiroko, calm down. You should be okay." I tried to calm her down without any guarantee why she was okay. Giving some quiz to each other was a last-minute cramming for us for the Tokyo Teachers' Screening Examination.

In addition to the Japanese National Elementary School Curriculum in math, literacy, social studies, science, music, P.E., arts, and home economies, you have to memorize the Japanese and World's Education History, Famous Educators and psychologists' work, Teaching Pedagogy, and current events, if you want to become a teacher in Japan.

This was only the screening stage. Don't forget about the labor intensive additional test, too. This ridiculously lengthy test process would define your persistence and accuracy in general. They would predict your laboring productivity and adaptive abilities in the new work environment by assessing your ability in several sessions of addition facts timed test. You really didn't have to worry about the interview for a while until you got your first screening test's winning ticket.

Hiroko seemed so panicked and overwhelmed. "It's too late to worry, Hiroko," I told myself in my head. At least I was relaxed, as I was able to focus on the lines in the book and give some questions to her. Since there was so much of memorization, I decided to rely exclusively on the Teaching Exam Monthly Study Journal. Hiroko had been subscribing to it for the last 12 months to prepare for this annual exam, so she should be feeling fine. My only subscriptions were the June and July editions. I knew that the last two issues right before the exam should provide the most meaningful and condensed information in order to pass the test.

So instead of overwhelming myself, I decided to intensively cram every item in these two issues from cover to cover, over and over until the magazines looked filthy. I brought a paragraph to Hiroko for a final memorization practice. I perfectly answered all questions last night. I did the same in the train with Hiroko on that day, too.

To prepare for the current events, I started subscribing to newspapers in my dorm room two months ago, which was the same time I purchased the Exam Study Journal. Shame enough, I wasn't aware of or interested in any hot topics or issues in any size community in which I belonged, like neighborhood, city, prefecture, country, and world. Maybe just because I didn't have a TV or I didn't have time to do anything besides school work. I didn't think I could afford to subscribe to daily newspapers until I realized a couple of months ago it was important for my exam. Newspaper became a great resource for me. They moved me from a level of ignorance to a highly engaged and curious person in the world. It was fun learning about other people's problems besides my small world. Now I felt pretty confident about what's going on in the nation and a little bit about the world. In addition to newspaper subscriptions, I started preparing for the "swimming test" in the second level of exam, just in case I passed the first screening test. I rounded up some of my fellow candidate friends, including Hiroko, at the college swimming pool every day. We were supposed to show our stamina from hours of swimming practices. The swimming was one of the second screening tests, too, in the most prefectures. A study group that I organized was held following the swimming and wrapped up with lunch at the popular café in front of the train station. Our senior year summer in our education-emphasized college was meant for studying after studying, including our dreams at night.

"Hiroko, this is the only paragraph I memorized. Don't be silly, you should not think I know everything," I tried to comfort her. She still looked hysterical but managed to respond to me, "You are right. I think I have studied longer and harder than you did. What you have done is to recruit swimming companions." I was not totally pleased about her comment, and I even felt offended by it, but I let it go as a matured woman would. Generally, Hiroko was a little bit spacy compared to our other friends. She was daydreaming and making funny comments that were very serious for her. She loved fuzzy pets and was optimistic and very caring. But her nervousness in the train was beyond her character of the normal Hiroko. I hoped she would not throw up during the exam.

"Good luck to you. See you after the exam," I waved goodbye to her. "You too," she didn't make her eye contact with me. Following the sign, looking right and left, my eyes reached my exam ID number on the sign outside of the room. "That's it." I had nothing to remorse whatever would happen in this exam. I did everything I could think of for this special day. I managed to fill out my name and exam ID number in blank boxes on the front page of the thick testing booklet, then I opened the first page with one big breath.

As soon as the first paragraph jumped into my eyes, I gulped my nice big breath. I couldn't close my mouth for ten seconds. I blinked my eyes three times and rubbed them. It was the exact same paragraph that Hiroko and I reviewed in the subway train! I couldn't believe my luck. See, my luck was turning the right direction! Feeling my heart pumping my blood actively, I took a deep breath again. "Well, all of my cleanest oxygen-contained good blood cells directly are shooting to my brain! I will pass this exam." And I did.

Following the first screening test, a twenty-five-meter swimming test, a group interview with two other applicants, and an individual interview with three committees came along. The entire exam process was finally over by the end of November.

In anticipation of receiving the passing notice or not, my classmates started talking about the graduation trips and parties after the winter break. One of the parties was called "the Appreciation Party" for the home room professor. It sounded odd, but since each department was specifically categorized by the grade level and subject, we had a home room professor just like the regular grade school.

Mr. Goat was in his 60s, a respected professional baroque keyboardist himself. The pomade products made his hair perfectly shiny with a comb. Behind his nice and gentle smile, I sensed some unpleasant, like fake, obligation, kind of feeling. His eyebrow hair grew straight up with the perpendicular angle from his forehead, his whole face reminded me of a goat. I didn't take his private piano lesson like some lucky students. Mr. Goat taught some classes, too, however, I was still nobody to him in his classes since my regular seat was quite often in the very back where most teachers don't care. Unless his eyebrows entertained me when I saw him on campus, he was practically nobody to me. So, it sounded odd for me to participate in the "Thank You Mr. Goat" party just because he was our classroom professor on the paper. All 54 senior girls in the Elementary Music Education Department were busy ordering party dresses, silk kimonos, making hair appointments, shopping for shoes, etc., except me. Grandma Fumi had made two dresses, a shiny blue green long sleeve dress and the other red with white ribbons patterned dress when I was in high school. For the festive reason, I knew I would wear red for my graduation.

My dress choice for a party was, therefore, the shiny blue green dress. It was not hard to choose and it didn't require any cost. Conveniently, I had a belt of large, silver metal chains that could go with my dress. My hair could be put up or put down by myself without paying a fortune to go to the beauty parlor. Honestly, I was reluctant to thank Mr. Goat without a genuine teacher-student relationship. But I was curious about the extravagant party food and the party itself at the four-star ranked hotel in downtown Tokyo. A party was for sure festive with colorful dresses, maybe a little bit too much. At this extravagant party, one of the girls looked and acted like the low ranked Geisha who used to work in the courtesan house. Her face was as scarlet as her gorgeous kimono. The back of the collar on her kimono was unreasonably pulled back too far down so her upper back was exposed intentionally. I could tell she was too drunk. She had planned to get drunk at the party anyway. So, I tried to stay away from her.

"We should go to the Hot Spring Resort for our graduation trip," Kaneko said. Geisha Girl was beyond excited and responded, "It is a great idea. Raise your hand if you are going!" Mr. Goat was supposed to be the center of this "teacher appreciation party," but his spotlight was hijacked successfully and completely. Sadly, in addition to the stolen spotlight, he was not going to be invited to the Hot Spring Resort trip. Somehow, I had saved enough money to manage the Hot Spring trip in addition to the week-long Indonesian tour. We laughed unstoppably, ate exotic foods, swam on the beach, and played UNO all night long. We all knew the end of a special chapter was about to end in our college life.

We would be the proud graduates in March. Another crazy party would happen after the ceremony. That would be the last party before my morning commute as a freshman teacher.

* * *

7:56 am – Entering School Building

As I push the entrance door, today's game, called "School," begins. Like other board games, I take each of my turns seriously. Especially when I roll my die, a little bit of excitement and a little bit of nervousness crisscross into my nervous system. Some people might have efficient techniques that make their die certain numbers, but one of the reasons why people enjoy rolling die is because, most of the time, it's unpredictable. Not knowing about the next moment causes me anxiety at times. On the other hand, I have a bit of positive anticipation that something great might happen with my roll. No matter what happens in the game or how the game ends, I prefer to have fun. I ask myself, "Am I ready to throw my die today? Am I ready to enjoy each moment of ups and downs during the game?" Walking down the empty hallway in the school building, I start thinking about major game players of the day and strategizing how and when I would use my cards. Oh, how I wished I and Ms. Aoki were the only major players in her game.

* * *

4-6 Years Old – Snow White on a Lily Pad

Typhoon Roll

I was four years old with thirty cents (a promotion!) in my hand, feeling a little older than the time I could only afford a Homerun Bar. I didn't have to be terrified of Grandma Fumi's arrogance either, because I was just waiting for my turn to purchase my favorite bread. It was the Wednesday Little Bakery in my school, not a general store in her neighborhood.

My friend, Hitomi, was standing before me in line. She comes to school with two long braids every single day without any exception. A vertical straight line on the back of her head parts her hair into right and left equally. Her hair smelled of grains of rice because her house is next to the rice grinder facility in town. Though my nose was tempted to get close to her head, it behaved itself. My nose already knew it was not a pleasant scent anyway. It was a unique and irresistible scent; however, my nose knew it would disappoint me if I actually inhaled it in through my nostrils. I tried to distract myself by holding my three coins really tight, fighting against yet another temptation. Should I touch her hair? No, I had no intention of pulling her beautiful braids. I just wanted to feel a tiny amount of the short and soft baby hair at the bottom of her perfectly straight hairline. Hitomi's mom cut half an inch off the bottom part of her baby hair because it was too short to be braided in. It turned out to be too short like a freshly mowed grass line. It was independently separated from the rest of the beautiful hairdo. I kept thinking, "It looks so strange, but I wonder how that short line feels."

Suddenly, "What are you staring at?" Miho said with her confronting voice. Hitomi turned around. "Well, n-n-nothing," I stuttered. Both Hitomi and Miho stared at me. I smiled apologetically, even though I was not doing anything wrong. Yet. Can they read my thinking bubble above my head?

Right before my left hand was about to reach her neck, Hitomi swiftly left the line with her bread. The fantasy crime was officially gone from my mind. My long-awaited turn finally arrived. I was lighthearted and feeling lucky because the Mighty Hard Bread was not a choice. Chipping my teeth by eating bread sounds awful and embarrassing, especially at school.

My demanding mother was nowhere near at this special moment on this Wednesday. And in fact, it was not the Donkey's Bakery anyway. Although I still missed the Donkey Bakery's Sweet 'n Soft bread that is still my all-time favorite, I had to let go of my past luxury. In fact, I sadly and happily admitted that a school bakery truck didn't deliver any kind of bread that the Donkey Bakery would carry.

"A cream sandwich please," I decisively said as I genuinely smiled. Ms. Aoki smiled back to me, but sympathetically addressed, "I am sorry, we have no more cream sandwiches today. Wait until next Wednesday. How about a typhoon roll?" I adored Ms. Aoki. Not only was she the prettiest and most thoughtful teacher in the whole galaxy, but she always knew how to solve the problem.

A typhoon roll, which looked like a real "eye of a typhoon" viewed from the top, could be an appropriate substitute. It would ease my disappointment from the lack of cream sandwiches. Its long, flat, square bread was rolled with some white whipped cream between the swirled bread. On the top of the crust, they spread a really thin layered chocolate icing. I reluctantly, but somewhat hopefully compromised to purchase a typhoon roll. While licking some white cream after unrolling my typhoon roll, I still dreamed about the yellow custard in a cream sandwich.

It was almost as if both the white whipped cream (real) and the yellow custard cream (the imaginative ingredient from the cream sandwich that I dreamt of) were melted onto my tongue at once. My imagination filled up my mouth with more than what I was actually eating. Miho asked me, "Isn't it good?" "Yes, it is more than good." Miho wondered why an over-victorious smile was on my face. Wednesdays had been special days for Miho and me.

On some Wednesdays, pre-kindergarten students were told to go home without shopping at the little bakery. The dark condensation hovered over the sky through the windows on this morning. They were about to drip some rain drops. Sigh... A rainy day equaled rain boots, a simple reason for why I felt blue. If only I had a choice of rain boots or regular shoes. My stubborn and unreasonable parents were single-minded in many areas, particularly in this. Technically, no flexibility had existed in my family. The family was exclusively dictated by parents, especially Father.

If you sneezed, you had to take some icky nasty powder medicine and go straight to bed. On the contrary, they never allowed us to have pain killer pills for headaches. Headache medicine contained bad chemicals, according to them. For stomachaches, suspicious black smelly herbal pills were the remedy. These fishy black pills were respected and therefore approved because they had grown in the Buddhist Temple where famous monks had trained.

A pair of rain boots was my parents' "must" item at the sign of rain whether a pair was cute or ugly. What an ordeal for a four-year-old child! I had my own reasons why I didn't wear boots. They totally refused to understand, or even listen to me because I was just a little kid. Nobody ever comprehends my parents' philosophy of the boots.

Accordingly, when the moist air fills in the air, kids needed to wear rain boots. I had to admit, though, that my rain boots were not the black ugly ones which my brother wears. But my silly looking rain boots humiliated me anyway when the sun came back in the afternoon. My whole body got clenched under the peer pressure. Someone would talk behind my back about how horrible I looked with my unreasonably stupid looking boots. Unlike my friends' boots, there were no flowers, stripes, or polka dots. The cancerous point of my boots was that they are too tight on my feet.

My mother was such a conservative shopper. According to her, she was the wisest consumer in the area, and never shopped for new boots until they are ripped. Being tight was not a criteria to shop for new boots. My school tennis shoes were a little tight, but at least they were red and had my favorite princesses on them. Just thinking about my boots made me nauseous.

Speaking of Creativity

First thing in the morning, Ms. Aoki played music from the boom box. "Who would like to create a movement with your arms from this music? Hiro, please come up to the front and show your movement. Everyone, let's copy Hiro's movement." Hiro held his arms up in the air and swung them. All of our arms were up in the air and swung from right to left, like the wind. Ms. Aoki was smiling, satisfied. After that, Ms. Aoki decided who should lead the next movement.

Of course, my hand was so straight and high. My fingers were so straight that they were almost arching out the other way. Unfortunately, the person chosen was not me. Ayumi, the fish market's daughter, held her arms up in the air, and swung from right to left. All of our hands were once again held in the air, and swung from right to left like the wind. "I can do something different," I blurted out with my arched hand.

"I need someone who is quiet when raising a hand," Ms. Aoki said while avoiding my begging eye contact.

The next person was up. Hideki held his arms up in the air and start swaying. "Are you nuts?" my heart screamed. I was totally tired of holding my arms up in the air and swaying.

Looking around, quite a few hopeful "I-wanna-go-next" straight hands and the "pick-me!" eye beams were somewhat ferociously shooting at Ms. Aoki. Finally, her eyes met with mine. Her beautiful smile made me extremely hopeful.

"Okay, that's enough for today. Let's do this next time."

Are you kidding me? Ms. Aoki, you will regret it if you don't see my special arm movement in your music! This disappointment in Ms. Aoki haunted me on and off through my entire pre-kindergarten career. Does she underestimate me? Does she underestimate me that I am going to do the same stupid movement? Ms. Aoki should be the person who knows me the best, maybe even better than my parents. Nobody can copy my completely complicated movement.

Perhaps she was afraid of what might have happened if she picked me. Earlier experiences of betrayal, disbelief, and realization of "Life is Not Fair" had been appropriately yet painfully seeping into my veins. Facing the reality was quite shocking and hurtful on my developing body and mind.

However, it seemed like that day turned out not so bad. A rigorously constructed clay snake and a couple of apples were showing off on the wooden clay board. Rich was making bananas on hers, while I wondered why as I kept rolling a snake as long as it can get, my snake got longer and longer, and skinnier. Maybe I could make the longest snake record. I carefully rolled one side, and held it for a second, and rolled the other side so I didn't break the snake. Soon it became longer than my clay board. I grinned triumphantly. My snake could be eligible to be a world longest noodle.

The most fun part was coming up. I was going to coil it up around and around and make my clay typhoon roll. I was almost there. When my snake was just about to reach the world record length, Rich pushed her desk by accident. Bang! "Sorry!" Everything happened in a blink of a moment. As Rich blurted out, my longest possible snake became one still-sort-of-long snake and one miserably-short snake. Instantly, my dream broke into pieces of a mosaic. With my fist clenched to avoid any tears from my eyes, I put two snakes together to make a hideous ugly rock which nobody made.

"Raise your hand if you make some animals," Ms. Aoki said. Someone showed her a mediocre snake proudly. "Wow, I have never seen such a long snake before!" Ms. Aoki exclaimed. That snake was not even half as long as mine. I was about to show my world longest snake and realized that I instead had a horrifically ugly boulder. Unfortunately, I totally ruined the only proof of the world record longest snake. It ended up being an unrecognizable humongous geological sample full of rage inside. It was very pathetic that I was so close to get the whole spotlight, yet I was not quite close enough. Maybe I just need to extend my patience a bit longer to wait for my spotlight moment until the school bus ride home.

We took off our art smocks and hooked them up. My penmanship notebook was ready on my desk. I was anxious to open my notebook because I just couldn't make the Hiragana letter "Ne" very well last time. I erased it several times, tried more than 10 more times, and then time was up.

Nervously, I turned my pages to get to the Japanese letter "Ne" page. I could easily find the page that was crumpled from being erased a million times. To my surprise, my "Ne" letter box was filled with red ink marked by Ms. Aoki. Not once, but over and over and over. It was clear evidence of her agony over the simple letter "Ne." I was so confused about which line she meant for me to trace. Soon my eyes caught the brand-new red ink letter "Ne" outside of the box. Her accomplishment finally appeared. She finally wrote her best "Ne" after several struggles in my practice box. Thanking her effort, I consciously traced Ms. Aoki's accomplished "Ne." Then, I did mine just like hers outside of the box although I knew she was not going to look at this page any more.

Ms. Aoki always wore a greyish dark blue smock along with the fellow lady teachers. Mr. Principal always wore a well-ironed white shirt and a tie without a jacket. He shaved his head every day because his other job was as a monk in his temple. This meant he must wear "Kesa" for funerals, burial services, and other temple related activities. It was kind of like Superman or Spiderman's life. Nobody knew the other half of his secret life. Technically, my pre-kindergarten was a small private Buddhist school where its temple became the convenient assembly hall.

Sambo among Us

When we came back from our summer vacation to school, teachers organized a "Black Contest" in this large temple hall. Kids competed against each other to see how dark they had become over the summer. Although I had tried really hard to win every summer, my competition always ended in the first round. To me, being dark was a way to make a connection to *Black Sambo* from the book. A champion of the Black Contest was always extremely dark, just like Sambo.

A black, smart, and witty boy, Sambo, somehow gets in trouble with tigers. However, he wisely escapes from them, and quickly climbs onto the top of the coconut tree. These tigers have no clue where Sambo went. The tigers keep running around the tree, looking for the mischief until they finally melt into butter. His mom and Sambo feast on pancakes with Tiger Butter until their stomachs cannot accept anymore.

I wanted to be Sambo. My imagination brought heavenly rich, golden yellow, and mouthwatering butter on top of more than the 25 slices of pancakes right in front of me. I strongly believed I should receive "real" pancakes with Tiger Butter as long as I became a Black Contest champion, perhaps as a prize.

Ironically, I also knew I was not going to win no matter how hard I tried because my home had a fatal disadvantage. Although my hometown was surrounded by the water, our home was not within walking distance to the beach compared to the majority of the kids in our school.

This year's champion was even darker than Sambo, in my opinion. Especially in the dark temple hall, he was almost invisible. We could only track where he is by carefully finding the white part of his eyes. I enviously and impatiently clapped my hands for another episode of losing.

At least Grandma Masu will take me to the pancake house next weekend. I knew I would l order two pancakes with a butter cube on the top. She would say okay when I asked to order an extra amount of syrup and lemon tea. As long as I was with Grandma Masu, I didn't really have to be Sambo to get tasty pancakes with melting butter.

Note: In a few decades, I would be shocked to learn about the controversy over the *Sambo* story in the multicultural literacy class in an American grad school.

Ninja at the Temple Hall

During the summer vacation, an overnight camp happened in the temple hall, too. We all lied down on the floor like people in a slave ship, the latter of which I would later learn about in world history. I was not kidding. There was no space between our bodies, and nobody was allowed to move from where they were assigned to sleep.

Technically, both sides of our bodies were touching someone's skin. If not someone's skin, it was a wall. To clarify, no one was able to move any of their body parts. The only thing about this was better than a slave ship was we only do this just for one night.

The reality that you had to sleep like this was shocking enough that your common sense was betrayed. And you could not remember to do minor things, even things as simple as remembering to be quiet after lights off.

Two seconds after the lights go off, I started hearing someone snoring. As I got familiar with the snoring sound as a kind of sounding rhythm, I, too, joined la-la land. At that second, a neighbor's leg attacked my belly. Ouch! I learned quickly that a deep sleeper's body was twice as heavier than their regular weight. My attempt to roll over was unsuccessful due to the limited space. The person on my other side was quite active, too. Her fingers covered my neck.

My mind kept swaying between reality and dream for a long time while I protected myself from the people's random body parts surrounding me. I got a kick to the top of my head, too. It woke me up instantly. This person already turned himself around 180 degrees. I remembered his head was touching my head before lights off. I wouldn't have been so optimistic and thought to sleep until the next morning if only I had known that the most terrifying moments were around the corner.

Something touched my right upper face. This object was hard on the outside but not terribly hard on the inside. Its pressure didn't stop until it gradually sank into my cheek.

"Ouch! You are stepping on my face!" I murmured with a dreamy voice.

"Sorry," Ms. Hori whispered.

Ms. Hori stepped on my face! She might have skillfully walked through tiny spaces before, like a ninja, however, she was not quite skillful enough to be a real ninja tonight. I was the primary practice obstacle for the master ninja-walking training.

Tonight, I involuntarily sacrificed my face for the ninja training. This kind of sacrifice itself was not a totally negative experience if you were a typical student in a Buddhist school. My sacrifice would benefit on someone's needs. Or was it a kind of an ordeal? Did I have to experience this to be a good person, just because it was happening in the temple hall? I simply wished I had a sophisticated definition of "sacrifice" during this overnight camp in the temple hall. Without any good answers, it was simply and physically painful.

This temple activity hall itself was the reason my school chose an elephant symbol for the bus; it was a symbol of Buddha. Sacrifice and ordeal were some parts of the Buddha package you had to go through, at least during a summer camp. Unlike its painful image, the children's classrooms sounded cheerful. The one three-year-old room was called the Plum class, the two four-year-old classes were the Stars and the Moons, and the two five-year-old classes were the Cherry Room and the Peach Room. We students were as adorable as the classrooms' names.

At the same time, our school often expected us to excel beyond our potential as if just being in the Buddhist school instantly made you a respectful Buddhist. An example of this was when we were not allowed to move while we stayed in the temple hall in the camp. Its tormenting discipline was the exclusive reflection of the painfully strict ordeals that Buddha has experienced himself. On the other hand, its educational beliefs, such as "compassion" that Buddha taught, were implemented and delivered by the loving teachers, like Ms. Aoki.

Compassionate Elephant

It was very obvious that every religious private school in the world tries to control students by using uniforms as the first step. Even the teachers, like their students, were required to wear a uniform to our school. This meant that the school tried to control the teachers, too. Differentiating between the teachers and students, by only a little bit of style and color, was the only mercy within the dress code for young teachers like Ms. Aoki, if it even existed.

The student's winter uniform was made up of slightly heavier materials that have a navy blue and white round collar. The sky-blue sailor collar and the white tie was the summer uniform. The summer uniform made me feel a bit prettier. My favorite part was the summer straw hat with the navy-blue ribbon. That was part of the summer uniform. Until June arrived, we had to drag ourselves to put on the world's ugliest hat. It was still a dark navy blue, but it was almost blackish.

In addition to this lousy color, we had to keep a black skinny rubber band under our chin. This made us unappealing and distasteful. It was unfair for us to wear the hat until we got to school. There should be some sort of mercy or at least some kind of flexibility or accommodation for students. No student was allowed to question the school policy. You must put your hat away on the hook as soon as you arrive at school. "Why do you care?" a teacher would say.

A yellow shoulder bag was put on one shoulder and the bag goes across your body. It had a handkerchief, a pocket tissue, and an attendance book. A teacher gave each student a sticker every day when we entered into the classroom. When we had no absences in a whole month, we get a special gold sticker. That was one of my favorite times. I walked up to my teacher as close as I could, and examined her bare knees that had white knee high socks. I had never seen lady teachers wear pants. Their bottom was always a tight skirt. It was always the same. My eyes followed from the bottom to top to reach to her eyes. "Good morning, here is your sticker for today." That sweet voice was coming from my teacher, Ms. Aoki.

Imagine Snow White.

Her hair was as black as coal, her lips were as red as a rose, and her skin was as white as snow. That was the exclusive description of Ms. Aoki. I had been dreaming about Snow White ever since my Grandma Fumi took me to the movie theater. My very first movie was *Snow White*. On my first day of pre-kindergarten, my jaw dropped. Snow White was standing in front of me. Even after she introduced herself as my teacher, I still could not believe my eyes.

Snow White was beautiful, no matter what, even in the ugly teacher uniform with bare knees and knee high socks. In the Moon class, we had the Snow White teacher, Ms. Aoki. My fellow Moon classmates and I believed and sometimes whispered to each other that Ms. Hori of the Star class might be an evil step-mother.

On the Lotus Leaf

It was not a perfect day on this specific Wednesday. To be honest, I had been a total loser all day today, however, my life went on, just like the elegant melody of Beethoven's *Fur Elise*. All kids put their heads down on the learning table and appreciated its mellow tune and melody coming from the classroom speaker. Every time I heard a black key my brain was pulled and lifted up a quarter an inch.

It was a unique and a kind of "mini" sensation that my brain responds to D sharp and G sharp, particularly. Therefore, while other kids might fall sleep with this calm Beethoven's piano piece, I was always swaying between my dream (often about being French) and semi-consciousness.

My brain didn't go away from my glorious moments of the day that should have happened. These moments, literally, could have been glorious. Unfortunately, life was not fair. Sometimes, it was almost brutal.

Good news was that my final chance to shine was still on my way. Ms. Aoki sat in front of the organ and started playing a goodbye song. All Moon class classmates sang riotously. In other words, they technically yelled to say goodbye without fine tune along with a pedaled air powered organ. The cord progression was simple enough, the repetition of I, IV, I, V, and I that I learned in Yamaha.

At the end of the song, with even more uproarious yelling echoed in the Moon room, "Goodbye Teacher, Goodbye Friends!" Kids swarmed like ants gathering around the dead worm, toward the entrance hall to change their shoes.

I was in the middle of group being guided by fellow ants through the hall. One by one, they got their shoes on and took off to the bus. I grabbed my rain boots from the shoe shelf and sat down. They were extremely tight as if my feet had grown two inches longer in last three hours. I continued putting my effort to put my boots on. All of a sudden, I realized the last person was gone. I was the last.

I was the only kid in the entrance foyer still struggling with these stupid boots. The bright sun was peeking through the cloud. I hoped my bus was still there. With the strongest force, I finally put them on. My right toes were not touching to the end. My left heel was in the air inside of a boot. But at least I had them both on my feet. I dashed to the ground.

There was no sign of the bus or people in the field. My eyes started welling up plenty of water. My eyes were big, but not as big as to hold in all the tears that kept coming. I missed the bus! I began hiccupping.

My nose started running. I repeated, "I missed the bus, I missed the bus, I missed the bus."

That meant I had missed my only and final chance to shine on this unlucky Wednesday. Nobody was going to listen to my jokes after all. I didn't know how to swear. I didn't know S-word or F-word. That frustrated me more. Turning around, I walked back to the building. I saw one teacher. Ms. Aoki! My eyes were welled with relief. "Teacher Aoki, I missed the bus. The bus was gone without me. I don't know how to get home. My house is kind of far away from here. Should I start walking?"

She replied, "Principal will make an extra route just for you, don't you worry."

Thank you, Buddha, I humbly received your compassion right here right now through my Snow White. This was how my "ordeal" Wednesday was compromised.

I rode the special bus trip all by myself with my principal. The principal's high pitch husky voice was somewhat soothing. I enjoyed the first official conversation with the principal. My vision was now myself being saved onto the large lotus leaf floating on the water. I even saw the beautiful pink lotus flower by the leaf in the pond by the school gate.

After all, there is always the flipped side of a coin.

Lunch Obsession

Opening the lid of my lunchbox was one of the highlights of the day, in addition to making my teacher laugh in the school bus. I couldn't stop thinking about lunch today because I knew what was in my lunch. My lunch box was not even an unfashionable aluminum bento box. It was a fancy yellow plastic basket wrapped by a pink handkerchief. My mother was halfway through her sandwich project when I came down to the kitchen this morning. Many pieces of sliced, exactly seven-millimeter-thick white bread were waiting to be sandwiched.

Last night, we stopped by the Andersen Bakery. Picking up the fresh-from-the-oven bread was our routine whenever we visit Grandma Masu. Margarine and strawberry jam were thinly pasted onto each side of the cotton like soft bread piece. It was too conservatory thin that you hardly tasted any sweetness. In fact, what I mostly tasted was the salt from the margarine. It would be a jackpot moment when the red chunk of jam hit my tongue. I knew she didn't cut any crust off, but I still dreamed about the joyous surprise of having no crust, just white sandwich bread lines in my lunch basket. Unfortunately, that dream would never come true. For now, at least I had something special in today's lunchbox rather than a tin lunch box with a red sour plum in the middle.

Besides, I brought sweetened black tea in my thermos instead of green tea. One of the few simple lunch rules here was that green tea should be the accompaniment of rice. Black tea should be sweetened and accompanied by bread. You could also enjoy your sweetened black tea with your breakfast toast. No other optional beverage was available, even water. Elders in the family always say, "You cannot drink water from faucet. You must boil it first. Otherwise, you will have a stomach ache."

Once she boiled the water, my mother cooled it off, then put green tea leaves or other Eastern medicinal tea leaves into the water. When you wanted to drink refreshing and keenly cold well water from the faucet, the best you could do was to sneakily snatch the water from the kitchen water faucet. But again, a water glass couldn't be seen on the dining table in my house, because water was not an official drink for a traditional family like us, if you called my family "traditional." If you were courageous enough to bring out a pop can or a glass of milk for your meal on the table, you would be shunned or even be treated like a criminal for the rest of your life.

Our refrigerator didn't have a variety of resources anyway, so none of us had ever been shunned. A few weeks ago, we had a rare outing to the steak house Sambra. The newly opened restaurant allured Father. I was overjoyed just going to the "steak house." We got to eat with knife and fork, not with chopsticks! It sounded like authentic Western food. Was it a French restaurant? A waitress brought a glass of water to each of us at the restaurant! A glass of water was an official drink today during our family meal for the first time. The restaurant offered the fantasized pleasure by serving water that differentiates from our "traditional" real life. As an accommodation, they boiled the water once and cooled it off without tea leaves for people like us.

Lunch menus at home had some non-negotiable regulations, too. I never had any opportunities to eat sandwiches for lunch or dinner at home. By the way, the American hamburgers were not considered to be or categorized as sandwiches in Japan. Bread was allowed in exclusively three occasions, such as breakfast toast, a breakfast sandwich, or school lunch. As eating a breakfast toast had grown to be modern according to the TV commercial, my parents tried to implement this modernization at home at their level. Here, Mother stirred Japanese traditional Miso soup along with a slice of toast every morning to serve her husband. The mixed up Eastern and Western fragrance from our kitchen confused my senses in the early morning every day.

Old folks in my region think rice gives you more power and a smarter brain than bread. If you saw the endless green rice fields in the countryside during summer, you would agree with these folks that rice was the best for the nation. Nothing really could be a substitute for rice, especially for older people. Bread was the food that the Western enemies ate. Even the young hamburger generation created the "RICE Burger" with a Teriyaki taste at the recently opened fast food restaurants.

One bread company was so desperate for clearing the negative image off of their face. The company composed a song to put into their TV commercial and played it over and over during kids' golden time consisting of watching cartoon shows.

We've grown up with bread so we are healthy and smart. We always get 100% on tests, no problem...

I was contemplating these claims and applying it to myself.

I thought that I was somewhat smart because I was eating a couple of slices of toast every morning. Am I supposed to get smarter if I would increase the bread consumption and perhaps eat more sandwich lunches than rice balls, or substitute bread meals more often at home? Am I just seeking the validation of which food was the more appropriate carbohydrate energy source for my body including my brain? Maybe my confusion among two carbohydrate sources was not as important as I contemplated. I wish I could choose what I eat because I like it, not because old folks label it as good.

Either way, I was simply and heavily influenced by the bread company's "Eating More Bread" promotion ads, as they expected. I loved bread! I was smart! I was one of the easiest targets among all afternoon cartoon generations even though I didn't have many opportunities to eat bread anyway.

My mother kept spreading butter thinly onto a pair of bread slices. Because the butter was too hard and the bread was too soft, she often made unpredictable holes on the surface of the white bread. She picked up a piece of almost transparently thin ham and a couple of cucumber slices, then, laid them over the miserable looking holes on the bread. The orderly lined sandwich in the yellow basket would make my day.

Sandwiched

Since there were three children in our household, I was supposed to be a middle of the sibling sandwich. I was supposed to be the best part, like ham, egg salad, jam, or even lettuce and tomatoes. I didn't think my sibling sandwich was well balanced in that manner. The oldest boy always took the best part. Then the left over was divided between me and my sister evenly. My sister and I were not as important as our brother in our family.

On January 1st, every kid gets New Year's celebration money called "Otoshidama" in Japan. My brother got $30. I got $10. My sister got $10. I complained, "It's not fair! Brother got more than me because he is older than me, but my younger sister's and my amount had no difference." My mother would say, "You will have no problem with money in your entire life because you were born in the Snake year. Why bother now?" "Because I am a child, that's why." My words were about to spill out from my mouth, but they stuck in my throat. I almost choked myself with my words.

When my grandma brought a souvenir from her trip, my brother got a black sword from the famous castle. I got a little necklace with a shell. I saw the same thing on my sister's hands.

In the meantime, Father recruited all of us and announced, "We are going to build a house in our new property. Follow me." About 100 yards from our house, there was an empty rocky property waiting for us. I saw a deep rectangular hole. Father proudly said, "It is our house. Now, pick up tools and dig more. Then, bring rocks and throw them in. We will put in concrete tomorrow." Whaaaaat? I screamed inside, but we did this physical labor that he said. It was actually a little bit exciting at a same time. We were building our own house by our own hand.

A few months after an outdoor pre-building ceremony in the community, our house was finally newly built. Another invitation had been sent to the relatives and community members for the open house party. This party was a real party inside of the new house. The luxurious cuisine and catering, served by female adults. Ladies with white smocks poured sake for the male guests or male guests pour sake for each other. All adult attendees with reddened faces entertained by taking turns giving speeches and singing the Japanese "Shigin" songs. My brother played with boy cousins. My sister and I played with girl cousins. After five minutes, my name was called from the kitchen. "Come over here and do dishes with your auntie," Mother demanded. "Why me?" I challenged. She irritatingly replied, "You are a 'big' sister." I grouched, "I want to play with my cousins. Why am I the only one working? It is not fair." My mother snapped, "Where in the world is the older girl playing with other kids in the family party? It's embarrassing! You are supposed to help around the house." I no longer talked back to her, but I couldn't hide my anger and frustration from my face and attitude. As long as I was in the kitchen and did the dishes, people were okay no matter how I felt. "It's not fair," I mumbled with a soapy dish by the running water. My auntie asked me, "What did you say?" I said, "Nothing."

Although I was constantly craving the special attention and recognition, nobody really noticed what I wanted. I didn't get any praise when I completed the highest mountain trail in the region without any help at age five, while my three-year-old sister received plenty of astonishing praises from every single adult. Yes, she hiked halfway by herself. But she was on a piggy back ride halfway back. I am five years old and completed the highest mountain!!!!! I wondered which was really more valuable. Let's say it's equally significant at each age level. No matter how I reason, my little sister gets all (I want!) and I get none.

Around the same time, my generous (by Father's word) sister recited, "Two times two is four." It amused my parents and neighbors. My parents often bragged about her, "My younger daughter memorized times table at age three." I memorized all two's table at the same time, however, it wasn't as amusing as my little genius sister's cutest 2x2=4. Though, my sister was not craving any attention because she knew she would get attention no matter what she said or did because she was the youngest and cutest among us. She was tired of frequent special remarks for nothing. My sister was pretty cut and dry, yet knew how her charm worked.

Needless to say, I complained often just because of these series of episodes. In addition to my parents' unequal treatment, I had another ordeal I had to deal with. This time, with my sister. She and I always had to follow my brother's unreasonable orders, just because he was an oldest male child in the family. Just because being born first in the order, he could make such idiotic requests like, "Scratch my back," "Bring me a pencil," "Follow me," "Go under the desk," "Call me your highness," "Be my dog," etc. It seemed like my brother's insecurity and lack of confidence would disappear while he controlled his younger siblings. He often threatened to beat us up if we didn't listen to him. He would beat us more if we revealed the beating incident to our parents. We were scared of him.

Imagine a sandwich structure. The first layer is the top bun, the second layer is the juicy meat and veggie part, and the third layer is the bottom bun. Our sibling sandwich was perhaps an open sandwich with double soggy buns. Although I had a right to shine in the middle layer, my selfish brother wanted to switch with the "juicy part." And he did because he was selfish; the older boy gets everything he wants in the family. I compromised to exchange my spot with my brother. The top bun now was me placed directly on the top of my sister bun, while my brother took over the juicy middle part and sat on top of two intimidated sister buns.

I was the older girl in the family who was supposed to sacrifice her childhood. I also had another responsibility that was to protect my little sister since I committed to be a replacement bun. Imagine this dysfunctional open sandwich. A Juicy-Part-Wanna-Be was boasting on the top of double pieces of buns without any recognizable qualification, but only as a bully. Yet he could not perform as the "real" juicy part.

I could've done just right, if he let me act as a juicy meat and veggie layer because I was in the righteous position. Since he was not what he was supposed to be, why could he be perfect? In fact, he performed pretty much everything poorly and disgustingly. My parents tried to save him every time he did something stupid, like stealing, misconducting, and bankrupting. He never had any consequences over his actions, but was protected instead. Every mistake he made, a fake juicy part (a.k.a., ego), collapsed and seeped into two buns in the bottom. The white bread pieces got contaminated little by little. "Help!" my sister and I screamed with our voiceless word.

Good news was that this agonizing situation was going to be over when my brother left our house after high school graduation. My parents announced that Brother was planning to be independent, living by himself a place across the water from us. Well, good luck.

Eventually, these sisters' soggy buns would become free. After Brother decided to move away from home, the buns would hopefully come back to normal. Well, I had to patiently wait for that moment. It would probably take another ten years. The bread pieces might be too dry like Panko (bread crumbs) by then.

Tragically, we had been a dysfunctional sandwich too long. I realized stains and scars on the buns' bodies over the years would never disappear. Would stains and scars take over me permanently? Can I take my juicy part back again? How? Gradually, a dangerous desire stepped into my mind.

I woke up one morning, noticing who I was. I, as a middle person, shouldn't act like a piece of bun anymore. I even shouldn't have acted as I did in the past. I am ham! I am jam with margarine! I have to act like a significant part of the sandwich because I am the righteous middle of the sandwich according to the birth order. Let me flap my arms with music in class! Let me tell some jokes to the audience! Let me wear what I adore like my favorite dress!

Unfortunately, no one was interested in my idea. Even if you like my idea, you cannot publicly agree with me because I was too young to speak up, and it was against the social rules in rural Japan. I had to be quiet and work hard just because I was an older child and a girl in the family. So, I decided to move out of my house.

In fact, I had a secret plan to reside in France. I could be a dream ballerina over there. But when? I already failed once when I sneaked out from the window with my favorite cream colored knit dress with frills. My mother got rid of my favorite dress after the incident. It would have been the perfect outfit for France! The dilemma came and went frequently in my little brain. It was quietly persuaded into, still immature, but a kind of certainty of my ultimate destination when I was just five years old.

Music in Me

Red River Valley was one of my favorite songs in Yamaha. It was a traditional folk song in America. This melancholy tune made me feel like I was in somewhere totally different than the place where I was. Goosebumps appeared on my arms when listening to it the first time. Yamaha Music Company wisely arranged this song so the young keyboarders could enjoy playing its main theme and some variations with ease. During the practice, I admired unknown places where I hadn't been before, behind my dreamy eyes. Whoever played, it sounded so cozy. Sometimes two kids got to play a duet on Ms. Nagaya's piano. Sometimes Ms. Nagaya played a duet with a student. I was stunned every time. Every tune is so beautiful.

"I chose *Red River Valley* for your graduation recital," Ms. Nagaya announced to me and a few other fellow Yamaha students. I could not believe my fortune. While other kids were assigned to other songs, this amazing news took me a trip to la-la land. *Red River Valley* was my song! Ms. Nagaya continued, "We have a great opportunity to play with a local community symphony orchestra at the Matsuyama Community Hall." It sounded so exciting! But what is a symphony?

The Community Hall was the place my Grandma Fumi took me for my first movie, *Snow White*. Grandma Fumi loved to take me everywhere she went for one reason. Grandma Fumi and I looked really alike, more than my parents. Wherever we went, 90% of the time, people asked her, "Is she your daughter?" "NO, no, no," with a waving hand motion in front of her face, then, she victoriously smiled and responded, "She is my granddaughter."

Grandma Fumi mischievously enjoyed every person's particular reaction. "You are TOO YOUNG to be a grandmother." She just needed frequent affirmation in her life. My grandma was like me, a victim of attention (a.k.a., proper love) deficit. We were both craving attention and love. Perhaps it was indeed in our blood. A long story short, yes, I remembered, it was a large concert hall. Playing a piano with a community symphony in this hall was a way more than honorable opportunity for a five-year-old.

After several sleepless nights of excitement, finally, I was sitting on one of audience seats, waiting for my turn to rehearse in the dark concert hall. There was a pair of grand pianos in the middle of the stage surrounded by chairs and music stands for the symphony instrument players. An enormous stage looked like heaven, only if it existed, tested by bright lights. Sometimes an incredible bright beam spotted the pianist's chair. Was I really going on stage and getting a spotlight?

Wow! Don't tell me you are just joking. My fingers became cold and shaky. It was more like tingly. What is this sensation? It must be a "stage fright" that my mother was talking about. I opened my small left palm really wide. With my right indent finger, I wrote a Chinese character "人" (person) on it three times. Then I cupped my left hand carefully and popped a letter invisible three "persons" into my mouth. As soon as I gulped it, I was supposed to be a stage fright free, strong, young musician.

Before I knew I was fear free, a nice gentleman with a dangling black bow tie from his neck walked over to me. He introduced himself as a concert master, a violinist. Sure enough, he was holding a violin and a bow in his left hand. "Wow, I have never seen a violin before. It is so real," I exclaimed. The violinist replied with a gentle smile, "Of course, it is real." Then, his right hand went into his trouser pocket. What I saw was a handful of candies! Different colored wrapping papers attract my eyes and appetite. If this was a dream, please don't wake me up!

I picked a strawberry candy and thanked him shyly. His humorous lecture about the recital excited me. According to him, he was going to use a special technique called a pizzicato on his and his fellow's violins for my variation of *Red River Valley*. He put his violin on his shoulder and wiggled it to adjust under his chin on the most comfortable spot. What is a pizzicato? To my surprise, instead of bowing, he plucked a string at a time. It was a sound of rain drops on my ugly yellow umbrella. "You play, 'Re-Mi-Ti-Re,' on your piano and we jump in like this, 'pluck, pluck.'" He demonstrated an amusing pizzicato right in front of me. "Do you want to practice with us?"

On the stage, I was surrounded by a group of string instruments. I patiently listened to the orchestra intro of my music piece. What amazing tunes! Not only one, but a whole section of string family was plucking their strings at the same time just for this little girl (ME!). While Mr. Concert Master was sending me a cue, I was still in heaven, absorbing the most intriguing sensation in my chest I had ever felt. Don't get me wrong, I was not ignoring his cue. I appreciated the music too much to play my part.

Mr. Concert Master gave the violinists a cue to stop. He stepped forward to my seat and whispered, "It is your turn. You can make our music more special if you join in with my cue." Nervously, I joined my part in the orchestra. This large group of adults played their music just for me. I was the main part of this beautiful music of Red River Valley with rain drops of pizzicatos. After my performance, I noticed that I had been on the spotlight. I squinted my eyes against the bright light full of contentment. Then, I turned my head to Mr. Concert Master to send a cue with my smile. "I did it."

Several hours after the successful dress rehearsal, I completed my best and last recital of Yamaha Music Academy. All in all, *Red River Valley* with pizzicatos was the most memorable event other than marching around the classroom with music and the human dominos. Complaining about every little thing wasn't wise and wastes your precious time and energy, comparing to the depth of glorious moments.

I now knew that there were some ways to impress Ms. Aoki other than flapping music arms. Maybe music? My self-confidence level was a couple steps ahead my fellow five-year-olds. I had developed a strong faith in me that someone in some place would recognize my potential in the future. I should be valued as the middle of the sandwich. A hopeful obsession appeared in my mind. In this vision, something good might happen in my life by someone who would be from France, when I would be a little older like eight years old. I was just contemplating when I was five years old.

Spring Goddess

Through the pre-kindergarten years, we had accomplished several incredible projects, like the origami album and the Future City. The seasonal origami album was an accumulation of monthly origami arts; cherry blossoms, frogs, hydrangea, irises, carps, snowflakes, bunnies, etc. Colorful 15 centimeters by 15 centimeters wide square papers came alive by little hands. Magically, sophisticated live plants and animals create their new world in the origami sketch book. These natural creatures began breathing in the background that I drew with pastel. What a wonderful way to appreciate changing seasons!

In another time, we discovered ourselves in the freedom of imagination during craft activities. My heart was dancing for the joy of building our Future City. The soap boxes, tissue boxes, seaweed boxes, and any kind of boxes were becoming, one by one, a hospital, a police department, a city hall, a floral shop, a temple, a business building, and more... in our Future City! In the meantime, I wrinkled my wrapping papers to form a suitable shrub for the Future City. While Ms. Aoki was talking about some other ideas about the city, I needed to complete my idea. Besides, no one except me could hear paper crumpling noises, I thought. "Shhhhh!" someone hushed me. I ignored it because I was not talking. "Shhhh!" another person hushed. All right. What's the matter with you guys?

Ms. Aoki looked at my hands, "You are making noises. Put it down." Her words were beyond my belief. No one should have ever heard my paper crumpling noises. I had never heard someone else's before. Or had I been just unconscious about crumpling noises? I put my head up and looked around the classroom. I saw Keiko over there flipping her wrapping paper. At that very moment, I heard her paper waving sound on her desk! Oh, my... Ms. Aoki revolutionarily broke a curse, a paper-crumpling-noise spell out of me.

If a "Selective Listener" existed, I had been the typical one. I had never tried to be a smart aleck or a sassy little girl. The paper crumpling noises had not been imprinted properly in my brain. Today was the special day. A day of discovery! I discovered myself being able to hear

Paper Crumpling Noise. Thanks to Ms. Aoki, selective listening disappeared from me.

Not only that, but I stopped breathing for two seconds when I saw the future town constructed with toilet paper rolls and empty soap boxes. It was the real twenty-first century city before my very own eyes. We built it together! I was a part of it! I wish I could live in this city. Would France look like it?

Origami and the Future City were just two of the good old days' glorious memories as soon as the graduation ended. Thinking about leaving the Buddha school distressed me. My anxiety level was growing larger inside of me each day, beyond my comfort zone.

In the meantime, a whole school including teachers, parents, and even little students were busy preparing for the final school play. Even though I didn't get the Spring Goddess role, Ms. Aoki assigned me a more important role. At least she said it was. By the way, the Spring Goddess' costume was a gorgeous long white dress. The Spring Goddess was supposed to dress like the Olympians like the Greeks with an olive leaves crown on her head. In the middle of the circle, she announced the spring to all creatures in the woods by holding the torch up high, "I am the Spring Goddess!" All the girls longed for that role because of the charming costume and the symbolic torch.

What Ms. Aoki assigned to me was a caterpillar. I couldn't hide my disappointment on my face until she told me her secret explanation about this role. According to her, I was supposed to start with being a caterpillar, however, guess what a caterpillar grows into? A butterfly! I had an important role that saves a dwarf's life in the woods by flying him back to his friends.

My mother proudly knitted a lime-colored, one-piece dress in the knitting machine and hand stitched a caterpillar on front. She also hand knitted a beret with a strong plant green yarn. She sewed a couple of black buttons as eyes and a couple of chains as antennas on the hat. The best part was the wings that Ms. Aoki found in the school supply room. I put each arm through in a circled rubber string and wore the wings just like a backpack. The transparent shiny wings with some sparkles were as beautiful as the Spring Goddess, who might be envious.

I was exclusively transformed as a transformed butterfly. I flew around the stage. I felt I was so beautiful from head to toe. My feet and legs were covered by the white tights which I initially didn't like, but I enjoyed feeling the smooth surface of the stage floor. With a dwarf on my back, I came back off the stage.

All of the sudden, I realized that I completely forgot something important on my back. My main beauty! My wings! I did not wear the butterfly's signature wings between the transition. Oh, no!!!!

I screwed up the entire show. I must have looked so stupid acting like a butterfly without wings. I wish I could hide somewhere no one could see me. Before long, Ms. Aoki found me upset. She put her hands on my shoulder and whispered, "Your hand movement was so graceful. I even didn't notice that you forgot about your wings. You were a beautiful butterfly on stage. Don't worry, we have another show. You will complete your final stage with your wings and elegant act. I look forward to seeing you tomorrow."

On the next stage, I double checked my wings right before I went to save the dwarf. I charismatically appeared on the stage to rescue the dwarf. I freely moved my arms and fingers up and down. I proved my arm flapping talent that I had wanted to show for a long time to Ms.

Aoki. Ultimately, Ms. Aoki already might have known it. I was ecstatic to see her tender smiles and endless applause that she was sending me behind the curtain.

Marching Buddha

The kindergarten's graduation was around the corner, yet, more events to come. We would be in the town parade with our special music marching band. There were some elementary instruments, like harmonica, keyboard harmonica, a big drum, and snare drums. My instrument in the regular band was an accordion thanks to Yamaha's superior music education. Yet, a reason I played an instrument which is half the size of myself is because I was the toughest and strongest among fellow five-year-olds. Well, actually I was the second strongest.

Kazu was my band pal who happened to be the strongest in the band. Although he had a baby face with red cheeks, his body was as large as a big kid, vertically and horizontally, like Pooh Bear. He was the only qualified player for a big drum, just because he was big. Fortunately, he was capable to keep the steady beat for the entire songs. Kazu and I were always together in the back row or the side of our band. My accordion was very heavy, but I couldn't complain. I just couldn't disappoint Ms. Aoki.

As the graduation march's day approached, I grew some anxiety whether if I could walk with this gigantic instrument. Soon I received grand news. I didn't have to play an accordion in the marching band. Yet, there was a catch.

"You are going to learn how to play a bell lyre," Ms. Aoki and Ms. Hori announced in unison. "It is not as heavy as an accordion. If you can play accordion, you can learn it really quickly," Ms. Hori said. The instrument they introduced to me was the vertical way of a glockenspiel.

Two teachers put the black belt around me. In front of my belly button, there was a super mini basket that was the bell lyre's handle holder. Ms. Hori put the bell lyre's handle into the supporter that belonged to my belt. "Here, why don't you hold it by yourself?" I held a red handle. Teachers said it was lighter than an accordion. Well, how do these teachers know it while they are not the ones who were holding it? I looked at Ms. Hori and Ms. Aoki without any word.

Finally, I opened my mouth. "It looks very cool (which was true). I like it (it was also true). It is easy to play because the bars are lined up like a piano (it was very true). I don't feel any weight because I am the strongest in our band." Oops! What did I say? If I played this instrument successfully, everybody would look up to me for sure, at least until our graduation. If I played this instrument really well, my teacher might call my name as an arm-flapping volunteer in music class.

When you wanted to accomplish something, you had to compromise in some way. It was almost giving up something in exchange for what you wanted. My priority was quite simple. Attention! I just wanted to be recognized like real sandwich meat. The juiciest part of the meal! I wanted to be recognized like butter and jam, even if they were extremely thin. Try me! I would melt on your tongue to make your dreamy smile. Someone would really acknowledge me for who I really was. Carrying the heavier instrument was no longer a burden. It was an easy trade with being acknowledged.

On the parade, my fellow music band members and I dressed with a white top with two red stripes on the shoulders. All girls wore pleated skirts, as short as above their knees with white high socks. Boys wore white shorts with high socks. A white trimmed red top hat was placed on each musician's head. It was fancily made out of a rolled white cardboard paper. Of course, I had to put the rubber band under my chin to make it stay.

Kazu asked me, "Can I try your instrument?" He carried my bell lyre with no effort. I was very envious. He continued, "You can do it. You are good in piano. You are strong like me, too." He gave me a matured, unlike five-year-old, encouragement with his Pooh Bear smile.

As soon as Ms. Aoki blew her whistle, the mighty music band started marching, following after a huge elephant on the float. It was a time for Buddha's birthday. The bell lyre was very heavy. I paid attention to each correct sound bar and timing that I was supposed to strike while my left hand held the handle very tightly. My focus might be even stronger trying not to drop my instrument rather than playing it. There were supposed to be a large audience alongside, however, I didn't even peek at it. It didn't matter because my parents were not there anyway. After huffs and puffs, an exhausted kid marching band came back to school. I heard teachers' complements. One of them announced, "Let's celebrate Buddha's birthday with a cup of sweet tea." But Buddha's sweet tea was not as sophisticated as my lunch special sweetened black tea. It didn't satisfy my gourmet tongue or recover my physical and emotional exhaustion.

Goodbye Ms. Aoki

I would miss the hyacinth bulb growing in the special vase in Ms. Aoki's classroom. Its roots grew every day. I could see it through the clear light violet vase. I admired every inch of the hyacinth's growth. The sunlight beamed on the purple transparent plastic vase to make a rainbow like a prism. What a mysterious scene it could make! I drew a picture of today's hyacinth on the top box of the observation paper and wrote about how long it had grown since yesterday on the lines in the bottom of the sheet. All of my classmates exclaimed, "Oooooo, ahhhhhh," when we saw a little bright green bud showing up on the top of the bulb's head. A science dude, Hide, measured its roots and leaves with a ruler. I stared at the bulb.

What kind of secret miracle did this little bulb keep inside? A few weeks later, its secret was going to be revealed. Little buds would start showing their color from the bottom of the stem, then it would complete the hyacinth miracle. I stared at the mysteriously attractive flower more carefully for a long time while it grew each day. It became beautiful because many people believed in it and admired its beauty. I knew I could be beautiful, too, if someone found my charm, stared at it, and believed in it. I, too, have a secret miracle inside of me waiting to open. Ms. Aoki put her hand on my shoulder and said, "I love your purple petals on your paper. They have grown just like you." I will miss the tenderness of Ms. Aoki, forever.

LESSON

2

Discovering

9:30 am – Mindfulness Circle

Every morning I welcome each student at the door. "Good morning, how are you today?" I smile at one student. While this student is thinking about his response (you'd be surprised at how hard it is for an eight-year-old to respond "fine" or not!), another child interrupts. "Mrs. Hallinan, I am excited because my grandma is coming today!" I am about to say, "Great," when another student comes in and says, "Good morning, I beat you!" (Meaning she said good morning to me before I could say it to her.) I see a girl who is often quiet and shy putting her backpack on the hook. "Good morning. I like your skirt today." She slightly smiles at me, but I seldom carry the conversation because another student hands me her "dragon" art she made. In the meantime, another student nudges me with his elbow and says, "I want to share my Pokemon book." I turn to the Pokemon student and ask, "Have you done the morning routine step 4? Why don't you go before the bell rings?" The morning routine is posted on the white board where students check in with their magnetic name tags. It says, "1. Good morning, 2. Name tag, 3. Homework to Blue Tub, 4. Bathroom, 5. Morning Task." He points his finger at the number 4, and turns around and says to me, "That's right." I notice the dragon student and pretty-skirt student are already in their seats working on the routine step 5. The thinking-about-the-answer-to-how-are-you student is putting his homework in the blue tub. The grandma-visiting student is zoning out at his seat so I have to tap his shoulders and point to his work on his desk. After a few more "good mornings" were exchanged, finally we hear the first bell. That's when I turn off the classical radio station and lights as the daily mindfulness practice, the Smiling Mind, follows. All students drop their pencils, make their still body, and close their eyes. The recorded guidance starts, "Today, we are going to work on kindness to ourselves. Breathe in... and out..." I wish I could have known this gentle voice and self-compassion in my high school days.

* * *

15-18 Years Old – Girls Should Be Girls

A Losers' School

The "Loser Girls' High School," it's publicly known name (but only the implicit understanding), is the famous private girls' high school I was about to attend. My house was far away from the central part of the city where my new school was. If I took a bus, I would have to walk for 20 minutes to the bus stop, ride a bus for 30 minutes, and walk to school for another 15 minutes. If I take a train, I would have to walk for 35 minutes to the station, ride a train for 20 minutes, and walk to school for 20 minutes. I would also have to carry about 20 pounds of books in my black leather school bag, along with my P.E. uniform bag and lunch. Also, the transportation fees would be beyond our family budget.

I proposed my commute plan to my parents. "If you buy a new bike, that cost is way less than other transportation fees for the next three years. It is a good investment." My parents surprisingly and easily agreed with me. It sounded like our family budget was surely tight. Also, they pitied me on going to the "loser's school." I got a brand-new three-speed bike for my commute. It would take 40 minutes from my house to school. My heavy school bags were bungeed onto the back seat so I didn't have to carry them by myself.

Now, my commuting pal had already been arranged since the high school exam results day. My mother's friend had a daughter, Yoshi, who was same age as me. Yoshi's mother called my mother on the phone. "Yoshi didn't make it. How about yours? Oh, I am sorry (she sounds sad, but really she was smiling at the other end), but Yoshi will be glad to commute with your daughter." Without our knowledge, Yoshi and I became instant commute to school friends.

At this point, I made my mind not complain for not passing the prestigious high school exam. I determined to focus my best in my new school. No more pity. No more regret. Move forward. At least in public.

Secret Social Detour

But Yoshi couldn't get over her failure. Unfortunately, it might take time to re-shift her thinking and attitude. I wondered if she knew it was her problem, not mine. Although Yoshi's whining about going to the "loser" school was annoying, the bike commute expanded my activity range. Yoshi and I were getting better at finding several unique detours that we could take lingering around after school. We also explored inexpensive hidden snack stops. Supermarkets or the stores exposed on the street were pretty obvious. We stopped by and got some ice cream bars on the hot and humid summer days and Mister Donuts on the random hungry days. At the convenience store, like Seven Eleven, our winter favorite was the Chinese steamed bun. The white and round buns were waiting for us in the small steaming box. Even though all buns look the same outside, there are several different surprising ingredients and flavors inside. My favorite were sweet pork and sweet red bean. Curry was a little too modern for me. Yoshi often ordered the same kind as I ordered. We carefully peeled the thin skin outside of the bun. We were so ecstatic for the very first warm bite. From a bite on the bun, a little white steam puffed out of my mouth. Soon we stored full energy for another four miles to get home. We smiled at each other to prepare for the four-mile ride home.

The teenagers' social network was only chatting in person or on the home landline phone. When we went to school, someone always knew about something hip and fun. It was not necessarily the same person providing information, but new information was always available each day. If you missed your favorite TV show, you would experience it as if you watched the show that you missed, right at school. The high school girl's expression is explicit and exaggerated beyond the generation. No exception.

Yoshi and I had saved our allowance to take our occasional secret detour thanks to our primitive and unwired network, in a 20th century style. All information was quickly and efficiently spread among teenage girls by the power of word of mouth. It was literally quick to know the affordable gourmet snack for hungry high schoolers. Another of our favorites are octopus balls in the kind of filthy shack outside of the popular supermarket, the Japanese pancake house where we made our own at the private grill on the table, and the fancy mini donuts shop that just opened in the Central Station area. Nutritiously speaking, our favorites were too starchy to be healthy. The only reason we didn't become *Biggest Loser* contestants was because of our young high metabolism. An energy boost from the daily bicycle commute, 80 minutes total both ways, balanced out our snacking habit.

My high school was nicknamed "Mammoth" because of its large number of students, which was over one thousand. It reminded me of my kindergarten's mascot, an elephant. Mammoth, unlike the elephant of my kindergarten, didn't encourage students to have any kind of religious practice. That's why it was chosen among two other private schools which required a "Chapel Time" once a week and a daily blessing. One of two was the strict Catholic school. Its students have so many more rules than other schools, and students must wear black stockings or socks throughout a year. Their uniforms were way uglier than ours. By the way, I hated the summer uniform in my school. It was a hideously old-fashioned ugly green pleated skirt and white open-necked shirt. Its design probably hadn't changed for 40 years. I assumed that it might have been the most stylish design back then. The Catholic school's uniform was worse than our summer uniform. Another Christian high school had a different story. Their uniform reminded me of "freedom" and a cover girl on *Seventeen* magazine. Students could choose tops and bottoms as long as they follow the color code. These girls looked so cute no matter how much they weighed. But this school charged very expensive tuition. It was evident that this school welcomed only wealthy and stylish families. Of course, my family couldn't afford it anyway. The mammoth school was the most suitable losers' school for me (and my family) among three private girls' schools.

Queen's English

During my first year of high school, the English teacher was the homeroom teacher. She looked a little bit like Ms. Nagaya, the Yamaha Music teacher, in her short curly unusual reddish hair, pale skin, shockingly red lipsticks, and somewhere between comfortable and uncomfortable fragrance. I wondered, "Is she going to open my door to the hopeful future?" She introduced herself as an English teacher and shared her English learning experiences. She had lived and studied in England for several years in the past. The "Queen's English" is her English, she explained. Unlike Mr. Excellent Field, a junior high Technology Home Economy teacher, Ms. Queen's English sounded so much more like English from the Radio English Conversation Class that I have listened to when I was in seventh grade. My friends and I believed that her statement, "studied English in England," must be true.

In fact, no one in our class had ever heard a relevant "L" sound, "R" sound, and "Th" sound in our junior high schools. We were so shocked how authentic the English language could be, if they study in England. Although all English teachers in my high school had studied English with their college degree in Teaching, they didn't necessarily speak English like Ms. Queen. Mr. Seaweed was a classic bad example.

His nickname was given by our class (me?) just because of his hair style. In his late forties or early fifties, he had hard time handling the only hair he managed to keep on his round and slippery head, like my third-grade teacher Mr. Lucky Sun. It was just even worse. Mr. Seaweed combed his hair from his left ear to the right, just like real rectangular seaweed wrapping over the top of a rice ball in a lunch box.

Of course, his nickname was our secret code. We never called him his nickname in class as a token of our dignity and respect.

Mr. Seaweed read the English text really fast as if that was the only way female high school students would admire him. It was a very bad plan. He didn't realize he could not be Ms. Queen. What irritated our ears most was his "t" sound that even we could easily make. His "t" sound was consistently "ts."

For example, in the lesson on infinitive, he would say, "It is important to use 'tsu' in infinitive. 'Tsu' is very convenient in infinitive. You have to learn when you use 'tsu' and not to use 'tsu' in sentences." Okay, that's enough.

Every recess after Mr. Seaweed's English lesson, we put our heads together and wondered why he couldn't pronounce a simple "t" sound. "Maybe his tongue is too short to attack the roof of his mouth," I brought up. My friend Miwa jumped in and said, "I think 'ts' sound requires the tongue length the same as 't.'" Miwa hit the point on the head. We concluded that Mr. Seaweed was disabled in making the "t" sound, until one day.

Mr. Seaweed was explaining something about ordinary and extraordinary situations. A Japanese word for "ordinary" sounds like "futsu." The air froze like the Arctic Circle all at once when he sounded it "fu-**to**." We looked at each other, with only using our eyeballs. He asked, "What's wrong with you guys?" We were all in shock about the fact that he WAS totally capable of making the "t" sound! He was purposely driving us crazy every day! What kind of teacher was he? At least that we reached to our conclusion of the mystery on that day.

New World, New People

In the first week of freshman year in high school, we were assigned a seat by Japanese alphabetical order of our last names. I was the second from last in that order. My seat was by the wall on the hallway side. Teachers usually called students' names by their last names, for example, "Good Morning Miss Suzuki." Within one minute entering the tenth-grade classroom, I quickly learned the girl behind me had a same last name as mine. Because her last name is as same as mine, Ms. Queen had no choice but make an exception in our class. Instead of calling us by our last names, she made the exception and called only my friend and me our first names.

One of the girls sitting my left side, Mika, attended the school where Grandma Fumi's nephew, Issa, went. Issa's mother was one of Fumi's sixteen siblings. I knew Issa very well—not only was he the same age as me, but he lived a next door to Mr. Turtle, the Fixing Joints Doctor, a kind of Japanese version of alternative medicine. Mr. Turtle could fix anyone who had bone-related problems, even broken bones. People seek their pain-free lives in his care. My mother took me to his office for several months after I left the hospital from my car accident. She wanted to make sure a crack on my skull was all healed and never caused reoccurring headaches in the future. A hospital discharged me because the problem was fixed, but it wasn't enough for my mother. Mr. Turtle's big, long, and strong fingers press into both of my temples. His mighty powerful fingers caused so much pain that I had never experienced in the hospital. Why do I have to have this unnecessary pain? I didn't understand how this painful treatment would make me "pain-free" while I'd never experienced any pain until now. It seemed like the "alternative" medicine was like a "mainstream" treatment for the older generation. Issa's mother and Mr. Turtle's wife were the best buddies among all sixteen siblings. I was also envious about Issa's dad being a professional chef. It was hard to imagine how any male figures fix meals in the kitchen. I asked Issa if his dad would fix meals at home. Issa answered, "He watches TV all the time and never stands in the kitchen." This explanation gave me a sophisticated understanding of a typical Japanese male adult. Issa's family dynamic might not be too different from mine.

Most of the new faces among my classmates were engaged in conversation, trying to make friends on the first day of high school. A tall, short-haired girl turned around and introduced herself with a beautiful smile. Yoshimoto, came from the same school as Mika. In front of Yoshimoto sat a girl from a sister junior high school with the local university. Her name was Miwa. She had short and spiky hair. She looked very friendly. She was very funny, too. We became instant friends. But I wondered how people like Miwa, who had attended a prestigious junior high school, ended up being at the "loser" school.

Although an enormous number of teenage girls came to this school with different academic levels and uniqueness, we (98% of us) shared one common fact. We all failed the latest entrance exams into the public high schools. All public high schools were all academically ranked. Depending on your academic level, you would be assigned to try out the particular school by your advisory teacher. If you maintained the high academic level in their junior high school, your teacher would determine you eligible to take the entering exam of the prestigious high ranked public high school. And if you were a low performing student, your future school would have low academic expectations. It really didn't matter whether you had a dream high school that you wanted to attend or not because you would not be allowed to choose your favorite school if your score was lower than your dream school's expected score. You would be strongly encouraged to take a lower level school's exam in the honor of their junior high school. Twenty plus junior high schools in the city competed against each other by the exam passing rate. However, this system didn't promise that you would pass the exam. They don't give much consideration to the fact that the exam day could potentially be simply a bad day for some students. In other words, if you screwed up for the exam on the very exam day, it's over. All of us were in different levels, but our situation was clearly the same—we had failed on the important exam. To summarize, our student body consisted of students with different academic levels who recently "screwed up" on the exam on the very exam day to join the "loser" school. Ironically, that phenomenon created our diversity and uniqueness in our school. The interesting thing was that no one seemed to care much or pity themselves among my new classmates, of course except my commute friend Yoshi. Everybody except Yoshi had no time to worry about the past.

There were 20 pounds of new textbooks, notebooks, dictionaries, and an academic schedule sitting on our desks. Teachers were eager to whip their students' butts in order to receive a higher salary and bonus by increasing the collage passing rate. It was an unusual experience for me to see 53 female bodies all at once in one classroom. It was even more powerful if you saw more than 1,000 girls all together in the humongous gym during the whole school assembly.

Everything looked so fresh, new, and overwhelming that I didn't think about myself a "loser" anymore. Besides, 50 out of 53 students were in the same situation as mine. I didn't have any reasons to pity myself in the first week.

But my bike commuter friend Yoshi dragged herself into a "loser" situation and purposely drove herself crazy. Failing the prestigious public school exam was her first and most difficult torment in her life. No one could save her but herself. I tried to distract her whenever she started talking about it. We, in our school, were all losers after all. Why did she have to cry forever? Yoshi dropped her eyes down to pedal her bike when she saw her favorite high school's uniform. I felt sorry for her, but I couldn't be her mom.

My mother's lunch duty restarted on day one in my first high school year. Technically, she had been making lunch for someone most of the time, for her son or her husband, at least. There was no more school lunch in high school. The school didn't have a cafeteria or kitchen. If you didn't have food, you just didn't eat. It was very cut and dry.

Going back to the lunch box routine reminded me of back in the good old days of pre-kindergarten. Yes, I took sandwiches in some days, however, my mother never wanted to make rice balls, even fist-sized, anymore because it was time consuming.

Teenager's Self-Talk

Around that time, I grew more self-conscious in my weight as a normal teenage girl. I had been away from the scale or mirror since eighth grade. If I didn't step on the scale, I didn't have to worry about the weight. If I didn't see the mirror, I didn't have to agonize over my double chin or even my ugly acne. Yuu, in junior high, made a pathetic Haiku poem about his weight gain. He was already big and heavy, yet cynical and humorous at the same time. With a description of the true feeling, and a little humor, he wrote the second line: *Afraid of stepping on the scale*. His voice was absolutely speaking to my mind.

"Because I am riding bike to school every day, I am not supposed to get overweight," one part of me would say. "No matter how many hours you bike, you will always be fat just like you were as a little girl," another

79

part of me would speak really loudly. It almost successfully traumatized me. I didn't know and I didn't want to know how much I weighed. I didn't know how much I was supposed to weigh as a healthy teenager. The body-sized mirror in our house was in my parents' room where I couldn't go in on a daily basis. That was the only mirror I could see my whole body. Without access to the body-sized mirror, the only another mirror was a small rectangular mirror in the washroom, which was the size of my face. I could check my breakouts on my face or find a tiny food scrap between my teeth, but not my entire body image.

Not knowing how I looked, I felt terrible about myself just because I had been a "chubby" character in my family as long as I could remember. Whenever Grandma Fumi and Mother measured my size for my skirts, shirts, sweaters, dresses, etc., they commented, "Oh, my, your butt is huge," and "Look at your thighs!" These were their expressions of exclamation and celebration for how much their kid grew, but I had been totally offended. It was as simple as saying, "If you are not skinny, you are fat." To tell you the truth, that was another major reason I decided on the bike commute over the train and bus.

Day after day, I rode my bike, however, nobody mentioned how skinny I was or never gave me any flattery: "You look like you lost some weight." So, I decided to cut a part of my lunch, "cutting carb diet" except bread. That meant that I simply decided not to eat rice every meal. My mother was conservative in the use of butter on the bread so I didn't consider butter as a lethal amount that would create more fat on my tummy. My Plan A: I would eat all of the sandwiches if she ever makes them. Unfortunately, the sandwich was neither a popular nor traditional lunch menu item in my household. If I had a sandwich lunch once a month, I would be very lucky because that was the only day when I allowed myself to eat my lunch in full. You must be wondering, "Why didn't you fix your own lunch?" That is a good question from the Western point of view. But if you knew the typical Japanese bento, you wouldn't blame me anymore. I wasn't able to even dream about fixing my own lunch. I have never dreamt to try. It was my mother's sanctuary that nobody could touch, not even her daughter.

My Plan B was to give away most of the rice in my lunch. Luckily, it was not hard to find a person who was willing to take extra rice from me. At lunch time, close friends put their desks together to make a table in the classroom. Since we didn't know each other much anyway, my neighbor girls decided to eat together. When we turned desks, both Yoshimoto and Naomi were on my sides and Mika was in front of me, in addition to three to four more friends in the group. About most of us were done eating our lunch when Mika blurted, "I am still hungry." It caught my attention immediately. She was the tiniest among us all. It surprised us. I offered, "I wonder if you would like to take some of my rice." Mika's eyes were wide open. "Are you sure? I will take it, if you don't mind." As I put my rice onto her lunch box's lid, I mentioned, "You can take my rice every day if you want to." My cutting carb (rice) diet started successfully. I was very confident in my eating habits because I was still eating the nutritious part of my lunch box, such as eggs, beans, carrots, etc. It was a well-balanced meal based on the food groups I had learned from Ms. Takahashi when I was in her fifth-grade class.

Adventures in the Woods

Less than a month after school started, a team building camp was planned for the newly entered tenth graders. We planned to hike, kayak, cook outdoors, sing songs, build a campfire, and to even sneak a midnight snack (which was prohibited, but it was still on our list). Getting lost in the wilderness was never in our plan. The main team building activity was orienteering in a beautiful green forest. With a map and a compass, each team had to find the posts at certain points that had stamps. When a team got all the stamps from all the posts, they could come back to the central cabin where we were staying. My proud team was the first one back to the cabin! "Congratulations, girls! Hmmmm, oops, that's not right," Ms. Queen said as she looked at our map and stamp book. She frowned her face. Her eyeballs moved back and forth from the map to our faces. She quickly learned that we had used more of our instincts than our map reading skills on the trip. Then, she coldly announced, "You are disqualified. It is quite obvious you guys cheated. Go back to the woods and start over." "Cheated? No way!" we argued. She continued, "If it didn't happen on purpose, you must try again. Read the map more carefully. Go out and play this game again. No one has come back yet. You still have a lot of time." We had no choice but to put our heads down and drag our feet back to the wild trail.

Here we were again in the middle of the woods wandering without knowing where we had to go. No one was confident enough to survive in the wild. We had been in "Examination Hell" (an expression of how hard the high school/college entrance exams are) but never expected to feel vulnerable in the wilderness. How pathetic! The sun was about to set. We hollered at the cliff dramatically, "Don't go away from us, sun!"

"Well, we have to go back before dark," one girl said. "I know, but how?" "Well, let's keep walking, I guess." Suddenly, someone else said, "Look! I can see the central cabin! Its lights are on!" We were on a tip of the cliff looking way down at the home base. We started yelling, "Hello!!!!! We are here! Do you hear us?" Surprisingly, a hopeful echo came back. "Come home now! Dinner is ready!"

"How? We are way up here and by the time we get down, the food will be gone!" "That's terrible!" "I don't want to skip my dinner. Waaaaa!" Some of the fellow girls started whining. After a few minutes of dramatic whining, my team reached a radical decision.

"Let's have a shortcut straight down on this cliff instead of following the trail." It was very steep and bushes were everywhere on the hill. But we had no other choice.

"We are going down now!" I began sliding with my feet sideways. Everybody followed one at a time. We were like forgotten stranded soldiers during WWII in the uninhabited islands of the Pacific Ocean. We looked at each other and asked each time we stopped, "How many scrapes do you have?" I counted and said, "Three." Another girl somewhat proudly announced, "Four." We had no Band-Aids with us, but we were still fine. "Lick your scrapes. You will be fine." And we kept descending.

About halfway down the slope, the campfire beckoned to us to help show the way back. "I hope they keep our dinner," I blurted. "They should," the others agreed. I encouraged my team as a self-selected leader, "We are close to the food. Let's keep it up." We cheered each other on to keep up our steady pace. We laughed about how pathetic our situation was. Nobody cried any longer.

At about one-third of the way from the bottom, the cabin seemed larger and we started seeing people as figures instead of as "dots." We also heard our classmates encourage us from the bottom of the cliff. "Are you alright? You can do it! Keep coming down!"

Finally, we climbed down close enough to identify the cabin structures and our classmates' faces waiting for our team. After a final leap, our exhausted team members landed on the flat ground. As soon as our eyes met our friends', we were doused with a shower of nonstop questions from them. "What have you guys been doing?" "Are you okay?" "Where did you go?" "Why did it take you so long to get back?" We didn't necessarily have all the answers. We were truly overjoyed about our safe return reunion. Of course, we were the last team to return, but our team was the most entertaining team among all. Ms. Queen smiled and sighed at the same time, "Finally."

Teachers and friends loved our adventure story in the woods. Although our bodies were exhausted, our adrenaline kept running to prevent us from a sound sleep. Of course, a few minutes after the lights were officially off, we started whispering about our adventure again. Instead of falling asleep, our eyes were wide open for another dangerous adventure. The "prohibited" midnight snacks.

Somehow, Ms. Queen discovered (smelled!) this secret mission of ours. She sneakily slipped into our cabin room and suddenly turned on the light. "Who is eating a snack right now?" We all squinted our eyes from the bright lights. "Show me all of the snacks you are eating right now. They are all mine now!" She continued yelling, "I am so disappointed in you after all of your adventurous accomplishments today!" We looked down and felt embarrassed. At the same time, we sent a secret message to each other. "How sad, Ms. Queen doesn't understand what teenage girls are about." "Anything else?" Ms. Queen interrogated. Ms. Queen was finally satisfied after Kazumi threw her unopened bag of chips back onto her cot.

Academic Elite or Sports Elite

My high school was traditionally strong in sports, all kinds of sports, because they recruited superior athletes from junior high schools and offered them free tuition. Unrecruited, regular students were welcome to join any kind of club. However, students in the academic elite class were discouraged to participate in competitive athletic clubs.

Being in the academic elite meant you could redeem yourself. You could reclaim your championship belt just like the movie *Rocky* and prove yourself to the audience who had put you down in the past. In a sense, it was revenge. Our teachers were the important trainers of our rematch. In fact, their salary was based on how many students went on to promising prestigious colleges and universities.

I stood by the gymnasium door admiring a gymnast on the balance beam. This would be my first and last chance to get involved in this sport because I might already be too old to start gymnastics. While I contemplated about joining the club every day after school at the same door for a couple of weeks, our teachers started to push us in a single direction. "Are you planning to be in the Academic Elite Class?"

It translated to, "Are you planning to get revenge, or to be a loser?"

Three hours of practice every day after school plus a 40-minute bike commute might kill my body and soul. Besides, when I got home, I would have homework and piano practice, too. When would I sleep?

I secretly admired my body's flexibility and strength that could transform me into a potential candidate for gymnastics. I knew this because my junior high P.E. teacher mentioned it several times. I had to make a big decision. I could not find any supporters to back up my potential or give me some guidance. "To get revenge or to lose" were two extreme ends. It didn't help untangle my complicated thoughts. I didn't know if I wanted to get revenge, but I didn't want to be called a "loser" again.

In addition, if I went to college, I wouldn't have to live in my house anymore. I could explore my opportunities in the promising land where

I would be. My thoughts swayed back and forth like a pendulum, oscillating between pursuing my current passion without support and moving towards future opportunities with proper guidance.

I still didn't know what was inside of my hyacinth bulb, but I felt something surely rumbling inside of me. If no one could find it, I had to wait until it ripened.

After two weeks, I quit standing by the gym door.

Broadcasting in High School

Instead, Yoshi and I knocked on the Broadcast Club's door the next day. Girls in the Broadcast Club created radio drama, announced school news during lunch time, and acted as an M.C. on field day, just like a regular professional radio station. Our team's radio program had just won first place in the National High School Radio Contest sponsored by the national radio station. Two of the senior students who were involved in this project and the supervisor teacher, Ms. Old Maid, had just come back from their award ceremony trip in Tokyo.

Yoshi was interested in mixing sound behind the show, and I was, of course, the front-runner of announcing on the radio. Although it was not a physically active club, it was still time consuming. Under the strict hierarchy of a girls' high school, freshmen didn't have real activities. Just observing the senior students' work in the small broadcasting room was a waste of my time.

In the meantime, I looked around the tennis court. All freshmen, whether recruited or not, stood behind the line picking up balls that senior players missed. During break time, these freshmen dashed to the court for the real practice for themselves. That meant freshmen didn't have any breaks throughout the entire practice. This did not only happen in the tennis club. Most clubs organized activities based on respecting seniority. I had no problem with looking up to elders, which was one of the typical Japanese beauties. However, it was not fair that those who had similar or better talent in a field didn't have equal opportunities to participate just because they were younger.

In the broadcasting club, I could read the news better than some of the senior students who were only one year older than me, but I had no chance to sit in front of the microphone. Seniority was the most important rule among school kids. "Things will be better next year," Yoshi encouraged me on the way home. "Am I too cocky? Am I too impatient? Why doesn't anybody have any protests against the system?" I asked myself. The social norm demanded that speaking up to elders was impolite. I had to be quiet.

To be quiet with reasonable doubt and to continue being tortured under the unfair circumstances were not my style. Well, frankly, I didn't know if I had my own style of life. But at least I knew what felt right and wrong beyond likes and dislikes.

Music Training

Coincidentally, at around this time, my surroundings at home became busier. My piano teacher, Mr. Clarinet, thought I had to learn more advanced piano pieces from a "real" piano professional. The connection between Mr. Clarinet and my family had started from my mother's trustful brother, Miki, when Uncle Miki referred him to us as my piano teacher. Uncle Miki was the only person in my family that I would consider a decent adult. Mr. Clarinet had built trust with my mother by being her children's piano teacher. His recommendation was relevant based on his well-established relationship in addition to his credentials. Mr. Clarinet introduced me to a voice coach as well as a new piano teacher who was a professional pianist. This arrangement was significant in order for me to prepare for music college.

Furthermore, if I pursued a teaching career, I would have to stay in the local teaching college. This new piano teacher might have a connection to the school. Playing piano and singing songs were my mother's dream come true. Growing up with a single mother in poverty, my mother had to give up many of her dreams. Pursuing a music career with local celebrity teachers would make her happy. Sadly, she was never allowed to dream about something for her own life. Mr. Clarinet was going to retire from being a piano teacher, but he offered me music theory lessons to prepare for the music college exams. Even though my mother and I didn't necessarily agree with everything in the decision-making process, we got along well enough overall to move forward. We never expected that having extraordinary musical techniques didn't automatically lead to effective teaching skills, though.

School, my daily commute, homework, piano lessons, voice lessons, music lessons, practices, and of course, house chores... The high school life was a once in a lifetime experience. I was going to spend most of my next three years just preparing for college exams in the Academic Elite Class. How pathetic! But I didn't know what else I could do to protest. I didn't even know what I was good at. I just would do what I could do, mostly what my parents would tell me to do. I simply couldn't add more to my plate.

I visited Ms. Old Maid, the broadcast club's supervisor, to announce my resignation. Being with Ms. Old Maid in the same room was scary enough, but talking about my resignation was scarier than ever, especially after hearing a terrifying story about her. According to our seniors, Ms. Old Maid had such a temper. She had a habit of grabbing anything close to her and throwing it at the student if she didn't like what the student was doing. They told us when Ms. Old Maid was getting angry, they tried to hide all pairs of scissors in a drawer before the teacher would notice. When I entered the room where she was, I looked around carefully and made sure nothing sharp would be nearby. To make her calm, I needed to avoid any complaints that might upset her. So I didn't mention anything about unfairness in the club nor my pathetic career plan. To my surprise, she was unexpectedly calm. I finally quit the broadcasting club to focus on music lessons and preparations for the college exam.

Seriously, a 40-minute commute (one way!) was too long just to pedal my bike. On the other hand, while other students could study on their commute (on their walk, on the bus, or on the train), we, the bike commuters, just got to bike. How could we study while biking on the busy street?

At first, I killed my bike commuting time by chatting with my commuting pal, Yoshi. But I had enough of her complaints about being in the loser school. I finally decided to be a solo commuter because Yoshi just couldn't stop her "loser" talk like, "If I were in the West High School, I wouldn't have to wear this uncool green skirt in summer."

After the midterm exams, she would ask, "What did you write for question 2 in math? What about question 4 in English?" I would tell her, "I don't remember a thing." In fact, I didn't look behind. I didn't have to answer everything right. I was somewhat optimistic and hopeful. I was done and couldn't change anything. I just let go of what had passed. Instead, I was crossing my fingers very tightly. Some teachers would miscalculate the total points so I would have a bonus. If some of the teachers were too sleepy to catch errors on my test paper, it would be another bonus!

Yoshi was too nervous about every little academic outcome. She was in the denial stage even after many months since high school life started. I would say, "Yoshi, it's done, why don't you forget about it? Let's talk about tomorrow's test subjects." Yoshi would agree in a moment, "I know, that is a great idea." But after a couple of minutes of conversation, she would go back to the topic about the last test we just finished. I became very exhausted.

The next morning, I decided not to wait for Yoshi. I felt great. I was free! I took a red pocket-sized English word book from the basket in front of the handlebars. The little book fit in my left hand perfectly. Mr. Seaweed picked 20 words each week for the word test from this book. Repeating the Japanese definition and the English words back and forth made sure I memorized them all perfectly. Mr. Seaweed picked only 20 words out of almost 40 words in his weekly list.

Other days had similar drills: Classic Japanese language, Chinese poems, Chinese characters, world history quiz, etc. Sometimes these demanding quizzes overlapped on one day. Soon I mastered how to maneuver my bike, my left hand holding the handle, and my right holding a mini-book or a notepad in a sophisticated way on the busy street. My bike commuting time became "cramming" time for the quizzes instead of time where I was the audience for Loser Talk. Let me say, it was a good move. Finally, I started pedaling at the green light.

Counseled High School Girls

"Hey, yo!" a high school boy called me from behind. The girls in my high school were not allowed to be friends with boys of any kind. If you were involved with boys, your future would be destroyed... That was the message Ms. Queen and other teachers repeated over and over.

"If you have time for boys, you must study because you don't want to be a loser anymore. You have to pass the prestigious college exams," they would say. Having a boyfriend was a crime in our school. Some of our friends had been sent to the punishment room with a closed door. Sarcastically, this room was called the "Counseling Room."

None of us had a good image about the word "counseling." That was the place where the troubled boy-crazy girls would end up for their punishment. These troubled girls would be our stars because immediately after they were released from the detention period, they would always report back to us. We were innocent yet curious about these teenage girls' mischiefs. The closed counseling room was harsher than what we predicted.

Here were some lectures from our favorite "troubled" girls:

- *If you go to the counseling room instead of the regular classroom, you have to arrive thirty minutes earlier than regular students and leave thirty minutes after school's out. So you will not be visibly identified as a troubled student.*
- *You have to copy the school rules 30 times a day.*
- *You have to carry two gallons of water in huge kettles in both hands from the water station to the teacher's lounge before the school staff arrives.*
- *You have to straighten your hair even if your hair has natural curls. You have to hem your skirt higher than your knee.*
- *You have to show your remorse (tears are often a good idea) about what you have done.*
- *You have to promise you are not going to see this specific boy or other boys again.*

- *You must not talk about anything that has happened in the counseling room.*

We would all exclaim, "Wow! That is amazing!" "You are so brave!" "What's your boyfriend up to?" "When are you going back to get your hair permed again?" Our lunch break chat would pass by so quickly with millions of Q&As. One of the girls stuck her index finger up and shook it. "Don't ever see the boys in your uniform within a three-mile radius of school property. Then, you will stay away from the counseling room."

After all of the incredible "live" lectures from "real" people, my head turned around to the boy calling me, "Hey, yo," in a school uniform at the intersection one mile from school. "Oh! Hi, Baby Powder. Good morning." I continued exclaiming, "You look so tall since I saw you last time. Glad you eventually started growing!"

This high school boy was Baby Powder who was my former classmate in Ms. Takahashi's class. He used to have unusual natural soft curly hair that reminded us of baby powder. To account for his baby face and his size, we called him Baby Powder in the fifth and sixth grade while we were jump roping. His legs were really white and skinny like Bambi's, extending out from his shorts.

One day after cleaning time, he slipped in front of the bathroom entrance. This accident caused severe trouble in one of his skinny Bambi knees. It showed not only blood but also the most grotesque flesh I have ever seen. He was transferred to the hospital with an ambulance. We, his fellow classmates, sighed, "Man, I wish I could be on the ambulance ride. Baby Powder gets to ride a cool ambulance with a siren." That was our kind of joke that we always had. While people were down and worried about something, someone always would cheer us up with something uplifting or funny to ease our hearts.

A few months after Baby Powder recovered from his knee injury, Ms. Takahashi announced, "Baby Powder is in the hospital again. This time, he has appendicitis."

Now, four years after our elementary school graduation, his head was shaved because of the athletic students' code. His beautiful curly soft hair was completely gone. His voice was as low and sturdy as the fish merchant, Peko. His face was still cute, but I was so jealous of the boys my age who were growing so fast and becoming taller than girls. And he was skinny! The no-rice diet was not necessary. I hardly believed that Baby Powder used to be a baby to us!

We caught up with each other until Baby Powder turned his bike towards his school. That was a close call. I talked to a boy in my uniform within a three-mile radius of our school property. After saying goodbye, I dropped my eyes onto my little red English word book and finished studying until I was ten feet in front of the school's gate.

Every day, a team from the Discipline Committee and their supervisor greeted us at the gate. At the same time, they checked the girls' attire to make sure that their hair was not artificially permed, dyed, or too long over their collar, and that their skirts were not too short or too long. On one October day, I was stopped by a teacher on the committee. I got off from my bike. He looked at my hands and said, "Why are you wearing gloves?" Yes, I wore gloves in October. My fingers were cold. My fingers' color would blanch to a pale-white color when they were exposed to cold temperatures. "What's wrong with protecting my fingers?" I asked him. The discipline teacher said, "October is too early to wear gloves, no matter how cold your fingers are." I obediently took my gloves off right in front of him. Then, I pushed my bike to the bike rack with my frozen fingers.

I was expected to be a very good student. I had no choice but to comply. Performing well was an expectation. Therefore, there was no compliment for doing well. It was a celebration for me, however, because no one had any reason to complain.

Generally speaking, people in Japan didn't praise kids just because they were good students. Only when they had done something extraordinary, like saving someone's life or winning the national contests, were their parents satisfied. If they missed from being perfect, their parents would make them feel miserable.

What would I choose? Being a quiet, good kid to make peace or bragging about how good I was just because no one noticed me? Although I desperately needed someone who would acknowledge the beauty in me, I never initiated any action. I was the heavy weight of a pendulum, swaying back and forth. Instead of using a purposeful force to stop, I just let my weight swing. I never stopped to ask questions. As long as I was quiet and obedient, the pendulum kept swinging. This made adults happy and peaceful. But it didn't necessarily work well for me.

Respect vs. Dictatorship

In fact, some questions had gradually grown in me. I started to see things that were not just right.

Grandma Fumi moved into our new house.

She yelled clear from the garden to upstairs where I was, "Get my tea!" I paused and wondered, "Wait a minute. Is she asking me for something she wants? And is she demanding this with an angry voice and without the magic word, 'please'?"

I walked downstairs and saw her. "Would it be, 'Please bring my tea' because you are asking me your own favor?" I challenged her. Fumi exploded, "How dare you talk back to me like that! You have to do what you are told to do no matter what." I sickeningly replied, "But I am not your servant." "If you disrespect your grandmother, you will be a rotten. Don't you ever talk to me like that!" Although Fumi's reasons didn't satisfy me at all, I had to boil some water in the kitchen and bring her tea anyway.

Another time when it was about to rain outside, Fumi yelled, "Take dried laundry in now," standing by the laundry poles outside. I looked her down from the upstairs' veranda. She was just standing, not even looking like she was trying to help with the dried laundry herself. I argued with her, "Why are you standing right there and doing nothing? I would love to help if you ask me, 'please help.' But why do I have to do everything for you? You are capable to do the same labor." My pure questions ignited her fireball.

Fumi ignored all questions or disagreement about what she said and did. Everybody younger than her should be obedient to her. And it was obvious in our family that everybody else was younger than her. It wouldn't matter if it was reasonable or not reasonable, elders must get what they want. No questions were allowed. This tradition was passed on from generation to generation and had poisoned the individual's voice. Well, nobody might care about this issue but me.

Father and Brother were definitely the candidates to be the next Fumi. They would make more arrogant demands because they were first-born boys in the family. I was barely breathing the thinning air around me at home. Speaking up often would cause such ugly endings.

I witnessed the flying rice bowl at the glass cabinet with uncontrollable rage. I was terrified by the classic tape recorder thrown down from upstairs' veranda to the front yard and miserably broken in pieces.

My sister reports the chainsaw brutally chopped off all of the trees in the yard shortly after some nasty word exchanges between Fumi and Father, with Fumi's screaming as the background. These were only a few of the examples when Father got out of control because someone challenged him. And apparently, he couldn't control logically so he decided to explode. I never appreciated it no matter what the reasons behind the situation. I couldn't grow my respect in adults who would threaten others by their anger.

Also, I questioned a society that would allow "elders'" selfishness. Some adults easily misinterpreted the difference between the true concept of "respect" and demanding others to exercise quite selfishly. I was scared of some portion of their blood flowing through my veins. I refused to believe it. I shouldn't be here, and I don't belong here. I had to get out.

Bike in the Rain

Rainy days were not my favorite kind of days, even without any ugly rain boots. It was pretty miserable for bike commuters. Wrapping up the school bags with plastic bags to tie on my bike, I put on my rain jacket with a hood. My rain jacket did not offer me full protection from the rain. Most of the time, I would get wet anyway during the 40 minutes of biking, especially my feet, with wet socks in the tennis shoes. My bangs were dripping all down my face. Also, it was not a good deal at all because my last minute quiz cramming method was not an option in the rain.

When a typhoon was close to our region, the situation became worse, as you could imagine. By the time I arrived at school with my mighty pedaling effort against the strong wind, my bangs were dripping and my skirt and socks were soaking like after diving into the pool. I undressed my rain jacket in the covered bike parking lot. Then I covered it over my bike like other students, hoping it would get dried by the end of the day.

If the sky cleared at the end of the day, I just folded it and shoved it into my bike basket. The problem was when the rain kept falling throughout a day even after the end of class. I had to put the wet rain jacket on again. It was not a cool routine for teenage girls. In the classroom, our fellow bike commuters looked and acted similar to me in the morning. We changed our wet skirt to P.E. pants so the skirt would get dried behind the chair by the end of the day. We assumed teachers would understand for the circumstances of why we would not be in full uniform. That assumption was wrong.

One Modern Japanese Language Arts teacher hated when girls "partially" and "inappropriately" wore their uniforms. She didn't like the combination of the school uniform and P.E. pants. Although it was obvious why we looked like this, she asked, "Why are you wearing P.E. pants?" One of us would reply, "Because my skirt is soaking wet." A teacher immediately raised her voice, "No matter how wet, you must be in full uniform to respect your teacher in class. Anybody who has P.E. pants on must stand on your desk during my lesson today." She was not kidding.

Five bike commuters who had miserably managed their soaking wet uniforms ended up standing on the desktop as a punishment during the entire lesson. There was no flexibility at all in her discipline. Was this punishment better than hitting your head? The public humiliation was damaging the teenage girls' self-esteem, as bad as the physical punishment. On the next rainy day, I would keep my wet skirt on and deal with the discomfort, even if I would feel water seep into my underwear.

It rained even harder after school. Even though I would be wet with my rain jacket, I would wear it anyway and pedal home. Strong wind hit my face continuously with massive amounts of rain. Not only skirt and socks, I also felt damp in my shirt. It was not a good deal. I had nothing to do but pedal.

About three–quarters of a mile from home, I heard the thunder extremely loud. I wasn't scared because my whole focus was to pedal. At that very moment, a zigzagged bright shining straight line of light dug into the water ditch by the rice field where I was riding by. It took less than 0.0001 second. The fantastic lightning show just happened right here by my bike. Wait! Was I about to get hit by the lightning? I was glad I didn't wear metal on top of my head. I was not ready to be a scientific experiment myself. The exciting adventure was great, but once was more than enough.

Assembly in the Rain

The next day, all of the mammoth-sized number of girls gathered outside for the Monday morning school assembly. Traditionally, the Japanese principals gave lectures every Monday in most of the elementary, junior high, and high schools, even loser schools, almost no exception. Our principal looked like a very frail old man. As he stood on the platform, all of the thousand girls in the mammoth school bowed to him for three seconds. I didn't pay much attention to what he was talking about, but it was supposed to be a "meaningful" lecture. Standing without any movement and talking was torture for only one minute. This lecture had been almost twelve minutes.

I noticed the shadow falling down in the sixth row from my spot. "Someone over there fell," I turned around to whisper Naomi. My eyes didn't meet hers. Her eyes were not focusing. She just nodded, though. Thump! Right behind me, my friend Naomi collapsed onto the ground. I waved to Ms. Queen to get help. Well, the principal's lecture was simply too long. "He needs to quit right away," I wish I could tell him right then. To my surprise, he didn't seem to stop his story.

Before another student fell, it started raining. First it was just a few little drops. Then it developed into a sprinkling, and then to a shower. The old principal was still talking in the rain. Buzzing here, murmuring there, a mammoth-sized number of girls were now out of control. "It's raining!" "When does he finish his lecture?" "My hair is getting wet!"

All of the sudden, a middle-aged P.E. teacher, Mr. Obana, grabbed the microphone and roared, "Be quiet! Shut your mouths! Stay still! There has been no rain that has never stopped in history!"

Every girl froze for one second trying to comprehend what they just heard. We were not as stupid as the P.E. teacher thought we were. He fell into contempt by receiving over one thousand girls' criticizing stares. The Monday morning assembly was lamely dismissed within one minute after Mr. Obana stepped down.

To the Foreign World

The Classic Japanese Literature and Chinese Poetry teacher, Ms. Bamboo, walked into our classroom. Wearing a navy blue silky sleeveless dress, she didn't seem to care about the private girls' high school's teacher's "dress code." One of the former counselor room convicts overheard about the teacher's dress code during her two-gallon kettle routine. "Female teachers should not wear any clothing that may potentially expose their armpits."

Ms. Bamboo often threw quite an irresistible sidebar talk show during class, which attracted the mammoth school's little birds in a cage. Perhaps she had been telling the same stories over the years to get her students' attention. "When I was a graduate student in Osaka, I fell in love with a guy from the foreign country," her love story always began with her nostrils wide open. It was hard to imagine our own teacher once fell in love with a foreigner. We were not even allowed to have boyfriends. I had never seen any foreigners in person besides my Chinese friend, Excellent Flower. People wouldn't consider Chinese as foreign. When Japanese made reference to a "foreigner," that meant Caucasian with shiny blonde hair and blue eyes, just like the figure I had longed for as "French" since I was in kindergarten.

Ms. Bamboo revealed her ex-boyfriend was from Budapest. We heard the word "buta-pesuto" instead of Budapest. Budapest was a very foreign sound to all of us. It didn't sound attractive to us at all. In fact, the sound of "buta" means "pig" and "pesuto" means "plague" in Japanese. We developed our imagination of Ms. Bamboo's ex-boyfriend's home city as the unsanitary muddy place where ugly animals roam.

At least Budapest was in Europe, so he was considered to be a foreigner.

Her favorite line soon appeared to be, "I followed after him to Budapest with only one suitcase. I didn't think about anything else but him."

Long story short, Ms. Bamboo dramatically reunited with her boyfriend in his territory, but her love and passion for him were not quite strong enough to overcome several cultural challenges. Dragging her broken heart, she decided to leave him behind. Moving back to Japan was not hard at all because her only belongings were contained in one suitcase after all. Ms. Bamboo completed the graduate studies and decided to dedicate her life to classic Japanese literacy and high school girls' education.

Love at first sight must have drained too much energy out of her. The Budapest guy was Ms. Bamboo's first and last guy in her love life. She preferred not to afford another one.

Crazy Rules

"Well, you are smart, so you will find out your way anyway," said my friend Taku straddling over his bike, and it somewhat comforted me. But it sounded irresponsible because he didn't have to have an answer for me. What he did was to listen to me and find a phrase that could get the seriousness away from me through our conversation.

His regular stop at my house perhaps started sometime in my early high school years. He visited and caught up on some gossip with me on his way home. He was exhausted from the rigorous physical training on the high school volleyball team. I, too, was exhausted from academic pressure and demands from teachers.

Taku had been a good friend of mine since fifth grade when we were the leaders in the volleyball club once a week. Coincidentally, we had the same birthday. His dedication and love for volleyball were extraordinary. His attitude toward this sport always was my inspiration, although I had never mentioned that to him. Taku had diligently practiced and developed his techniques as a setter in a junior high boys' volleyball team. His outstanding skills lead his team to the greatest victory in the Regional Championship.

Their volleyball coach, by the way, had such a short temper. He beat every player up after their winning game because he didn't like how they won.

Of course, his teammates were just as great; however, I knew it would take extra effort to keep up with the highest level, especially when he was the shortest on the team. As his own training, he had delivered milk on his regular route every morning, rain or shine. Except eighth grade, we had never been in the same class, but we had been good friends over the years.

It's nothing like best friends or soulmates or anything beautiful like that. If you really want to name our relationship, it could be called a "brain-dead" relationship because we never "discussed" things seriously.

He didn't completely understand my stress in the academic elite class. I didn't completely understand his pressure on his volleyball team. Instead of looking for each other's advice, we just shared what really sucked about a day. He would want me to set up a blind date with some girl in my school. I would want him to set up a fun party with some boys in his school. We never arranged, or even tried to arrange, each other's wishes anyway. These brain-dead topics were so appropriately stupid for us at the end of the day. Besides, I was safe to see a boy, even under the "counseling room" code, because my house was way further than a three-mile radius from my school.

Our school rules were cruel and totally against human nature and human rights, but fighting over or challenging school rules took too much time and energy.

That was what I had learned in Ms. Queen's class long ago. I wouldn't have been caught, but I wanted to be adventurous anyway on that specific day.

When I happened to see a group of boys from my junior high in my uniform near my school, my hair was unbraided. It looked curly and wild. The wild hair girl was in her school uniform, happily giggling and chatting with a group of boys in their uniforms. That was the scoop Ms. Queen got from her spy.

The very next day, Ms. Queen called me to her office. "Do you have a perm on your hair? Were you talking to the boys with your permed hair yesterday?" She kept pressing me. I pretended to be surprised and even made little teary eyes. "I am innocent. I have never had a perm on my hair. I just happened to see some old friends. I might have been a little loud because I was too excited to see my friends I have not seen for a long time." Ms. Queen sighed and said, "I believe you, but don't unbraid your hair until you get home next time."

The rumor was that if you report someone who was suspicious against the school rules, you would get a cash reward from the teacher in the counseling room. Who the heck was reporting about an innocent student like me and getting extra credit? The witch hunt was exercised in Japan, in my own school. I was terrified.

Another time, the broadcasting club assigned me to cover the story on the Japanese fencing in the Regional High School Sports Competition. I had no idea what to do for my first assignment in a different school. I was just standing at the nearby table and looking for my team. One of the student ushers looked at me and began talking. "Are you okay? Are you Hiromi?" He peeked at the players' list in my notebooks assuming I was Hiromi.

Chatting with him relaxed me a little for my nerve wracking job. On that very night, my mother freaked out. "You have a phone call from a boy!" "Hello," I said suspiciously. "Do you remember me? We saw each other at the competition today." It was the student usher guy. "How do you know my phone number?" I asked astonishingly. "I borrowed your school roster from my friend. I just wanted to say hi." Was I dreaming? This handsome student usher, a Japanese fencing player himself, too, was interested in me. Wow, this was the very first person who was interested in me personally, besides my teachers. And it was a boy! I was not even sweet sixteen yet!

Unfortunately, my dream days didn't last long. A few days later, three senior students dropped by my classroom looking for me. One of them stared at me with her knife sharp eyes and told me, "You must come to see us after school behind the gym." I asked myself in my head, "Are these girls going to beat me up? Why? Isn't it against the school rules?" I had to find out really what was going on.

These girls surrounded me and interrogated me. "A guy who is dating you is my ex-boyfriend. You will be dumped miserably if you continue seeing him."

"Okay, wait. First of all, I am not dating anyone. I am not seeing anyone. I just talk to someone over the phone sometimes. In fact, the last time I saw him was at the competition." My voice was shivering.

That was fact. But how did they find out I was chatting with this guy on the phone, anyway? Was my home phone bugged? It was a scary enough experience.

Taku said, "Why don't you dump him before he does you?" I said, "But we are not even boyfriend and girlfriend. How do you confirm to dump someone who I am not dating?"

The conversation was, of course, brain dead and a dead end. I had to solve my own problem. Mr. Student Usher and I exchanged some melodramatic letters despite our "nothing" relationship. He was even whinier than me. "I wish you could be my girlfriend, not just a friend," he wrote. "C'mon, me too. Maybe if you volunteer to take care of the senior scary gang girls' whining and jealousy. I guess you must go back to her and we can keep our own peace. It was fun chatting with you, though. I'm done," I wrote back to him.

I gave up on my first possible love with Mr. Student Usher even before I learned if I liked him or not. He would turn out to be the last person who was interested in me over the next couple of decades. How pathetic! The real-life lessons were too tough and cruel for this vulnerable teenage girl's heart. That's why girls go so crazy!

Blondie in Life

This crazy high school decided to accept the first exchange student from America. Charlotte Wesley was going to be our classmate for one year. Staring at the blonde hair for three seconds was enough excitement for ordinary Japanese people in their normal conservative life, but we got to see our own blonde for a full school year. I volunteered our family as her host family, so it could be an even longer staring time; however, this Yankee girl from Connecticut didn't prefer the 40-minute bike commute every day. Her host family must offer her a car ride for safety. Didn't she need any exercise?

One day, Charlotte appeared in our class escorted by Ms. Bamboo. We were all stunned. Yes, she had "real" blonde hair, blue eyes, and her size is, without a doubt, vertically and horizontally, American! She would soon regret that she didn't choose mine as her host family because she would probably keep growing without the daily 40-minute bicycle workout. Hopefully her diet would change from McDonalds to the Far East Oriental, somewhat medicinal, cuisine that would make some differences.

In the meantime, I was still keeping in touch with my English pen pal, Michelle. She sent me a couple of pictures of her and her new boyfriend hugging and kissing. I felt like I was watching a rated R movie in my very own room at home. Assuming all the Caucasian teenagers had boyfriends and girlfriends, my first question for Charlotte came quite obviously. "Do you have a boyfriend?" She said she didn't. She added something else, but none of us followed what she said after "no, I don't."

That was the exact phrase all of us had learned in Lesson 2 of seventh grade English class. Our English communication level seemed forever at a plateau regardless of how much time we spent on the English text and how much complicated grammar we memorized for the midterm exam. The communication skills could not be learned with paper and pencil, for sure.

Charlotte was very open to us. She was always available for us to explore new English communication options. She, too, was interested in the ways and perspectives that Japanese people interact with each other. Charlotte's huge smile often broke the tension among us over the different languages and cultures very easily, only if that kind of tension existed.

We loved watching her pleasant smiles. It became trouble on picture day. A photographer told us not to smile. Smile was traditionally considered to be disrespectful and lack of seriousness in the group pictures or the driver's license. Charlotte tried to be as serious as she could, but it turned out to look like some weirdo-figure-from-America awkwardly sitting in the front row with other "no-smile" experts.

The group pictures looked like a group of prisoners, including one Caucasian illegal immigrant in the Asian branch of a female correction center. We loved Charlotte and had a great time. She was never alone. Someone was always around her, which she didn't necessarily appreciate. The next couple of days, she stayed home sick; she was tired of being surrounded by people all the time. She desperately needed for her own space.

"I wish I could be an exchange student and go to America," I mumbled at home. "You are more than welcome to try, but are you smart enough to be selected?" my parents asked. I should not have expected a fruitful, meaningful, and inspirational discussion in my family.

Just because I was not smart enough, I didn't think I could achieve anything. At least, at this moment, the exchange student opportunities were available for only people in the "smart" category within the random public opinion. Unfortunately, I was not in that category, according to my parents.

Since Charlotte had been so popular among us, I hadn't had enough time to get to know her personally. After one year, she said, "Sayonara," to our class. Like something happened behind a magical and chaotic fog, poof! One day after her speech, Charlotte magically disappeared from us without her mailing address. I lost the opportunity and hope of the American connection. "Oh, well, I still have my Yorkshire, England, connection," I grouched.

Fishing Girls in the Pond

The private girls' high school was a heaven for the single male teachers. It was like a few fishermen dropping their line in the fish farm. He could catch within one minute. If he didn't like it, he could throw it back into the water and tried again until he caught his favorite fish. Was it ethically acceptable?

According to our gossip source, at least three male teachers were married to the graduates in our school. These teachers were not even attractive! Why were the single male teachers allowed to browse girls in school for their bride shopping while all students were prohibited to date with boys? No one could explain why it was okay for girls to be recruited by a teacher, but not teenage boys. Technically, our school's control was promoting sociopathic disorders among the students. Girls could never learn age appropriate courtship, which was pretty traumatic.

Sadly, teachers didn't know about it. They even didn't try to understand the miserable consequences of the future generations from extremely unreasonable school control. Our frustration was now targeted towards the heavenly single male teachers. One group of girls made up somewhat innocent but unrealistic rumors that one single female teacher was dating with another single male teacher. Before one of them entered the classroom, we decorated the blackboard with something like "Campus Love!" When he or she reacted, we would win.

In another time, someone put a feminine toiletry by a piece of white chalk. It was a really bad joke, we thought, but what the heck. Teasing teachers was our revenge. We were the little birds totally caged, but don't you underestimate us. We were age appropriately defiant. I never grew much respect towards male teachers in my high school years.

Female teachers looked more vibrant and sparked out their hefty self-confidence, including a love hegira to Budapest. Ms. Bamboo was a typical example. She was not necessarily my favorite teacher; however, she had the certain halo above her mysterious dignity. So, we couldn't ignore what she would say.

Sign of Luck

When Ms. Bamboo asked me to her office, I was so afraid. She asked me, "What is it?" showing me a package. The box was addressed to me at the school's address. I answered, "I don't know, Ms. Bamboo. Honest." She gathered her vertical wrinkles between her eyes and continued, "Look at the sender's address. Do you know the company 'Recruit'?"

Now I got it. Yoshi, other bike commuters, and I stopped by the College and University Fair three weeks ago. This company, Recruit, organized the fair. Each booth had a representative from a different college or university explaining their school and answering our questions.

Our school was lacking resources about colleges, although their focus was the student's passing rate. Thus, this fair was extremely important and beneficial for our future. During the fair, I remembered, there was a box to enter names for drawing some prizes. I didn't pay much attention to what I could win, but you know me by now, at least enough to know that I entered to hopefully win anything anyway. Here I was holding a box in front of Ms. Bamboo.

"Ms. Bamboo, I think I won something." Ms. Bamboo asked me to open. I unwrapped the paper, and then I recognized the word "Sony." From the box, the brand-new Walkman appeared. Sony just started selling it as their new product a couple months ago. Ms. Bamboo was the one who was the most astonished to accept this fact, "Oh, my goodness. You won the Walkman! Well, don't show it to anyone. Just put it away." "Okay," I replied.

As soon as I came back to the classroom, I blurted out, "Guess what happened? I won the brand-new Walkman! Look at this. Isn't it cool or what?" Surrounded by my friends with their full attention, I finally reached the glorious moment. The teenage girls' yellow envious tones of oohing and aahing echoed in my head forever.

Taste of Hungary

The beautiful blue sky was stretching out its arms wide open. It was a sign calling us for summer fun. That was happening outside of our school building. Sadly, we had no way to respond to this beautiful blue sky's invitation. Wiping my sweat on my forehead with a handkerchief, fanning myself with a ruler, and flapping my skirt up and down under the desk, whatever possibly could give us some break from the heat was what the girls were doing in the classroom.

The Chinese poem, *Struggling against difficulties for the sake of vengeance,* was often referred to as the promotion of the students' perseverance. The story behind the original poet was about an injured Chinese soldier who survived a long-term difficult situation because he had endured himself for many days by sleeping on the hard surface of firewood and licking an animal's liver because there was no more food left.

Ms. Bamboo recalled this poem often during summer. "The summer heat is nothing like this guy's struggle. You don't have to sleep on the firewood. You don't have to lick a bitter liver every day. In fact, you girls have more than enough calories!" She might have been right, but we would still appreciate it if our room was cooler than right now.

Before we were about to leave for summer vacation, Ms. Bamboo announced, "I open my air conditioning apartment for your summer study. If you join, I feed you the Budapest meal."

The summer vacation was not really a vacation for the most senior students. We were expected to attend the summer school literally every day during the summer break. We were to spend a few weekends to take mock exams to see what academic level we were currently at. If we were lucky, we might have one or at most two weekends to sleep in late. What else could we do besides enjoy a luxurious extra sleep on our weekends off, especially since most Saturdays were work days?

Several curious girls couldn't resist the temptation towards Ms. Bamboo's memorable Budapest food. They, including me, agreed to attend "Ms. Bamboo's Summer Study Party with the Taste of Budapest." Ms. Bamboo put three rows of long low tables on her tatami mat room. Her air conditioning was working on maximum power. "Come on in and start studying. I will fix the meal," she said, wearing her apron on her belly, and then she disappeared.

About two hours later, she invited us to her kitchen. What we smelled and saw was indescribably shocking. A pot of soup with a unique aroma, which we had never smelled before, maybe that was why we thought it was stinky. Inside the pot was something like meat and some vegetables, which were unidentifiable. Each of us got a bowl of Budapest cuisine.

We sent secret messages at each other's eyes. "Why did we stupidly come here to eat this?" "It is TERRIBLE!"

Not knowing teenager's nonverbal communication, Ms. Bamboo offered us seconds. "Have another bowl. I made so much soup for you today." We were not sure if we could finish the first bowl. How could we have the second? One girl finished hers earlier than anybody. She said politely, "Thank you, Ms. Bamboo." Ms. Bamboo offered more, "Would you like second bowl? I know you do. You eat it so quickly. You must like it. Don't hesitate. It's okay to have more if you want."

This poor girl tried to tell Ms. Bamboo, "Ms. Bamboo, it is really good, but I am too full now." But Ms. Bamboo picked her bowl up to serve another bowl for this student. Immediately, we all slowed down to complete our bowls to avoid seconds.

Being curious was a key trait in our learning. But being too curious could be fatal to our life. Think before you jump into the Budapest experience.

Donkey Debate

One of the Team Budapest members was Rie. Rie grew up in a different town, but she knew the Donkey Bakery. A Donkey had visited her town, too, she said. I finally found the person I had been looking for! We sang together, the Donkey Bakery's theme song.

"*Jam bread, cream bread, what about something sweet and yummy?*" Rie stopped.

"The song wouldn't go like '*Jam bread and cream bread.*' I think it is '*Melon bread.*'" As our bread argument heated up, we found out that we were not the only Donkey fans. More girls started joining the Donkey circle to provide different breads' names. Our discussion kept going. We substituted possible bread names at the specific point in the verse. Over and over, different bread names, but we never reached an agreement.

All of the sudden, she broke her news. "I am going to take an admission upon recommendation in Kyoto. It is the Christian private girls' college. The principal's name is Sister Mary Michael Tashiro." Wow! We were all in shock, not about her admission, nor Kyoto, but the principal's unnecessarily lengthy name. "What kind of nationality does she have?" We wished her good luck on her upcoming entrance exams and interview anyways.

As followed by the typical stereotype of gender and subject, only a few girls talked about majoring in pharmacology in college. Science was for the boys and literature for the girls. No one could change it. These private colleges, especially out of our area, were outrageously expensive, just like the music university Ms. Matsui attended. No matter science or literature, the financial burden was the universal problem among many of us.

The high school homeroom teachers often gave their students some recommendation in college choices. Ms. Bamboo gave me some of her recommendations, too. Unfortunately, I needed to turn down all recommendations Ms. Bamboo suggested because these private schools were not far enough distance from my house. Also, these schools were all girls' schools. I had enough girls' life in high school. I had to catch up with true "youth" in my life before it was too late. Lastly, why did I, who didn't even open books to read, have to study in the literature department? Because I was a girl?

My parents wanted me to go to the local national university for their convenience. The national university's tuition was way more affordable than any private school. It sounded okay, however, I didn't have a desperate desire to go to this local school. If I went to the local university, I could get family and relatives' approval of winning status, but it still could not erase my past failure of the public high school. It meant, all in all, everything finally would be squared away.

But why did I have to have somebody else's approval on everything and please everybody around me for my future choice? Flipping pages of the career books, I wondered what I should do and which school I should pick. Since I had been in the hospital for three months in second grade, I had grown a little interest in the medical field. It was a "science" field.

My parents said, "If you want to be a doctor, you should be 'really' smart." The true meaning behind it was: "You are not smart enough to be a doctor. Don't waste your time thinking about it. But you might be able to look into a nursing career."

Yamaha had a special technical school that had created many qualified and certified piano tuners. If I didn't play good enough piano as a pianist, it would suite as another path considering my music background. But nobody considered this Yamaha technical school as the same status as other colleges or universities.

Ms. Bamboo advised me, "They are completely different directions. You have to choose medical field schools only or music schools only. There are some girls' schools in Osaka, and commercial major in local private colleges at your level."

Her advice was not helpful or attractive because my interests in these options were not strong enough to become "passion" in my career choice yet. Evidently, there wasn't enough guidance to explore and determine which way was the best for my ability. College choices were based on the percentile results that appeared in the several commercial standard tests. I had no confidence to continue to study and pass the exam with uncertainty. It happened once at the high school entrance exam. Failing the college entrance exam was not an option. I had to make it if I wanted to wipe out the prejudice of "loser" in my family.

Feeling desperate, but I didn't have any brilliant solution yet.

In the meantime, I had to go to the book store. Our academic elite class required the *Monthly Radio Study Journal* other than the textbooks. I picked it up and paid my bill at the counter.

Unexpected Invitation from Future

The *Monthly Radio Study Journal* wasn't bad at all. It was rather a friendly and explicit study guide book for the 30 minutes college prep program on the radio. Every student was encouraged to listen to this program to cover their college requirements. Of course, Ms. Bamboo highly recommended listening to the program. Ms. Bamboo often used the *Monthly Radio Study Journal* as her classic Japanese and Chinese poetry materials.

First thing I did was to organize the whole book when I purchased the new issue. Precisely speaking, I flipped page by page and creased really well in every opening page. Then, I started tearing all the advertisement pages one by one. I had to be careful whether to note if both sides were advertisement pages that I could get rid of. The brand-new magazine quickly slimed down to one-third of the original thickness. Feeling the page reductions and seeing the discard piles made me feel relieved. I felt less overwhelmed with the amount and hopeful for my future study load for the month.

This ripping routine became a habit as my stress reduction. I tore my fat World History textbook and Japanese History textbook as well. Although textbooks didn't have any advertisement, one inch thick books were too heavy and overwhelming. I tore these textbooks by chapters so I still could cover before and after lessons in the small handmade booklets of my own. Teachers glanced at my extraordinary thin textbooks on my desk but they pretended to ignore it. Or they just didn't pay attention as long as I had the correct pages.

With such ecstatic triumph of tearing accomplishment, I admired the shiny cover page of the *Monthly Radio Study Journal* and enjoyed its smooth texture as each new issue arrived in the bookstore.

One ordinary day, I picked up the newly issued magazine and flipped over to the back cover.

There was an impressively large sturdy tree trunk with several branches outreaching to the air filling in the full background screen. The leaves on a tree were of course all green, but not totally the same greens. Dark sharp green, softer yellow green, some other greens in between were balanced and scattered on the tree brunches. The tender wind kindly guided its direction to the leaves, but individual leaves seemed like they represented their own lives, too. Gradually, I was drawn into this photo as if I were watching a movie scene. Even after realizing this was just a simple college ad, I was not disappointed. I was empowered.

Under the college name, some key phrases spark in my view: "Elementary Education," "Teaching Certificate," "The highest teacher's exam passing rate," "Secondary Music," "Scholarship Available," "Admission upon Recommendation Program." And this was a co-ed school. I might not have to wait for the fine man at the prestigious college gate every day!

I heard "click" with a little light bulb in my head. "That's it!" I found the school where I would attend.

But there were so many obstacles mounding up high in front of me until even before I took the exam. I marched into Ms. Bamboo's office with the manually trimmed magazine in my hand. Ms. Bamboo reacted in her surprise. "Well, I don't know if you can try this school because there is nobody who has tried or been accepted to that college from our school." I challenged her, "How about I would be the first one from our school?" Ms. Bamboo was very cautious because it sounded like a gamble. If I failed, it would destroy her successful reputation in her guidance career. The school wanted to avoid any risky attempts on college entrance. They wanted to keep boasting only good records among students in the community.

Informal Parent Teacher Conference

Based on the national standards scale, this college level was slightly higher than my current level. The Admission upon Recommendation program might be an even smaller window for me. Yet Ms. Bamboo didn't have enough resources to convince me not to take a risk. Ms. Bamboo asked me about what my parents' opinions were.

"I don't know, but I am sure Father would not like this idea. To be honest, I need your help, Ms. Bamboo," I said as I looked into her eyes. "We'll see what I can do," she responded plainly.

Next morning, at the end of the Classic Japanese Language Arts class, Ms. Bamboo beckoned me with her index finger to the hallway. "Tell your parents that I will be visiting your house tomorrow after school. Hope they will give me a ride."

Not knowing exactly why Ms. Bamboo was visiting them after school hours, or because of their total denial or ignorance, my parents were simply overjoyed for their daughter's very own high school teacher's personal home visit.

"What time do we have to pick her up?" "Does she drink?" "Do we have to buy fresh fish for sashimi and sushi?" Around 7:30 pm, Ms. Bamboo and Father started the parents' conference party over fresh sashimi and countless glasses of vintage sake liquor. Often Japanese business people make their deals over the extravagant quality and quantity of sake and tasteful exotic cuisine. Instead of hiring a Geisha, my mother served all the delicious plates one by one and poured sake before their sake glasses were empty.

With her face red and breath so toxic from sake liquor, Ms. Bamboo brought up the main topic.

"All in all, your daughter is NOT going to pass the exam anyway, but she wouldn't feel the closure unless she experiences it. Why don't you just let her go to take the exam, so she no longer would argue with you? Remember, she is NOT going to pass, anyway."

Right before Ms. Bamboo and Father got too drunk to look at each other, Father agreed, "Okay, Ms. Bamboo. You are right. My daughter is going for just taking a test. She is NOT going pass into that university."

Trip to College Exam

One chilly morning in November, I noticed myself chewing a piece of juicy steak listening to a sublime classical music station at Auntie Kumi and Uncle Makoto's house. "Don't you worry, you will pass no matter what," Auntie Kumi told me. "Well, my teacher and parents think I am not going to. That's why I am going to take a test." Auntie Kumi made a puzzled face, of course. "Why do you have to take the test if you already know you are not going to pass? That's a waste of money and time." I responded, "That is my family's crooked and absurd way of dealing with situations."

After I finished chewing the last piece of steak, I tied my shoelaces extra hard and picked up my backpack. Although I was an expert bike commuter, I was not familiar with the bus or train commute including a few transfers, especially in the big city. I couldn't imagine how crazy morning rush hours are in Tokyo until yesterday.

I felt, though, very confident today because I practiced riding all transportation systems I had to go through. I left Auntie Kumi's house early enough so I didn't worry about the time. After almost three hours of journey including 25 minutes of walking, bus, yellow train, grey subway train, and another blue-lined train, I finally got off the train. Because I was too afraid of missing the station, I didn't take express trains. That made my trip extra-long.

Walking with a map for fifteen minutes, the quiet residential area of houses, apartments, home gardens, monthly paid parking lots, and empty lots kept passing by my sight. Most people were power walking in a different direction than mine, towards the station for their own destinations.

At the same time, some high school uniformed people like me were making their move toward the same direction as mine. Some took different turns, which made me confused. From the middle of the bridge, I noticed the long rectangular sign. It was written in the sophisticated traditional Calligraphy, "The Examination Center for the Education Department Candidates" standing by the University's gate. I inhaled the chilly air of Northern Tokyo and hurriedly went across the bridge. I was so hopeful to believe the imaginary door at this side of the bridge would be connected to my future door. Today, I would grab its knob with my very own hands. And pull open with my full force.

Hoping the examiner wouldn't ask me to play D major or A major in the piano scale, although I had drilled all scales restlessly over two weeks until being able to play by blind touch, I preferred many flats and sharps. My fingers loved flawlessly crossing over each other and climbing up and down on the several black keys. Only one or two black keys were tricky for me. But I played perfectly E flat minor for the examiners. Then, I played the piano well in the assigned etude. In the next classroom, I noticed the music theory was pretty basic, therefore easy, thanks to Mr. Clarinet. He was right. He taught me everything he had to. I had the absolute perfect pitch thanks to Yamaha, so I had no problem with singing notes at sight reading without any accompaniment.

"You are through. You can go home," announced the examiner. I stood up and bowed for three seconds. Wow. Is that it? I thought I did well on the morning tasks of multiple choice tests in English, Japanese, Math, Science, and History. At least, there was no tricky questions that I had to rely on my creative guesses. I knew all the answers. I sensed I could pass.

Outside of the building, there were so many solicitors from the existing clubs like baseball, theatre, basketball, puppets, comedy, cartoons, band, etc.

These college students offered to report your result because most candidates were traveling in from a long way like me. I was caught by one short guy before the bridge. "Are you interested in Result Reporting Service?" He explained his service and said, "I will give you a call if your name is on the bulletin board on campus. At the same time, I take a photo of your exam number to send you before the official mail, and this extravagant full service is only five dollars." Without hesitation, I cheerfully responded, "Yes, I would like to sign up for your service." I took his clipboard and filled out my information. "Hope to see you in April," he smiled. I hoped so, too.

A week later, an envelope came from someone I didn't recognize. I had a hunch, though. Yes, it was from the photography club in the University. It must be from the Result Reporting Service. It said, "Here is the photo of your number. Congratulations!" I broke this exciting news to my family. "I passed into the school I am not supposed to!" "Really? What are we going to do?" My parents looked happy and confused at same time for my accomplishment, but their words were not so encouraging.

My mother lectured me. "Don't be too happy. Now you have to focus on the common primary for the national university in less than two months." Pathetically, I had to study more after this glorious moment and intensive study period.

The morning of January 15th arrived to my life much quicker than I expected. I also didn't expect how I would be reluctant and exhausted. "Mother, I don't feel good at all," I complained. My mother responded, "Well, you have to go to your test soon. Take your temperature anyway." It read 104 degrees Fahrenheit. Great.

"I will drive you over so do your best," my mother still wanted me to go, even though my body was clearly refusing to go. A math test packet was handed to me. With my drowsy, foggy eyes, I really couldn't comprehend what was written in any of the problems. Hoping I could solve one of them, I kept flipping pages. On the very last page, I told myself, "Okay, I might not be as smart as I wished, but that should not be the only reason I have no clue of every single problem." That was when my "guessing" exercise began in the multiple choice questions.

I completed filling all the bubbles with my hazy brain, for all of the subjects the national universities require. I was the first person (maybe the last) in the family and clan who took the National University

Screening Exam. I really didn't have to pass into the school that I didn't wish to go anyway. I honorably discharged myself from the "loser" trauma.

3

Exploring

9:45 am – Teaching Reading, Teaching Writing, Teaching Math, and More Teaching

Once I roll my die, my game begins. The game should be fun, right? But what am I supposed to do when the game isn't fun? I wish I could throw a tantrum and say, "I don't want to do it anymore!" I know that I cannot say it and I won't. At the same time, as a teacher, I don't want any players to give up because reading is too hard, math tasks are too complicated, or a friend is too difficult to deal with. At the writer's workshop, I am going to teach personal narratives. I say, "Let's list some of the moments in your life. What kind of small moments in your life do you remember vividly? Have you had a camping trip during the summer?" Immediately I hear many pencils scratching on their notebooks. Great sign. I see these kids engaged. Everybody's head is down. With my triumph, I start walking around to check what kind of events my students are listing in their notebooks. I start taking notes in my clipboard. *My Cousin's Birthday Party at Casino*... Casino? A kids' birthday party? Well, it is still a pre-writing listing stage, so I let it go. I will find out more details when she decides to start her draft. *When My Brother Fell from the Stairs*... Ouch! It will be a good descriptive flashback entry if he chooses to write about it. *My Aunt's Anniversary*... I hope it really relates to his own life. So far, the topics they are listing are not too far away from what I told them, although their topics are not necessarily what I had envisioned in their notebooks. I grew a little remorse. I should've presented more specific examples of "small moments" before we started. What am I going to do? I don't know yet, so I keep walking. At least, all of my students look engaged. In fact, this one little guy is so into something. As soon as I look at his notebook, I freeze. He is drawing Pokemon characters all over the place! "Do you remember what you are supposed to do?" I ask. He continues to draw another Pokemon and replies, "I know, but I don't have anything to write about." Up until this moment, I thought my game (of school) was going well. But actually, this player needs proper guidance in order to keep our game going. I drop my pencil and clipboard on the reading table. "Boys and girls, the topics you are listing are something you remember well, and you can tell all about it including rich details." The Pokemon guy blurts out, "Like what?" still looking down and working on his doodles. I take a big breath. Then, I say, with my finger lining halfway over my bangs, "Like the time my grandma chopped my bangs too short on the day before my first-grade school year started." His eyeballs finally met mine. That was when I began my small moments.

* * *

6-12 Years Old – No Shortcuts, No Excuses

First-Grade Makeover

Graduating from Yamaha and kindergarten made me feel so old, yet quite far away from eight years old (the estimated age that I could become a French person). My mom took us to Grandma Masu's a day before the first day of my first-grade year. She was my favorite grandma because she was the only one family member who let me sit on her lap. I had never dreamed that my favorite Grandma Masu would've ever gotten involved in doing something terrible in my life. My mother and Grandma Masu agreed to trim my hair before first grade without my permission.

It turned out my bangs were three-quarters of an inch above my eyebrows. Additionally, my beautiful daily-braided, long, black hair was miserably chopped. The back of my hair ended at the bottom of my ears. I was trying to make sense of all of this. First, my grandma was not French. My grandma's house was not in France. I was not quite far from eight years old. My bad luck happened just because I was not yet eligible to be French. Or was this actually the most recent authentic French style? I bit my lower lip and tried as hard as possible not to cry. "Why do you cry? You look fine. Your hair will grow quickly before you know it," my mother impatiently addressed.

No one understood my broken heart and pain just because it was the wrong person, wrong place, and wrong time. What I knew is that I would feel so embarrassed with flapping my arms in front of my class with my "extreme" made-over hair. Wait a minute. I would not even have that opportunity anymore. I just graduated kindergarten. I was quite heartbroken.

Moving up to the first grade was a big deal in Japan. Mine was not exceptional. The elementary school uniform made me look like a "real" student. On the top of a white shirt and dark navy blue pleated skirt with suspenders, I wore a dark navy blue jacket without collar. On the left chest, there was an embroidered school logo. Under the logo, I wore a cherry flower shaped name tag.

My mom put my name on everything—a shiny red leather school backpack, a yellow tote bag, a pen case, an eraser, every single pencil, new shoes, indoor shoes, a P.E. uniform, colored pencils, pastels, a math kit including all manipulatives, textbooks, and even my underwear! She is sophisticated and old fashioned in several ways, but writing the name is a ritual for her, using black ink and a brush in the traditional Japanese calligraphy style.

Grandma Masu bought me a red school backpack. That paid off all of her terrible haircut costs. I think I have to forgive her. Auntie Eiko, an employee of Father's company, gave me a red electric pencil sharpener that has three different power ranges.

School Lunch Dilemma

The best part of being in the first grade is to get school lunch with a shiny silver metal tray. Graduating kindergarten means graduating from home lunch. I was excited about the school lunch, but at the same time, I was nervous. I had to prepare for something critically important prior to my first school lunch. I needed to start training to drink milk. The school lunch was supposed to be accompanied with milk. Green tea or similar quality tea was not available at the school like any of our home meals. Nobody drank soda, apple juice, or orange juice for any meal occasions, no matter where you were. In fact, soft drinks were exclusively prohibited in my household, except Father's beer. But milk was a must for the school lunch. It was the only exceptional drink in my life—and my first hurdle.

Any other alternatives were also prohibited in my household. If you were drinking water for your meal instead of green tea, people wondered if you were desperately wishing for something, like your son passing his college exams, or your wife's illness being cured. Some people pray to their spiritual symbol to sacrifice their daily needs like tea as a trade for their significant wishes. You would say this for the trade: "God, by my exchange of sacrifice on not drinking tea, please make my wish come true."

Here was another example. Green tea was an exclusively important drink for Japanese meals. You could see your future by how the tea stem floated in the cup. It was like a turkey's wishbone. Well, a turkey meal happened only once a year, but a fortune-telling tea stem happened almost every day. If you were a week-old newborn infant in Japan, you would be introduced to some tea along with miso soup

I was not a milk drinker like many other ordinary kids. I even refused to drink artificial powdered milk, formula, when I was a baby. The reality was that the other kids drank tea during their meals at home. But they also had an ability to drink milk whenever it was available. I didn't know what kind of trainings they had had to drink milk. My tongue did not cooperate with taking the white dairy liquid.

This time, I needed to make a decision. School lunch was not an ordinary home meal; therefore, they served milk instead of tea. I had to choose between school lunch along with drinking milk, or just staring at the milk container. Thus, I would miss recess just by looking at milk. My teacher wouldn't let me go to recess with leftovers in lunch. I had to pay the price in some way to get over this conflicting situation. My decision was reluctant but clear; practice drinking the white devil.

My milk drinking training began. Step one, just lick. Step two, one sip with pinching my nose. Then, gradually increase the amount, one tiny sip at a time. Then pop a rice cracker into my mouth with each sip. By the day my school lunch would start, I should be ready to drink 200 milliliters of milk. I looked at the milk bin with confidence. I unwrapped a purple plastic paper and pulled out a round lid. A glass bottle was in my right hand. My left hand was proudly stuck on my left hip. Voila! A whole 200 milliliters of white milk was beautifully gulped down my throat within four seconds.

In the meantime, I found another fortune on my tray. I saw a utensil that I had dreamed about, yet, had never seen with my own eyes. It looked like a regular silver spoon, but its top was separated in three ways so you could use as a fork, too. This was my dream "watermelon" fork! I just couldn't believe my luck. I got to eat watermelon in the first school lunch. How big would one piece be? How many pieces would I get? Could I get seconds?

I couldn't stop fantasizing about my dream of watermelon while I was eating lunch, although I didn't see any sign of watermelon on my tray. Though, I was so optimistic. School lunch people were so smart. They even didn't show all the food at once because kids would go crazy as soon as they find watermelon. What a creative idea for the school lunch to do; bring the watermelon as dessert after the main meal like French style.

However, the watermelon never appeared by the end of lunch time. Was it some kind of joke? Why were lunch people mercilessly flirting with me in this way? By the third day, I couldn't be patient any longer.

"Ms. Kawamoto, where is the watermelon? I have been waiting for it for the last three days."

Ms. Kawamoto stared at me with surprise. "Why watermelon? Oh, this utensil, I see. Our school uses this utensil for everything, not just for watermelon. So you now know all about elementary school lunch."

Yes, the school lunch successfully ripped the brand-new first grader's dream into several tiny pieces.

During all these times, I was looking for my kindergarten band pal Kazu and best friend Miho. I found her on the playground playing with someone I didn't know. She blended into her new class, having a blast. I even hesitated to say hi to her, even just being three feet away from her. Kazu was nowhere near. I visited the other two classes to ask teachers. "Do you have Kazu in your class?" Neither teacher said yes. Where was my secret love, Toru? He was the cutest and Ms. Aoki's favorite.

I wish I could've talked to him on the black phone just like we did in our kindergarten class. He was my shy partner at the other end of the line when the phone company generously brought their real phone experience to the class. Our conversation was as lovely as this:

"Hello, Toru. What's up?" I initiated.

"I don't know. I guess I am talking on the phone," he replied.

"Do you want to play at recess today?" I asked.

After a few silent seconds, "I don't know," he mumbled.

He was kind enough not to say, "No, I don't want to, idiot!" Toru was cute and compassionate.

On the other hand, I was relieved by the fact that I didn't see a boy named Noriya in my new school. He was short and skinny, but a terrible bully. His eyes and chin were as sharp as shark teeth. Although he didn't hurt me directly, I couldn't stand his angry yelling, kicking, and throwing at times. But the first-grade year without Noriya's familiar mischief was an apple pie without cinnamon.

Thinking Bubbles

School work was extremely boring and I was always frustrated to see some kids who didn't finish the work on time. I raised my hand forever. Ms. Kawamoto avoided making eye contact with me and called out somebody else. It was worse than the arm flap performance in kindergarten. Definitely my life was lacking the stinging-tongue-hot-spice-like perky pace that kept my brain cells activating.

One homework assignment over the weekend was "volunteer to do one chore for your family." Regardless if I volunteered or not, I had so many chores already. For example, tofu shopping. Holding the metal cooking bowl and some money in my pocket, I walked down all by myself for ten minutes to buy fresh tofu. "Hello, please sell me a tofu," I literally yelled at the small general store. A large shopkeeper lady came out and smiled, "Sure." The shopkeeper lady put her big hand wildly into the water of the tofu tub and scooped a large tofu up gently, then filled the bowl with water up to the top. It seemed like she still had quite a few tofu by the end of the day. I paid, and then the challenge began. The easily carried empty bowl was now filled with heavy, large tofu and water. Both of my hands were tightly stuck by the rim of the bowl. The bowl was at my eye level, so I could see it was not spilling. To keep my balance, my feet wobbled here and there. I easily spent an extra five minutes on the way home.

When I was back to Ms. Kawamoto's Bamboo class, I had to make up a report paper about the tofu shopping. Instead of a complete report in some paragraphs, Ms. Kawamoto wanted us to draw pictures with the talking bubbles in the comic strip like format. My talking bubble was only "sell me a tofu." Most of my chores didn't require any talking. I was supposed to be quiet so I was done as quickly as possible. I drew my figure in each box. Only the third box had a talking bubble. Ms. Kawamoto asked me, "How about talking bubbles in the other boxes?" I hesitantly replied, "I didn't talk in these scenes." She said, "Well, then, make your character talk."

Question marks were all over my head. If I had to add the fictional talking bubbles, why did I have to experience the real chore? Of course, it was a secret personal question that will never be asked because we are expected to be obedient. I picked up my pencil and started imagining what I would say in each bubble. I added, "Mother, I would love to shop for a tofu for you today," in the first box. The second box was completed with, "Wow, what fun, helping out for my family," by the picture of me walking to the store. The third box was unchanged, "Please sell me a tofu." Lastly, I wrote effortlessly, "I am not going to drop my bowl."

The completed comic strip report looked very nice as Ms. Kawamoto wanted. I admitted that. But why was I still unsatisfied? My stomach was feeling sick sometime during the day. I told Ms. Kawamoto. "I have a tummy ache, Ms. Kawamoto." That was when I learned how to escape.

Ways to Escape

The school nurse's office was clean and smelled like a hospital. It made me feel hopeful. I was a refugee, an angel with broken wings, and a desperate attention seeker. I had been behaving well enough to make any adult believe me that I was really, physically sick. No one was available who was supposed to take care of your mind in school, like a school counselor. I must be physically sick to be eligible to be in nurse's office. At least, I had to look like it. I was really good at it. At least I kind of felt sick.

There were two curtain stand dividers. One separated between beds. Another divided the bed section and the main room. A school nurse pulled open the sheets. I slid my body into the fresh white cold sheets. I felt like I was going to be really sick in this bed. I closed my eyes. The nurse's slippers' sound went back and forth. It was very annoying but that was the price I had to pay. She never came to check on me. So why was I here? If you didn't pay attention to me, I should change my plan.

In the meantime, I heard some people coming in. It was louder slippers' noise. Mr. Fukushima began talking about his third-grade class. Then another teacher responded to him. Man, third grade sounded fun. I wished I could've been in the third-grade class with Mr. Fukushima if my brother was not in his class now. I grabbed a blanket and pulled it off of me.

"Hello, Mr. Fukushima. I am a sister of your student. How is my brother doing in your class?" All three teachers looked at me in shock. This little first grader carried a conversation like an adult. He called me, "Too Mature to be a First Grader." I hoped my brother was well behaved for Mr. Fukushima so I would look good as his family member. Mr. Fukushima was very wise and innocent. "Your brother is trying." That meant, evidently, that he was not well behaved.

From out of the blue, a feeling of responsibility raised in my mind. I had to rescue Mr. Fukushima from my brother's unacceptable school performances. "My brother hasn't admitted to himself yet who he really is. He must be the top of a sandwich bun, not the meat or tomatoes in the middle. He is not able to act like the juicy part of the sandwich," I was about scream out loud, but it stuck at my throat.

Instead, I promised Mr. Fukushima, "I will tell him to do better in your class. That's my job." Mr. Fukushima warmly smiled at me.

Lame Placement

Ms. Kawamoto was a grandmother-like teacher with buck teeth. Her front teeth were more bucked than Ms. Nagaya. Her short hair perm was often overdone. The day after her beauty parlor appointment, her hair sure looked like a double ice cream on a cone. Ms. Kawamoto rigorously pedaled a keyboard organ, like a station bike, otherwise the organ would not make sounds. The organ sounded pretty old. In fact, we could hear air coming out with each sound like huffing and puffing. Do-psh... re-psh... mi-psh... It sounded like an exhausted marathon runner trying to tell me something desperately. After all of Yamaha's extravaganza, Ms. Nagaya's beautiful river current, stream-like piano, the extraordinary double keyboards, Electone, and full orchestra band, the first-grade music sounded exclusively cheap and droughty. However, I tried to fit in the Bamboo class well rather than being cynical. I tried to be a good student. I tiptoed on the wooden stairs so someone would tell me I looked like a tall second grader.

I wished my birthday would've been in April or at least in May. My friend Rie's roster number was always one because her birthday was April 2nd. There was a rumor about her being born on March 31st. According to the rumor, her parents adjusted her original birthdate on the official birth certificate and submitted it so Rie could be the oldest and strongest rather than the youngest and weakest in her coming school years. Rie's parents evidently knew what "number one" in the class roster means to kids. They are even well educated to be accustomed to the famous Chinese proverb, "Be a rooster's beak, and rather be a cow's tail." It encourages you to be a top leader of a small or inferior group rather than the bottom of larger of superior organization.

My birthday was in October, so I would never be a beak or a tail. My roster number was ten or eleven out of 20 girls. It was in the middle of a whole girls' roster. Being in the middle was pretty lame. When we lined up in the assembly, shorter person was a line leader. I was in the middle of that line, too. Unless I was recognized for some awards in the school assembly, no one paid attention to the people in my position. I saw someone get help quite often because they fainted in the middle of the assembly. A principal talked too long for little students, of course, including first graders. I was strong enough to carry and play an accordion. Besides, I was too afraid to pretend to faint in the whole school assembly. All tests I brought home were 100% so that my parents would think I could survive without extra attention.

On the contrary, my parents decided to hire a tutor, Mr. Harada, for my brother. Although Mr. Harada was my brother's tutor, technically and unofficially, he became a baby sitter for all of us siblings. In addition to the new piano teacher, Ms. Yashima, I looked forward to seeing Mr. Harada who didn't seem to mind answering my questions.

The Third Door

Our school buildings were anciently old made out of wood. I was very afraid that one day a wolf was going to blow them away and we could no longer go to school. I just started my first year of this school. I had a sense of urgency for our school's exterior improvement.

The toilets were the creepiest and the stickiest, although they were technically clean. The bathroom building was attached to the main building. We had to step down from the main hallway to the concrete ground to change our shoes to the bathroom wooden slippers. Walking through the breathe way, there were seven old-fashioned wooden doors.

"Don't go in the third one," my friend whispered. "Why?" I asked innocently. With her serious face, she continued, "Because the third potty is cursed!" "Oh, no!" another friend and I screamed. "If you use the third bathroom, the dead woman's hand will come out trying to grab you. In fact, several first-grade students fell down into the hole in the past. Luckily, they were rescued."

My spine shivered as I said, "I will take the first door," and looked at the hole. A black hole. I couldn't see anything down there. "I think she is right. I am glad I didn't take the third one," I said, but my knees started shaking from squatting over the potty hole. The dead woman's hand might change its mind from the third to the first door today. I didn't want to see the hand!!!!! I frantically pulled up my underwear and quickly slammed the first door.

At the sink, I took a deep breath. I was safe after all.

Boss of the Class

On Class President Election Day in the second grade, I greeted as many friends as possible. I couldn't buy their vote with any special candies like Nellie Olsen in *Little House on the Prairie*. Even if I got the most votes, I would not be a president because I was a girl. A girl's position was always "vice president" in my school. I could still act like a president as being a vice president. A president could act like a vice president in my scheme. That should be what was going to happen. I determined to make it happen.

Masa was a second son of the traditional Japanese confectionery store in town. He was too sweet, short, and quiet for a president. People voted for him because he was a model student. I was too outspoken. "I will make your dream come true!" My message was pretty simple; if you didn't pay attention to me, I would make you. After a victorious speech, Ms. Hashida officially announced me as a class vice president. She handed the president button to Masa and the vice president button to me. "Please do your best job for our class," she said. I was elated to be a line leader of the girls' line every time we went outside of the classroom. I was no longer placed in the mediocre part of the line, at least for one full trimester.

Ms. Hashida often saw the other side of my coin. On the other side of the victory was my ongoing uncertain loneliness. She noticed my nails were long. That was a typical sign of neglect, or for a better word, ignorance from parents. "Come here," she invited me with her tender smile. She opened her top drawer to pick up a large teacher-sized nail clipper. Next, she held my left hand gently and started clipping each of my finger nail. "They have grown really well," she whispered softly. Right after the final fingernail, she opened the same drawer again and picked up a smaller shiny nail clipper with stars on top. "It is going to be yours now. I will be so glad if you learn how to clip your nails by yourself." I replied, "Yes, ma'am." My heart warmed. I determined I would please this warm-hearted teacher as much as I could.

A Reading Reflection Contest was in September after the summer vacation. I had read *Rip Van Winkle* in *the Mother and Child World Folk Talk Series* that Father invested in for his children. He didn't believe in the public library, so he had to buy books that he read. He had to do the same for children. His responsibility was over, though, after his purchase of children's book series. In fact, I had never read books with him. I had never really enjoyed reading books. I wouldn't have read *Rip Van Winkle* if I didn't have the summer homework.

Sharing excitement from the books with Father was just time consuming, unproductive, and disappointing. He would just say, "Good," in his best mood. A regular response would be, "Okay," which was not too bad. I told him once, "Don't you imagine how fun it is if you become as tiny as Thumbelina? You can hide in a tulip. I don't like to see the mean mole lady, but I want to ride on the butterfly. What would you like to do if you are tiny like her, Father? " His eyes were on the newspaper. "That is just a story. It will never happen to you in the real life. I cannot imagine anything at all."

Despite the not-so-fruitful reading experiences, some of the literature naturally rang a bell to stimulate my imagination. *Rip Van Winkle* was a time trip story like *Urashima* in Japanese folktale. Both stories were quite entertaining. Urashima forgot his time passing by partying under the sea as gratitude for the saving the turtle. Rip did something similar but by going bowling with barrels of beer. My plan, compare and contrast strategy, came naturally in my writing work.

Writing Agony

Ms. Hashida was so excited to read my book report. She told me that she selected my writing as a grade-level representative entry. My first draft which was handed back to me by her was absolutely overwhelming. There was the evidence of Ms. Hashida's agony all over my paper. She had re-written over and over with her red pen and finally decided how to revise. Let's say, it looked similar to my kindergarten practice book that Ms. Aoki lost her control over. Red marks were not really a comforting color. It just made my heart beat faster.

While I was writing my final draft, I felt guilty because it had changed too much from my original. I might win in the contest but I felt like I was cheating. I shared my feelings with Ms. Hashida. She explained that she had never changed the original content that I wrote. It looked like changed a lot, but she said she added just a few extra words. Feeling not completely digested, I turned my final paper. My paper won with no doubt. I read my paper through the intercom to the whole school during lunch time. Ms. Hashida was joyous that she contributed a winning paper from her class. My feeling of awkwardness was not so important, it seemed. I successfully pleased my teacher. That was important.

My campaign "Please Ms. Hashida" continued. During the teachers' daily morning meeting, I volunteered to teach the class. It was like a "Play School" with 35 fellow classmates. "Please open to page 12. Who would like to answer problem number one?" I called on one boy and wrote his answer on the chalkboard. For another question, I challenged another boy, "Did you really read paragraph 2 on page 10?" As soon as he looked down to the floor, Ms. Hashida walked in. "Teacher, we have done page 12. You don't have to review it." She thanked me and, literally, did not review the problems which we had already completed.

Big Round Eyeballs

The school open house was coming up. All teachers opened their classrooms to show parents a lesson or two. While some teachers organized an interactive lesson with the family members, most teachers planned a "showcase" lesson to the parents. Parents were mostly moms who were housewives. If you saw someone's dad, all the "guest" housewives would start gossiping. "Whose dad is he?" "What's the matter with his wife?" "Isn't he working?" Shame enough, some teachers like Mr. Fukushima would say, "Parents, be quiet."

Ms. Hashida's showcase lesson was the literacy comprehension with some vocabulary review. The story was about a girl who adopted a stray kitten. She looked for her missing kitten and finally they reunited. "How did this girl look for her kitten? What do you think it means to *make her eyes like dinner plates*?" I wished I could've known the answer. Nobody raised their hands. Ms. Hashida's face was turning blue with desperation.

I had no clue how to help her, but I raised my hand anyway. "'She makes her eyes like dinner plates' means her eyes become as round as dinner plates because she is frantically looking for her cat. Her eyes should be as round and as big as dinner plates in her search like this," I repeated "dinner plate" in my speech, then, stared at my teacher with my eyes as wide and round as large dinner plates.

I turned 360 degrees so that my friends could see what I was talking about. Some kids started copying me, then so did almost everyone else. This lesson became a staring contest with strange looking little children. Parents had a blast. Ms. Hashida's open house lesson was more than successful. I was certainly regaining my soul at school during the second-grade year.

Saturday, December 15th

Ten days before the end of the second trimester was Saturday. Saturday was a half day. I still had to go to school. The dark clouds in the sky fearfully reminded me a tragic memory of missing the bus. It brought a very similar indescribable worrisome atmosphere. It didn't matter if it was almost Christmas or New Years. Although I no longer had an elephant bus to miss, dark clouds slowly crept into my nerves. "Don't forget your umbrella!" my mom said as she beckoned the umbrella holder at the corner of the entrance hall. I picked up a yellow umbrella and marched off to school. Like other unpredictable weather, this Saturday would turn out just like the day when I missed my bus.

By noon, all the clouds had been swiped away. How could the innocent normal second-grade kid remember her umbrella with this smiley sun? I was skipping to home dreaming about my Saturday lunch which would fill my hungry stomach. "I'm home!" No one answered. My mother was still working in the block factory with her husband.

When I was about to step into the entrance after taking off my shoes, I realized I was missing something. "Oh, no, I forgot my umbrella at school!" I knew my parents would give me a hard time about how irresponsible I was over the umbrella. I rushed over to the factory and yelled over the obnoxiously loud machine noises, "Mother, I'm going back to school. I forgot my umbrella." She replied, "Okay, watch out the cars."

My mother often told me I was an easy baby. As long as I was fed, I was sleeping or watching TV in one spot without moving. The baby's brain synapses activate from numerous sources and disappear when it's not used. My synapses were constantly activated without any rest. Countless information from TV had imprinted into my brain successfully. People are usually amazed by the songs I remember by heart. These songs were animation theme songs, game show introduction music, and love songs that I was not supposed to know their vocabulary and contents. Some common lines from a soap opera got stuck in my memory, too, like "Where am I?" when the main character miraculously woke up from a coma.

I grabbed the handles of my red bike and pulled it out from the bike rack. I swiftly jumped onto the saddle and started pedaling. It was an early afternoon on Saturday, December 15th.

Criminal Investigation

When I opened my eyes with a slight discomfort in the late afternoon of December 16th, I saw some people looking down on me. "Where am I?" I mumbled. I felt so successful for having such perfect timing to use the famous line from TV in my own life. Evidently, I was in a bed. I couldn't move. Someone said, "You are in the hospital. Do you remember that you had a car accident in the intersection of Norimatsu General Store?" But I didn't remember any of the events people explained to me. The father of my classmate Takuya owned a construction company. It sounded like the company's van hit me at the intersection.

The company didn't want to get a ticket so they didn't call 911. Then they transferred me to a nearby hospital. But my condition got worse, and that's when they called 911. They transferred me to the better-equipped hospital. When the ambulance arrived at the hospital, my head injury looked critical from the fast and bumpy ride. After all, the ambulance transported me to this larger hospital without a siren. That was the story.

I was so disappointed. A white van? Was I in the ambulance? I didn't remember anything about that. I felt like a total loser. How could I miss such a rare opportunity? Even more shame, I did ride in the ambulance, but I didn't remember anything at all. "A doctor told us that you might not wake up," my mother told me with teary eyes. She was still in the dirty factory clothes with oil spits on her face. I was now as perky as being able to criticize myself for not remembering the ambulance ride, although initially I could've slept a little longer. At a same time, I feared if I continued to sleep, I really wouldn't have woken up forever.

Shamelessly true, I grew some kind of triumphant feeling. It said I was promoted from being hit by the donkey to by the van. I was officially the victim of car accident, like on a TV show.

The next few days were just like the drama that I have seen on TV. Nurses came and went to check my temperature and write something on the clipboard. A doctor visited and announced, "You must stay in your bed for a month. You should not move at all." The grievous double-bass and large drum sound echoed in my head, *dan, daaaaan*. "One month? You are kidding me!" Okay. I got it. Things got gradually serious.

An undercover detective knocked on the door. He handed me his business card. "How are you? I am a detective. I come here today to ask you some questions about your car accident," he explained. "Did you say 'Detective'? Are you Colombo? Where is your trench coat? Don't you wear sunglasses?" I just couldn't hide my excitement of meeting Colombo. I wished I could've told Colombo all about the crime scene, but sadly I didn't remember anything about what really happened.

I remembered I was going to go back to school to get my umbrella which wouldn't have anything to do with this case, however, he carefully took notes on his little note pad anyway. I vaguely remembered that I opened my eyes slightly like waking up. Yet I could not wake up because I was too sleepy. I thought it was a dream that I was on my mother's lap in the van. I saw my mom looking down holding my cheeks. I was afraid that she might have gone if I woke up. I saw the street, buildings, and trees that were passing by very quickly through the window. I thought sleeping on mother's lap would only happen in my dream. It was impossible to be with my mother alone. But in this case, it was happening in real time. I wonder what would have happened if I had forced myself to wake up in the van with my mighty effort. Might I have been dead? That thought chilled my spine.

Not So Practical and Proud

A few hours later, nature called. I pushed a nurse call button and asked, "Please help me to go to the bathroom." She responded, "All right. Please wait for me for one second." A nurse appeared in my room with a toilet-lid-sized, oval-shaped gadget. I squinted at the "thing" in a nurse's hands. "What is that? I need to go to the bathroom," I panicked.

"This is a 'bed pan' you use for your bathroom on the bed. As your doctor said, you shouldn't move from the bed. You even should not sit up on the bed. You have to lay down 24 hours a day for a month." A nurse opened a three-by-three vinyl square sheet. She swiftly and gently lifted my bottom and put the sheet under me. Then she set a bed ban on the sheet. When my undressed bottom cheeks finally met the bed pan, my bottom greeted the pan, "Yo, you are cool! Oops, I mean, cold."

Another nurse came in and encouraged me. "Relax. Think about if you were in a diaper." There were three or four adults around a girl who had her bottom naked on a bed pan. How in the world could I relax even if I remembered the diaper change? Yes, I remembered my Auntie Michi once changed my diaper. My bottom was nice, dry, and fresh, full of baby powder. My bottom cheeks met, at that time, a spunky fresh and dry cloth that was going to wrap up my little buttocks for a next few hours. What a heavenly experience! The bed pan was completely different. My bottom cheeks didn't prefer it anyway.

Finally, the nurse left with a certain dignity, saying, "Maybe you can do it with your grandma. Good luck." Good luck didn't happen, even with just my grandma. I really wanted to pee, but my pee was too afraid to come out in this unique setting. I soon began taking constipation medicine, too.

When I wanted to move my head, I had to ask someone to move it gently. Whoever was available held my cheeks and turned my head to where I wanted to turn it. When I was thirsty, I sipped from the tiny water jug like a mini teapot. It was always green tea or some kind of tea. My head was turned to someone who fed me. Literally, my life turned into my infant life that my mother once described to me. I watched TV if it was on. I slept if it was not on. I was good at sleeping with the TV on, too. I was more than catching up on TV programs and commercials all day long, every day, for a month. Great deal!

Soon it turned out to be just my delusion. The doctor told me, "You cannot watch TV for a long time because it will overstimulate your brain." He added that the x-ray showed a crack on the left back side of my skull. His treatment options were to undergo surgery for a day or stay still for a month. The first option didn't make my parents feel so pleasant. My month-long-no-TV life had begun.

After a few weeks, finally, I received a permission to sit up on the bed. I could feed myself. Grandma Masu visited me often with Holland pancakes. They looked just like Japanese pancakes, but you were supposed to eat Holland pancakes with ketchup and mayonnaise sauce. My tongue had never met such a sensational flavor before.

Masu put her right hand over my head and closed her eyes. Once a week, she performed the Eastern alternative healing practice, Reiki, on me in the modern hospital. Ms. Hashida visited me with some magazines that would kill my time. She also delivered me sympathy letters from my classmates. Every one of them said, "I miss you, come back soon." I hoped their words were genuine. Takuya's dad visited to apologize to me with a huge fruit basket. I felt awkward since I didn't remember anything at all.

My little sister visited me to ask if she could eat some of the items in the basket. I was too indulged by being spoiled to remember the beauty of sharing. I coldly told her, "No. They are all mine." I admitted that I was a total jerk, an oriental version of *Nellie Olsen*. The consequence came before I knew it. I threw up all the sweetened tangerine orange that I ate without sharing. I was truly remorseful, but it was too late. The worst thing was that no one blamed me because I was the poor, restricted little girl on the bed suffering from nausea. Who would? Only a proper punishment could reduce the level of my guilt. Spank me! Yell at me, please.

Miracle Clara

After few regretful hours, I noticed a little person with a mysteriously bright halo at the door. Is Buddha standing in my hospital room? My guess was not correct, but not too far. That was the high-pitched voice principal from my pre-kindergarten! He appeared to transform my agony to compassion with caring words, without harsh punishment. He brought me comfort and left a miracle.

Shortly after they principal's visit, a doctor announced that it was time for standing and walking. My legs were as weak as a newborn fawn's. I was so afraid of putting pressure on my feet. It was hard to believe I could stand and walk once again since I had been lying and sitting for so long. The floor tile was too cold on my toes.

A nurse and Grandma Fumi were holding my arms from both sides. My feet were now officially touching the floor, and I attempted my first step carefully and slowly. "You did it!" Cheering supporter number one was my nurse who looked like Heidi from the TV show. Number two supporter on the other side was Grandma Fumi, a.k.a., Heidi's grumpy grandpa, and I was, of course, Clara, absorbing the joy of walking. The best of all, Clara was the prettiest one in the whole story. I wished we could've been on the top of the Alps. My favorite France was the other side of the boarder!

It had already passed one month. I was still in the hospital. I twisted both of my ankles at different times and caught a cold a few times which had delayed my discharge a few weeks. My mobility regained freedom in the hospital. First thing I did outside of my room was to make sure that I was not in the room number four. I checked each room number one by one. Sure enough, after number three was five. This hospital was safe. I would be better pretty soon.

Uncle Long Legs

One day after the regular nurse's morning routine, she brought up the adult patient next door. She asked me if I was interested meeting with him. Since I was starving for socialization behind these closed doors, whoever wanted to talk to me was very acceptable. A giraffe tall gentleman in his nightgown walked in with his crutch. His right leg had a cast. He told me that he had been here even before me. It made him a senior in the ward of this hospital. This gentleman resembled *Curious George's* Straw Hat Man. He might have hidden a monkey in his room. I followed the crutched Straw Hat Man with my wobbly steps next door. His wife greeted and welcomed me. Soon he crouched to reach the bottom of his bed. What he pulled out blew my mind.

It was a glass showcase with a wooden frame full of butterflies! I couldn't believe my eyes. They were huge, black, orange, and exotic butterflies that I had never learned about in science. Each butterfly was pinned carefully and labeled in the display glass case. I wondered if they laid eggs on cabbage like Japanese native butterflies. Were their caterpillars green? Where did he catch them? My questions flew out one after another like water in Niagara Falls. He answered all of my questions.

My eyes widened, perhaps, as round as dinner plates. Your eyes got as big and round as dinner plates when you frantically look for something. I was learning that the same thing happened when you discovered something new or various knotted mysteries were untied.

He flipped open his bed skirt. There were 20 or 30 more glass showcases of his insect collections under his bed. Who would've expected the vintage collection of insects from all over the world? This room was an unbelievably unique and amazing museum with a 24-hour associate tour guide. Why did he bring them to the hospital room anyway?

I named him Uncle Long Leg because of the astonishing length of his legs in addition to his height. I didn't remember his real name. My visit to Uncle Long Leg became part of my regular routine. He knew all about wonders of insects. For example, there are no cockroaches in Antarctica. There are more than 1,000 different kinds of ants. All these facts mesmerized me. I was quite envious that Uncle Long Leg had been different places all around the world. Had he visited France? Some of my stays were longer than other stays. Pretty soon nurses found how to keep track of me. They would say, "She is probably visiting next door," when my visitors couldn't find me in my own room. I enjoyed dreaming about visiting somewhere cockroaches do not exist. I had been disgusted to fight over these dirty, shiny insects in our kitchen every night during the summer. The flying roaches terrified me.

I walked around my ward every day to make new patient friends. Most of them were pretty old. When I found the appendix surgery patient looking at the window, I was excited. She was about my age. But she did not stay for long. When I caught her attention, she had been there already for four days. Her last recovery phase was only three days. People came and went.

My doctor finally made a discharge announcement one day in March. I went around the whole floor to catch anybody to tell them I was leaving soon. Most of the elder patients congratulated me, except one. This grumpy man scolded me seriously. "Don't share your news with me or anybody around here. Many of us cannot go home yet." I thought he was little bit too harsh on me, but I also admitted how unthoughtful and selfish I was.

I apologized to him sincerely.

He looked shocked because he didn't expect my apology. I didn't feel totally awful. Rather, I experienced something inspiring. Perhaps I was developing my compassion through him. This guy and other patients were the butterflies pinned in the showcase. They were tendered but could never fly out from the case. I was flying away, but I couldn't save anyone like I did in the kindergarten school play. Numerous thoughts were churning in my head trying to justify what was right and wrong. This unfriendly guy might have been a genuine Buddha, giving me a lesson.

Turtle Treatment

I returned to my school, however, it only had two more weeks to the end of the second grade. Reluctantly (I had to say goodbye to the princess treatment) yet hopefully (I liked school, after all) I went back to the regular routine except a few follow-up appointments with a doctor, brain wave tests, and the oriental alternative treatment that Fumi's brother-in-law practiced in addition to Grandma Masu's Reiki treatment.

One of Fumi's sisters married for love, which is rare in her generation (most people went through an arranged marriage), to this guy named Mr. Turtle. His parents wished him to live as long as a turtle when he was born. If your name includes "crane," it has the same meaning, too. Cranes and turtles are symbols of longevity. As they say, "Crane lives for 1,000 years, Turtle does for 10,000 years." I didn't know whether that was scientifically true. Most wedding kimonos made of magnificently embroidered silk included these two odd combination of animals for their future bright wishes.

Mr. Turtle looked old enough for his name's sake. It had some kind of holiness and discerning atmosphere surrounding him like Gandhi. Mr. Turtle awaited for me in criss-cross-applesauce. As soon as I fitted my bottom onto his lap, his two thumbs pushed deep into temples behind my neck where my head was supported.

"Ahhhhh," I groaned in pain. It was just the beginning. His other fingers quickly shifted on my skull and pushed with his maximum pressure. "Ahhhhhh, it hurts, stop!" I pleaded helplessly. Mr. Turtle sternly replied, "NO."

Gradually, all of his fingers were sinking into a canal between my skull and spinal cord with extreme pressure. Then, my head was lifted under Mr. Turtle's control. My two eyeballs were about to roll down by my nose trying to get out. I didn't know whether this exercise would do something effective to my head, but he was Fumi's brother-in-law. I was already discharged because my injury was fixed. Why more? You couldn't have any doubt.

My mother took me to Mr. Turtle twice a month for the next six months. During these six months, my sister injured her knee cap and sprained her thumb. His painful treatment performance on my little sister was difficult to observe each time. Though, no one could challenge his dignity. At least my sister got a cold and wet poultice with a sticky vinyl bandage over a cloth bandage after his treatment. Hopefully a medicinal poultice compensated for the series of indescribable painful agonies for my sister. Not only relatives but also local people came to seek for help from him without any advertisements. That was enough evidence of his medical credentials and reputation. I wished I could have learned more about his secret oriental medical training and naturally engendered spiritual dignity.

Lucky Sun Rises

Despite my long absence and new peers, I was re-elected as vice class president in April as a brand-new third grader. My new teacher was nothing like my previous tender teachers. My first impression of him was an old guy straight from the military with several medals on his chest pocket. "Earthquake, Thunder, Fire, Grumpy Old Man" was the Japanese phrase interpreting what ordinary people are scared of. Originally, three natural phenomenon were chosen, then, the last word was added because the word Oyaji (old man) rhymed with Kaji (fire). This is simple word play but it's true—old Japanese males always seem grumpy. Mr. Lucky Sun was not an exception. His dazzlingly bald head was a typical Japanese stubborn male who interfered in anybody's business. His barking commands terrified most of us on the first day.

When I peeked at his raising vein on his neck, my spine shivered. I instinctively decided to be a teacher's pet by taking advantage of my vice president position. So, I should be able to survive in the military class harmoniously. I obediently did everything he said. I gave my fellow Mr.

150

Lucky Sun's students some lessons during his morning faculty meeting as I did last year. I asked the class to be quiet. I told him page numbers before the lesson began. He liked his new teacher's pet very much. He smiled at me. He gave me special stationaries. He even allowed me to write an exceptionally rude poem about him.

My teacher is bald and round as the sun. His name is Lucky Sun. His yelling is rainy. His smile is shiny. I can't stop looking at his head. My teacher is bald and round as the sun...

I didn't get in trouble by mentioning his bald head because my poem had some rhymes.

My third-grade year brought Ms. Fountain into our school music program. She was a heavily bucked-teeth teacher like Ms. Kawamoto. She wore a little bun on the top of her head. I became a convenient teacher's pet with her, too, because I could play piano. She gave me accompaniment assignments so the class sang songs with her conduct. Ms. Fountain often showed an uncontrollable temper at what she didn't like. As her pet, I had less opportunities to be yelled at than the majority population. In fact, there were only two occasions in three years that she yelled at me.

When I focused too much on my own fingers on the keyboards, I couldn't look at her conducting baton often. I didn't notice how fast my accompaniment was going until she screamed, "Stoooooop! It's TOO FAST!" Another time, we were singing around her grand piano. I glanced at her planning book on the attached stand. She stopped her piano all of a sudden and slapped my head. Bam! She yelled at me, something about sneaking, but I couldn't remember. It hurt my head very badly.

I was too dizzy and naïve to quite comprehend. I was traumatized for a couple of months. Though these frightful experiences didn't stop me from learning music. I was a new person every day. Besides, I learned Ms. Fountain was my new piano teacher Mr. Clarinet's neighbor. Ms. Fountain recruited me for her honored choir even though I was younger than anybody else.

Also, she signed up my name on the special field trip to the symphony orchestra. I was drawn into its mesmerizing sounds of symphony. The guest marimba musician stroked her marimba bars with multiple mullets in each hand with the orchestra. My spine shivered in a different way compared to the introduction of Mr. Lucky Sun. My hands were sweaty from the excitement of the phenomenal sounds. Ms. Fountain published my reflection paper in the symphony orchestra's newspaper. Only a teacher's pet deserved the VIP treatment, even after being yelled at a couple times.

Ms. Fountain organized a marching band that my parents never enrolled me in because of its cost. It was not like Buddha Preschool marching band. Ms. Fountain's band instruments were REAL wind instruments like trumpets, trombones, and tubas. That told how much she loved the marching brass band music. She played Souza's marching songs from her record collections. Someone suggested, "Let's march around the room with *Stars and Stripes Forever.*" The trauma from the first day of Yamaha crept back into my mind. I nervously stood up and started marching by my desk, but my trembling feet couldn't go forward. Pathetically, it was a scratched record disk, playing the same part over and over. I looked down at the floor and marched in one spot until Souza was over while my classmates were proudly marching around me, not knowing what was going on in my mind.

Little Ambassador

It was kind of complicated to learn about Mr. Lucky Sun. Although he looked, acted, and talked like a military soldier, he had beautiful smiles and tender approaches at times. I didn't want to be the cause of his anger, of course. But it was unpredictable when and how Mr. Lucky Sun would react in a certain way. I just did my best to please him.

On one afternoon, we all packed up and were ready go home. We always waited patiently until our teacher walked in because we respected that teachers had meetings and miscellaneous things during our recess and cleaning time. But that afternoon was a little different. I successfully conducted the closing meeting, and reviewed what we had done that day, positive behaviors that someone experienced, and horrible events that someone witnessed and never wanted to happen, etc. I even checked everyone's planning book to see if they had written all of the homework in their notebooks. Five minutes passed. I put my elbows on my red back pack and sighed. Ten minutes passed. I looked around and saw that everybody else was doing the same thing. Fifteen minutes later, someone blurted out, "Where is Mr. Lucky Sun?" That was everybody's question. By twenty minutes, the classroom sounded like a buzzing bee nest full of anxiety of not being able to go home.

In thirty minutes, we concluded, "Mr. Lucky Sun totally forgot about his class still waiting for him maybe because he is too old. Since he forgot about us, we can dismiss us by ourselves."

I organized my fellow Mr. Lucky Sun's third graders by their home directions in lines. Then, one by one, I let them go home saying, "It's okay. He would understand. Take care. Bye."

When the last three groups, including me, left school, it was about four o'clock. At the fork, I stopped. "You guys are going to walk another three miles. I think I will accompany you." Instead of going with my original group, I said goodbye to them and joined the three-mile group. After about a half mile, I was huffing and puffing on the hilly road that I was not used to hiking on. As soon as I was about to give up on the steep country road, a dad of one of the kids was driving by our troop. He offered a ride. All of them hopped into the back of his truck and said goodbye to me. I was so relieved that I completed my mission, which evidently was not mine.

The last group was safely home. Luckily, the way back was walking downhill. My school was again close to my sight. I pointed to a couple of students from a different classroom. "Hi," I friendlily greeted them. They looked at me in surprise and said, "Where were you guys? Your teacher was steaming and boiling mad."

Oh. He remembered us after all.

But it was too late. Everybody was home safely under my supervision. I had to take the punishment if he was planning to punish someone. I hurried home, ripped a page from my notebook, and started writing the apology statement for tomorrow. It should be okay.

Mr. Lucky Sun called my parents at home a few nights after the "self-dismissal incident." I was terrified he was going to fire me from the vice class president role because of the agitated mass distraction that I engaged. Mr. Lucky Sun might have felt so offended by the whole class' disappearance.

Instead, my parents broke the news from Mr. Lucky Sun. A new student was coming to our class from a foreign country in a few days. I just turned eight. I had a feeling that my longtime fantasy of connecting to the world was finally come near me. Mr. Lucky Sun requested that I write a welcome message and practice reading it for the welcome ceremony.

A new student was coming from China in two days. Unfortunately, she was not from France, but I was just fascinated by the sound of "a new friend coming from a foreign country." How many people in this rural community got to see someone from different countries?

Japan is a group of small islands surrounded by water. Old rulers banned contact to and from other countries for more than 300 years. Shogun government was afraid of people being influenced by the foreign ideas. Shogun thought as long as the country is isolated, people would obey the government. Of course, and fortunately, this dictatorship didn't last forever. However, even after more than one century since that inconvenient rule ended, seeing foreigners was not a popular event in rural areas like ours.

Her name was revealed by Mr. Lucky Sun a day before her arrival. Her name in Chinese characters represented "Excellent Flower." Excellent Flower anxiously encountered her first day in her mother's graduated elementary school where she didn't understand any words people spoke to her. I was the designated helper admirably appointed by Mr. Lucky Sun.

The local TV station brought their light, camera, and interview crews to catch a local scoop. I proudly read my letter to our new friend who had no idea what I was saying.

My eyes met hers. I smiled at her. Excellent Flower smiled back. Then, I grabbed her hand gently to guide her to the seat. My flashback memories chimed right in.

Yes, I could communicate with my creative musical waving arms. I could learn Chinese if I wanted to. I wondered if Excellent Flower drank green tea or sweetened black tea. Either way, I had accomplished something no one had done before. This was how the instant young ambassador slash adventurous interpreter without the language acquaintance was born.

Mr. Lucky Sun purchased the newest Japanese-Chinese dictionary and flashed it in front of his students. Despite his wish, I was able to find what Excellent Flower wanted to say before him, even without a fancy dictionary. My confidence was soaring fearlessly in school.

I was becoming officially and proudly the sandwich meat. I didn't have to worry or complain about the unfairness between someone above me or below me. That was why I wanted to come back to school even after the luxurious princess period in the hospital. In the eighth year of my life, enlightenment was in my sight, even though it was far away from where I thought I should be. It was such an incredibly uplifting feeling.

Unexplainable Family Saga

On the contrary, my dilemma continued at home. Countless miseries were happening out of control of my power. No one protected me from the disastrous situations as if our parents were purposely throwing the fatal and cruel events at their own kids' faces. They might have wanted us to prepare for the worst scenario in the future. But it still didn't make sense. Intentionally traumatizing young kids could be a deadly trauma of their lives, but it was not a solution or a lesson to prepare for their future.

Our new house was attached to the business office in the southern part of a half-acre rectangular-shaped property. The east side of the property was the factory building, materials, and finished blocks that my parents made. Two iron machines were extraordinarily loud, powerful, and dusty, which might have been toxic.

Mother put the dirtiest shirt, pants, and short apron on before she went into the factory with her husband. A navy-blue bandana was tied on her head, hopefully, to protect her hair from the dust. She always came out from the factory with oil stains on her face at the end of the day. There was a speaker in the factory so you could hear the telephone ring when the microphone was kept on in front of the office phone. Most of the time, one of us little siblings, office-sat and informed the telephone ringing by the microphone. "A phone call for you. Please come to the office." My voice echoed in the busy factory. My parents barely heard it there.

This factory also had a boiler room and cooling room that made them even sweatier and filthier. Father often boasted about how the blocks he made in his factory were feeding his family. He was the, founder of this business and ran it by getting himself dirty, which was true. That was all he always told us. But he never looked at the people around him to acknowledge and appreciate them.

In fact, after a full-time work day, Father usually went to clean himself in the hot bath that his children prepared, and watched TV with a glass of beer while his wife fixed dinner, did laundries, and other chores after the exact same full-time job that her husband did. Mother ate dinner with her oil-stained face.

The north end of the property was a jail-like caged dog house and a vegetable garden with a chicken coop. The middle aisle from the entrance gate to the dog house was made out of concrete, wide and long. It was good for the bike practice as long as the damp tracks with sand and rocks were not coming in and out. We had to watch out for a forklift and customer's vehicles on the property. All of our outdoor activities on our concrete property included running, tagging, biking, hiding, and seeking. These activities mostly happened during the traffic-free time, often after the factory's closing hour.

Not only bike practice, on this day, but Father wanted his wife to learn to ride the 150cc motorcycle that he purchased recently. I didn't know why he wanted her to ride the motorcycle. She just learned to drive the family car so that she could shop and transport three kids. Also, I wondered why Mother looked terrified. Brother, my sister, and I anxiously stood by the stacks of blocks. My mother's motorcycle started moving toward us. I thought, well, she was pretty good for her first time. As her motorcycle continued getting closer to us, we kids spread apart. A two-wheel vehicle swirled around on the concrete ground. As soon as we heard her wimpy helpless voice saying, "Oh, no, what am I going to do?" an unfortunate tragedy was witnessed by all of her family members. Bam! All of the sudden, her bike crashed into the block stack and she fell off the motorcycle. The motorcycle's tires were still spinning on the concrete ground.

Underneath the motorcycle, one of my mother's legs miserably laid covered with blood. Her husband viciously yelled at her, "What are you doing? You must stop!" Mother hesitantly mumbled, "You let me start without teaching me how to stop." He squeamishly picked up the motorcycle and checked if there were any scratches on its body. Mother pulled her bloody and bruised leg with her best effort. "Are you okay, Mother?" we anxiously asked.

We were in shock witnessing her brutal accident and her husband's despicable reaction. Our own mother crashed and was terribly injured right in front of us. Her bright red blood and disgusting looking flesh on her knee gave me much more pain than the scars that I had gotten in my own bicycle practices. More blood was oozing out from the minor scrapes from her arms and hands. I really wanted to confront Father and ask, "Why didn't you teach her how to stop?" But I couldn't. I was afraid. No one was courageous enough to stand up to him.

Mother stayed in bed the next morning and early afternoon, though her recovery was unbelievable. She fixed regular dinner and poured green tea into five tea cups by the early evening. Next, she served a bottle of beer into a glass that her husband held as if nothing had happened the same time a day before. It was so uncomfortable at the dinner table in the awkward atmosphere.

Nobody talked about this despicable accident at the dinner table. To be honest, the accident happened, so the accident itself was not necessarily despicable. The truth was that people revealed their true human nature by how they handled the situation. It might have been developed by the mixture of instinct, inheritance, living experiences, and environment. I was relieved that, although no apology was made from husband to wife, at least that her horrendous first motorcycle practice ended as a last practice. She didn't deserve unnecessary pain.

Fishing Chicks

I wished I didn't know about "Fishing Chick." It was a merciless and inhumane game at the village fair. Most vendors at the fair had friendly and pleasant games or items that were appropriate for all ages, like cotton candy, yo-yo picking, toys, takoyaki (octopus pancake balls), goldfish scooping, and shaved ice. I didn't quite comprehend why you had to buy a chick by catching it with a fishing pole. Brother dropped his line that had a worm at the end into the pond-like circle. He pulled up his fishing pole swiftly as soon as a chick bit the bait. The chick helplessly peeped and squirmed around in the air, but it was too late.

The old and wicked-looking vender emotionlessly grabbed the chick, took the hook off of its beak, put it in the paper bag, and handed it to Brother. Brother didn't have any plan about what to do with the chick, even after he opened his prized paper bag at home. He thought he was a pure winner. He would have been, if he took his responsibility for this creature seriously. "Consequence" was not in his dictionary. Or his father had marked off the word for him. Brother didn't even have to worry about the chick's living space because the wooden framed chicken cage magically appeared right the very next day by his father's magic wand. Father willingly tolerated whatever his oldest son did because that was how he had been treated when he grew up as an oldest boy in his family.

One day, Brother was in big trouble from shoplifting a toy in the toy store. A day after he was viciously, physically, and intensively punished of this crime by his father, he played as happily as if nothing had happened. The last time I had seen him, he was miserably tied with a rope on the column like a prisoner in the movie. How did he become free from Father's anger? Did he forgive Brother? Father's anger hadn't gone. As soon as Father saw his son, his rage erupted. Unrealistically, Mother was beaten by her husband instead! She untied Brother's rope when her son wanted to go to the bathroom. She didn't tie him again. Father was enraged to see his son without a rope on his hands when he got home. His father rescued him by placing the responsibility onto someone else, instead of his son. His oldest son knew how to manipulate his doting parents by taking advantage of just being the oldest son.

A chick started to look gross in a transformation from a chick to a chicken. It was not my pet after all, so I quit going to the chicken cage for a while. Brother caught more chicks and there were three chickens in the cage before I knew it. When we first found an egg in the chicken cage, we were so excited. I fed the chickens and gave them water when I was asked, hoping I could find an egg. But I couldn't stand their smell. When they tried to come close to me, their uncoordinated neck movement grossed me out. I was disgusted by their eyes, beaks, crests, and especially sharp-nailed feet while changing their water. I avoided looking at them. I quickly finished the chore, tried to keep them inside when I came out, and shut the door immediately. I begged for my resignation from chicken duty at the dinner table because I was terrified of them. I couldn't take it anymore.

Luckily, I made a deal by adding the extra chore at home. Next day, my sister, an animal lover, reported, "A chicken ate an egg." The chickens became malicious day by day. Another report of my sister said, "One chicken got hurt. It has blood." It was very evident some bullying was going on in the chicken cage and it was uncontrollable. They were not happy. I didn't know how many times Brother took care of them. They were not loved. Had they been fed properly? They were all uncontrollably savage now.

Finally, Father stood up and said, "Bring the butcher knife." We all followed him as he ordered. I dragged my feet holding my sister's hand, trying to catch up to the group. He opened the chicken cage door and grabbed the neck of the bully chicken. I closed my eyes with my sister. When I heard the last ruthless squeaking from this creature, I opened my eyes. A headless chicken was running back and forth in the vegetable garden. I felt so sick. I closed my eyes again and pulled my sister's hand and said, "We have to go home." Father bragged about his malicious and victorious chicken murder story to his wife. His son applauded Father's victory.

Father added that he put the chicken body into the meat machine to make chicken burger meat. The bulldogs that lived next to the chicken cage ate it for their dinner. This whole process was beyond disgusting. Father confidently declared that there were no more bullies in the chicken cage. The next day, one of the remaining two chickens was violently attacked by the other. Father repeated the same procedure on the new bully. His bulldogs were joyous. His daughters were traumatized forever.

Little Kid Handler

About one hour after the factory's machines turned off, the bulldogs were out from their dog jail (a.k.a., cage). They roamed around in the large concrete property. Buying, breeding, and selling dogs were initially Father's hobbies. It became his obsession, but all the dog chores like scooping poop, feeding, watering, and trimming were on his children's hands. Mother became an instant mid-wife when a dog delivered babies as well as a casket builder.

The first male bulldog was named Taro. The Japan Kennel Club issued him a doggy birth certificate identified as a son of champions. Father took him and me to the dog shows on the weekends. We traveled many hours in the car. Grandma Fumi sewed my new pants and corduroy jacket before the dog shows. Sometimes I slept with Taro in the backseat although he smelled stinky and drooled on me.

Prior to my debut at the dog show, Father gave me some lessons on how to walk Taro and how to show him to win. In addition to owning a champion breed, Father thought that the dog show judges were normally easy on little kid handlers. That was how I became a handler. Taro's head should be up all the time. I held the leash a couple of feet straight up from his collar to be able to control his movement.

Taro and I walked side by side about a foot apart from each other. When the judges stopped me from walking in the circle, I took Taro to the center with fellow bulldogs (sometimes with different breeds) and their handlers. My left hand kept his leash up the whole time to pull his chin up. My right hand was placed in his crotch under his tail. In between my index finger and middle finger, and between my middle finger and ring finger, I had to feel each of Taro's testicles so I could maneuver and adjusted his whole body straight.

A full awkwardness spread over my right hand, maybe because my age was still one when I hadn't learned a male's anatomy quite yet. When finally his body looked straight and tight, we froze for a moment. The three judges put their heads together and whispered about the best in show. One of the judges pointed his pen to show an action. "You are out," he said to one dog and another.

Taro was one of the final two and kept himself tall and still. A mustached judge brought a three-foot magnificently tall golden trophy. Then, he put it down conscientiously in front of Taro and announced, "The best in show is Taro and the little kid handler!" Taro swept trophies in every show we went to until one day my mother found his body hard and cold in his dog prison. It was the hottest day of the year. He was dehydrated, according to my mother who now was an instant canine funeral manager.

Mad Animals

Our trophy cabinet was too full, but Father's ambition never stopped. However, despite his effort and dedication to the dog shows, other dogs didn't win as big as Taro had done. Mariko and Lana were too emotional and nervous in the show. They were girls, after all. Around the same time, Brother brought a stray cat home.

During the bulldogs' roaming time, he intentionally threw this little kitty in the middle of the bulldog pack. The kitten's hair instinctively stood up and shocking "fffff!" sounds came out through her teeth to show her feistiness. Her eyes were wide open. Suddenly, the cat showed her claws to scare a bunch of scarier looking bulldogs. Sure enough, the dogs were scared away. Brother triumphantly went outside and picked up his cat. His cruelty was unexplainable.

A few days after that incident, he brought home another stray cat. This time, the new cat was even smaller and frailer than the first kitten. She barely licked milk with any enthusiasm. Our compassion poured heavily onto this weak kitten. Needless to say, the first kitten didn't like the attention given to the new comer at all. This caused another tragedy. She held her breath, hid her claws, and pretended she was not interested in the other cat or even us until no one was around the fragile kitten. As soon as the humans' eyes were away, the cat's jealousy exploded. It brutally tore the fragile kitten apart.

If there was a place called "hell," that must be it. The first cat had brutally attacked until the newest kitten hardly kept her breath steady. Our family was all upset over this brutal bullying. Father decided to get rid of the bully cat. He put her in a box, drove to the fisherman's wharf, and speculated, "She will never remember us over her favorite fish." The young kitten recovered in a month.

One day after her remarkable recovery, she was caught in an action of stealing. It was evident that one of the dinner fish that was on a plate was now in her mouth on the kitchen counter. Mother shrieked, "What a stupid thief cat! You bite the hand that feeds!" Her destiny was the same as the other one. Hopefully the unlimited fish supplies successfully distracted them so they wouldn't find each other in the fisherman's wharf.

More Dogs, Tragic Ending

In the meantime, Father switched dog breeds from one to another like changing shirts, just because he couldn't find such a treasurable winning dog like Taro. The next breed was the beautiful long white hair Maltese, and he found Mimi and Koro. Koro's grandfather was the champion Maltese whose name was Sheik-a-Dancer from England. Their bangs were tied like a baby ponytail so they could see well. Combing their hair took time thus required patience. Eventually instant barber, Mother cut their hair short so no one had to comb anymore. They looked funny but no one complained because no one wanted to comb their hair in the first place.

Mimi and Koro's baby, Momo, named after the popular singer, went to my cousin's house. She looked decently cared for whenever we visited her. Although Koro was a champion's descendant, he never won in the dog show or he was not even allowed to compete because he was unfortunately born disabled, with one testicle. That was the true reason why the dogs' hair was mercilessly sheered. They were useless in dog shows.

Mimi was disqualified as soon as she came to our family because she was too old to maintain her shiny white coat. Father was desperate to find another breed: poodle. A female dog he brought home was called Monroe by the previous owner because she swung her hips like Marilyn Monroe. Taking care of poodles' hair was somewhat easier than Maltese because it was more like brushing than combing. Monroe and Mark started to breed the next generation.

Sometimes poodles went to the doggy beauty shop and came home shaved on their necks, faces, legs, and bottom of the tails. Somehow, the pink exposed skin parts had a grotesque impression. As the dog population grew at home, the southern room of our new house, 100 feet across from the factory, became a doggy apartment. There were three dog cages stuck up in three columns.

Overwhelmingly for us, yet selfishly, Father kept purchasing new dogs, breeding with other champion-blooded dogs, and we ended up having fifteen dogs living in the doggy apartment at one point. There were Pekinese, Pomeranian, Sheltie, Shiba, and the largest breed, Great Pyrenees, "Summer."

Father tried to train the Sheltie, "Beauty," and me for the dog shows, but Beauty did not perform her obedience like Taro. That didn't mean she was a troublemaker. She just purely loved to run, enjoyed her freedom, and wanted to talk to people.

Shetland sheepdog, known as Sheltie, was supposed to run the enormous green field to watch the sheep herd. Beauty didn't like to walk with the leash. Besides, she didn't prefer running to walking with her shiny light brown and white hair blown by the wind. This astonishingly friendly Sheltie often came onto my back. I lifted her up to give her a piggy-back ride. Her long face was by my ear. She even talked to me in my ear. It was evident that Beauty was not for exquisite dog shows. So, Father's interest was no longer winning at the dog show. His ego, though, grew in depth by hearing people talk about how many different great dogs with pedigree he owned in his house.

The Great Pyrenees was extremely large as an adult with beautiful white hair that didn't require frequent combing. Summer was born the same size as other grown dogs and grew up with other adult dogs in our house. Poor Summer, she wouldn't realize how big and strong she was even though she was still a baby. Although she was almost as big as me, she still wanted to play just like a baby with others.

My little cousin Ken was very curious about Summer who was way bigger than he was. They played both like puppies until we heard terrifying screaming. "Help! Stop! Help!" Auntie Michi dashed outside and screamed, "Summer is dragging my son!" Summer was just having fun and didn't know it could be fatal play. Summer and Ken's almost-deadly play finally ended with Ken's multiple physical scars and trauma that would haunt his entire life. Summer was sold within three days.

We were so dismal and felt unfortunate to see her go, but we also knew that it was way better and humane than malevolently becoming hamburger meat.

* * *

10:15 am – Two-Minute Ninja Break

"Champions?" I call my students at the end of the partner sharing in Writer's Workshop. Their heads turn to my direction and reply, "Yeeees?" I smile and announce, "We are going to have a two-minute Ninja Break. What is the noise level during the Ninja Break? Yes, maybe 0 or 1. Clean up your desktop and enjoy being a Ninja." The kids immediately put their writing notebooks in their desks, then scatter around in the classroom. One kid whispers to another student, "Can you split your legs like me?" and both students become instant dancers. In the different area of the room, two students put their palms together make a bridge. A couple more join to make a longer bridge. Three more students come and walk under the bridge. "No noise, guys, we are Ninja," said one of the bridge persons, warning the walking students. After Ninja students go through the bridge, the Bridge students become Ninjas. A group of visitors from the district ask one of the Ninja students, "What is a Ninja Break?" Ninja Student 1 proudly answers, "Ninja is a kind of spy in Japan a long time ago. They have to be quiet to complete the secret mission. That's true because my teacher told us a story. She used to live in the castle!" Ninja Student 2 interrupts and says, "No, she didn't live in the castle. There was a castle in the place where she lived. I think her grandpa was a Ninja." The adult visitors look at each other with confused expressions on their faces. Ninja Student 3 now joins. "You guys must listen mindfully. She didn't say her grandpa was a Ninja. But maybe her great-great-great-grandpa was." Now Ninjas 1, 2, and 3 and the Bridge students are no longer on noise level 1, which is a whispering voice. All of the sudden, a timer rings. It is an ending sign of their break time. I am glad the break ended before the adult visitors put my name on their black list. Ninja student 2 raises his hand as soon as everybody comes back to their seats. "Are you a Ninja?" I crouch my back and get close to the students. Then I look around at each one of my students' faces and say, "No, I am not. But guess what? I have done so many adventures on the road where the real Ninjas worked for the Samurai Leader. I was even younger than your age."

* * *

0-4 Years Old – Family Roots under the Samurai Castle

Donkey Bakery

Wednesday was an unusual day of the week because nobody in my private preschool was supposed to bring their lunch. On some Wednesdays, we had to go home before lunch time. On other Wednesdays, a teacher on-duty opened the little bakery in the office foyer to sell us some bread. On these Wednesdays, a little truck rolled in through our school gate and unloaded pastries into the building. I only wished it could've been my favorite Donkey Bakery.

If it were the Donkey Bakery, a real donkey would haul a bakery trailer full of pastries through the narrow aisle between the classroom buildings and the common temple hall building, while the catchy Donkey Bakery Theme song followed it. This song reminded me of Ferde Grofé's *On the Trail,* of course, with the sight of the enormous Grand Canyon's sunset. With this tune, your mind would travel to the donkey's back, holding the reigns, swaying your upper body, and bumping your bottom while traveling on a rocky surface.

Sometimes the donkey lazily neighs. This somewhat idiotic sound that was skillfully played with a violin perfectly fit in the movement of the gorgeous symphony, *Grand Canyon Suite.* The Donkey Bakery theme song sounded just like *On the Trail* music that instantly took me to a dream land that I had never been to.

One day, I heard a Donkey Bakery song at Mitch's house across from our house. My heart began racing. It allured the three-year-old's genuine temptation. I happily inhaled the irresistible aroma that came along with the silly donkey melody. Just visualizing my favorite Sweet 'n Soft Steamed Bread filled my mouth with water. All of my five senses were successfully stimulated by the Donkey Bakery.

I had to get permission and money from my mother so I could get something yummy! My mother's regular bet was a square shaped Mighty Hard Bread that is sweet but as hard as a rock as it would almost break your teeth. If you didn't want to chip your teeth, you had to suck it for a long time so that it would get soft enough to chew. Usually, my mother was not going to buy a Sweet 'n Soft because it didn't last long enough to entertain a short-tempered preschooler. Mighty Mighty Hard Bread was my mother's best friend; it could be a long-time-period babysitter. Kids would suck it for a long time until it would finally disappear. But I begged every time anyway. "Will you get me a Sweet 'n Soft Bread?"

I couldn't wait any longer. I declared, "Mitch, I must go. Goodbye!" Pushing and opening Mitch's door with my strongest force, I slipped my shoes on for the perfect run across the busy Main Street.

My old neighborhood had been a crowded and busy town with the commercial and industrial merchants. Many small business owners and their descendants had developed and passed on their businesses over the years underneath the Japanese Castle during the Samurai era. In addition to the business buildings, people, bicycles, some motorcycles, and cars were all sharing the Main Street. This small Main Street itself was a little community.

Were some things in my way across? Unfortunately, I was too short to observe things that big people could see. But I didn't care. My focus was just on the direction of my house where I would dash to. I estimated about five seconds to get home. I darted toward my house like a bull. But, in the middle of the street, something tripped my feet and hoisted my little body in the air for a second. Then my little body fell on the hard concrete ground, flat on my tummy, just before I enjoyed the flying sensation. Thud! "Ahhhhhh!" I'd just run through a donkey's feet!

I laid petrified on the ground like a dead frog under the donkey's cart that was ignoring and passing by me. There was a filthy looking canvas bag under the rider's seat where the donkey's droppings directly fell into. What an amazing idea this canvas sack's spot was! My eyes caught the huge amount of donkey's brown baseball-like dung.

The double shock of falling down and witnessing a poop sack paralyzed my entire body as well as my mental function for a long time on the hard ground. By the time I finally stood up by myself, the Donkey Bakery's theme song was far away from where I was. The thoughtful wind carried an almost echo-like music to a miserable child. In the distance, the trailer became a tiny dot which became smeared in my wet eyes.

Heartbreakingly, I dragged my feet home. "What happened to your dress? Oh, no, your knee is bleeding. Did you fall? What happened?" Holding my baby sister in one arm, Mother looked terrified. She washed my bloody knee. "Here, why don't you eat your snack," she comforted me.

In my hand, there was a piece of Mighty Hard Bread leftover from last week. It sneered at me, "Hehehe.... Eat me! I am your destiny." Madly I started biting it. It wouldn't budge. Then I realized I had to give up before my teeth broke; I had to suck it just as usual.

It was my typical snack time. I often fought, but most of the time, I withdrew, then ended up obnoxiously sitting in front of the TV in the house where my family and Grandma Fumi lived.

Town's Corner

Grandma Fumi's house was spotted through the narrow aisle between the Yoshino Family (rice merchant family) and the Koresawa Family (Grandma Fumi's maternal home), fifteen yards in from Main Street. It was exactly where I got hit by a donkey.

Yasu and his parents, an honest watch technician/merchant couple, lived in front of Fumi's house. We kids often conveniently passed through Yasu's house. For instance, I would say hi to Uncle Watch. Generally, the older male figures were called Uncle and the females Auntie for respect and friendliness, even though they were not technically family members. I entered his store carelessly from the Main Street entrance.

After I socialized with him for a few minutes, I picked up my shoes and went up two steps into the living space right behind his store. Compared to the commercialized bright and shiny watch store, their living area was unintentionally as dark as a cave. Neither the crowded buildings nor the sole window helped to bring in enough sunlight. Then I greeted Auntie Watch and mingled a little more, perhaps nibbled on some candies, and played with their son Yasu for a while.

Occasionally, Yasu made incredibly imaginable and creative vehicles out of Legos for me. If my whole body was the size of Legos, I sure could blast off to space with one of his space ships. Finally, I excused myself through their back door to my home. This shortcut didn't really work as well as it should. Ironically, going through this shortcut would take longer than the regular route just because this hunchbacked couple and their Lego-genius son always welcomed me without exception, unlike the Yoshino Family.

In fact, I had never visited the Yoshino Family's house. The keloid-faced man was Mr. Yoshino. The dark purple blotches were clear on the dark skin under his glasses. The house fire was quite unfortunate, but he was fortunate because he at least survived from the terrible inferno when he was young. Even though I knew his past, his facial features scared me away while Uncle Watch's hunchback didn't bother me at all. I had no interest in learning about him. He was probably not interested in me either.

On the other side of Uncle Watch's building, Ms. Sato's yarn store was pretty popular among the town's housewives. In fact, these two businesses shared a building. Unlike the watch store, Ms. Sato's yarn store was dark. Her colorful knitting displays tried to cheer up her business space and created a friendly atmosphere. Some projects were on the wall, and a complicated patterned sweater was shown on the mannequin doll. Often, neighbor ladies gathered around a small table to chat and share their knitting projects. This was my mother's favorite store. Ms. Sato had a huge smile and welcomed me anytime I visited her with my mother. But I didn't visit as often as I did with Uncle Watch, because her space didn't have the shortcut to my house.

In Fumi's maternal house, Fumi's mother, Tama, and her first son's family resided downstairs and the second son's family upstairs. All of them were living together in this unique living arrangement under one roof.

These residential buildings (Tama's, Uncle Watch's, and Ms. Sato's spaces are all somewhat connected), Fumi's and the Yoshino Family's houses, were both separated by less than three feet of space between the buildings. Sadly, that caused unpleasant lawsuits amongst family members and close neighbors.

Huddling together at the corner lot, the buildings still standing there barely survived the inferior bombs dropping from the sky during the war.

The American military planned to exclude the Japanese historical buildings like castles, temples, and shrines from their "destruction" list. However, the surrounding towns happened to become their targets as a consequence. Unfortunately, Fumi's town was a typical target.

After her husband was drafted, Fumi came back from Osaka, 217 miles from home, with three little children all under five—in fact, the youngest was a newborn infant. The respectful visit to her in-law's house turned out to be her worst choice. No one wanted their daughter-in-law or their grandchildren. They, too, were barely surviving during the difficult war time. "We don't need any more mouths to feed," her father-in-law coldly announced to her.

Luckily, Fumi's parents extended their arms openly, even though, at that time, Fumi's parents had about 10 children. (Fumi is the first child of sixteen siblings.) This extended family ate together, worked together, played together, and evacuated together under the incendiary rain. The survival from the fatal war itself was a miracle. Keeping their house and property was another miracle. There could have been hundreds of people who died on the street where I got hit by a donkey. The whole town's rapid recovery was indescribably miraculous.

Fumi's kitchen had a special underground room to store food. I suspect it used be an evacuation unit where family members hid when they heard the frequent war siren. Now she used it as a punishment dungeon for naughty children. My blood froze immediately when she touched the knob on the floor, even if I didn't do anything wrong.

Grandma Fumi's bedroom was on the other side of the kitchen. I often sat on her bedside to ask her to tell me a story of a Japanese folktale, the Peach Boy. No one in our neighborhood except Fumi had their own modern western-type bed. It was way softer and bouncier than a futon. I wished I could've slept in a bed someday.

Every evening, the majority of the neighbors took out their futon and cot from their paper sliding door closet. In the morning, they folded them nicely and put them away into the closet. Although, owning your own bed would reduce daily physical tasks, owning a bed was something too modern for the general population of her town at that time. Besides, as an honorably deceased Japanese soldier's wife, the western items were things you did not consider owning. But she did what she wanted.

When I visited my grandma's maternal home by stepping on the seven flat stones outside of her house, Fumi's first brother's white spitz dog, Chiko, greeted me with high pitched barks. I made it through the sliding door entrance only once in five tries without any troubles because of Chiko. Grandma Fumi's first brother, Chiko's owner, became known as Uncle Chiko, and his wife as Auntie Chiko.

Uncle Chiko was one of only two boys from 16 of Fumi's siblings. The other boy was Uncle Koma. Koma means "small and young" in the regional dialect. Technically, there was another boy between Uncle Chiko and Uncle Koma along with several girls. Sadly, he deceased at age one. His name was Issai, which means "One-Year-Old." This was one of the several family wonders: Why did his parents name their new born child Issai in the first place? It sounded almost like a curse on the innocent and unfortunate child. That was what the neighbors and even Issai's siblings gossiped about behind Tama's back.

Fumi's father used to be a famous inventor of carpentry tools. When someone stole his innovation, this greedy thief got a patent with quite a large reward. Despite this nasty fraud incident, Fumi's father retained a solid reputation among customers as a carpenter to be able to feed his wife and their 16 children. He was the one dignified family man until his secret love affair was revealed by his devastated children several decades after his death.

To reveal another family wonder: How did the two boys, Uncle Chiko and Uncle Koma, live together under one roof while they never got along with each other in their entire lives? I had never seen both uncles together talking or laughing with each other, like regular brothers would, on any occasion, even during the wedding of Uncle Chiko's daughter. The boys' ongoing battle never ended, even after the judge's rule in the court 40 years later. It eventually settled a few years after Uncle Chiko passed away.

Outskirt of the Castle

In addition to the little corner lot of Fumi and her relatives, there were so many different places to explore in this town. You could practically go anywhere on foot, even to places beyond the daily needs stores, like the original Samurai Period merchants' stores: the children's clinic, the otolaryngology office, the dentist, the electric store, the rice store (Mr. Yoshino), a couple general stores, the yarn store (Ms. Sato), the liquor store, the clock store (Uncle & Aunt Watch and Yasu's house), the tavern, the Old Castle (Mitch's house), the floral store, the traditional Japanese confectionary store, the street car station, the meat store, the fish store, and the Lutheran Church that had a concrete block fenced playground where the neighbor kids often played. I was one of these kids, even though I didn't consider my family as Christian.

In the back of the living room corner of Fumi's house, a black wooden Buddhist altar was sitting at home with dignity. In the altar, there was a picture of Fumi's husband, his mortuary, two white candles, a scent jar, two vases, a gold teacup-like gong, a little rice bowl with a leg, and two tiny tea cups. All items in the altar represented appreciation and respect for the family's ancestors. It was the heir (usually the first son in the family) family's responsibility to take care of the altars and graves in the temple. People believed that their ancestors' spirit would bring good luck and health to the family if they practice the consistent ritual.

Every morning, freshly made rice and green tea were served at the altar. Offering them to the altar before anybody had their meal was a way to respect ancestors and elders. The candles and green scent were lit accordingly. Mother did this routine most of the time.

Putting her hands together in front of her chest, she hit the little singing bowl twice, closed her eyes, put her head down, and mumbled a ritual chant for a long time, maybe ten times longer than what her kids did. When she was satisfied with her long prayer for the day, she put out the candlelight by waving her hand to send wind. "Don't blow the candles," she scolded at me. Blowing breath at the altar is exclusively prohibited because it's considered to be rude. It showed enormous disrespect against the ancestors.

All in all, it sounded like some kind of a joke that this apparently non-Christian family was sending kids to the Christian Sunday school almost every Sunday. Interestingly enough, my mother, the most serious altar prayer with her long ritual chant, attended the Sunday service with her kids sometimes. Each child sat on the bench holding 10 cents in their right hand for a donation, watching as the donation basket passed through people's hands.

The gentle speaking pastor's wife asked for a volunteer to read a part of the Bible. A big girl's name was always called. Not only did she never ask me to read, but she also ignored my confident hand shooting up in the air. I sadly conclude that she didn't know me well enough.

The best part of the Sunday school was the imaginative and entertaining activities. Last year's Christmas play was one of them. Though I didn't always get a significant role at this church, I truly enjoyed holding the baby Jesus doll in my arms between rehearsals. I ended up performing as a "tree" in the real play. Another activity I loved was the old newspaper dress contest. Teaming up with a couple of other kids, we created a dress with old newspaper and toothpicks. Surprisingly, our dress didn't look filthy despite the materials we used. It looked rather gorgeous. And what satisfaction and accomplishment we shared! After the dismissal of Sunday school, most kids directly met up at the tiny playground. The church playground had big toys, a swing set, and a sandbox for all ages. Until I went there, I had never seen a jungle gym before. Climbing up it was like conquering a castle. I, the king, governed one part of the jungle gym, and the other side was the other king's property. My mother let us play there any time we wanted without supervision, even after a visit to the doctor. By the way, nobody in town ever made any appointments with any doctors. They couldn't. Most of the medical facilities were walk-in only.

Anyways, it was hard to ignore the playground in between our house and the clinic, especially after having painful shots on my butt. I was very thankful to have such joyful memories and places in this town, even after I got hit by a donkey. I wondered which discipline brought me my good fortune—using church facilities or Mother's diligent daily prayer to the Buddhist altar. It might not be either one. It might be both. It might be a coincidence. Did I belong to one particular religious group? I didn't even understand the meaning of "faith."

Family Wisdom

"We are moving," Father declared one day at dinner. Within a month, my family was no longer living in that small and busy merchant town anymore, except for Grandma Fumi. Fumi looked disgustingly at her own son and threw her words at him. "I am not moving."

Father decided to move his family to a new house attached with an office in which he was going to start a new block production business.

Fumi preferred to live in her own house that saved her and her three children from World War II. Even though this house held countless memories of various horrendous wartime incidents, she was proud of herself for surviving on her own. She rarely talked or whined about her honorably drafted husband who died somewhere in the Pacific Ocean.

Back then, she had no choice other than to be tough. Living in this house represented the feistiness and resilience that she had refused to give up many times. Besides, regardless of her age, she still desired the maximum amount of comfort and support from her mother next door. Fumi had had special respect and trust with her mother in the traditional Japanese way.

Everything her parents said had been right in her life, even if Fumi disagreed. In fact, Fumi's mother was the one who encouraged her to have an arranged marriage. Fumi didn't want to marry someone she didn't know. Fumi and her mother sat on the tatami mat, face to face, silently. Fumi's mother lectured her. "This is the fifth visit in three months that his uncle came to ask us to marry you. You should feel honored to be wanted by this young man. You should not be stubborn anymore. It must be a good match."

Fumi gave in and married this young engineer who had an enthusiastic match-making uncle. At this point, no one expected this young engineer's fatal ending that would change his young family's destiny. I hoped she learned about him more after the marriage—Fumi loved her young husband. After all, despite of her son's declaration, Fumi chose to stay in this house, perhaps because she treasured a few memories of unforgettable and amazing times with her late husband.

When I visited Fumi's emotionally attached house, she routinely handed me one 10-cent coin to shop for something fun in the tiny general store. I could buy a prism shaped vanilla ice cream bar, a Homerun Bar, from a sweaty 10-cent coin inside of my fist. After I licked all the ice cream, I might see the lucky engraving, "home-run," on the wood stick. This means I could get another bar for free. Although winning a free ice cream bar is very attractive, the 30-cent chocolate coated ice cream bar looked even more extravagant. Since I only received one 10-cent coin at a time, there was no way for me to purchase the extravaganza.

Another unique treat was the lottery strawberry-shaped candies. Each of 50 some strawberry candies had a long sturdy kite string which was surprisingly untangled. If you were lucky enough to pick a winning string, you could receive a bigger candy than the others. I looked seriously at the complicated yet untangled strings in order to pick the biggest candy in this Ami's lottery. I always aimed for a large one. But a struck-gold moment never happened to me. I should have felt fortunate because there was no loser in this lottery. Instead of waiting for a random possibility, I became curious about the 30 cent chocolate bar called Ghana. If I got Ghana, I didn't have to gamble. Ghana itself was winning. Ghana was another luxury that I couldn't possibly deserve. Unfortunately, Grandma Fumi never taught me the "saving money" idea. Simply, I could save up 30 cents as quickly as three days' time if I saved my desire to shop and the actual 10 cents.

In my little brain, 10 cents must be used up all at one time, just like a church donation. A church wouldn't accept a statement like this: "Well, I won't donate anything today, but trust me, I will donate double the amount next time." They might not have allowed me to do any fun activities if I skipped the donation, even if I promised God the double donation next time. Besides, I would feel terribly uncomfortable during the entire service if I didn't donate at all. Fumi expected me to learn things by myself, regardless of my age, maturity level, and lack of life experience. Her lessons were all developed from her survival. "Do the best you can do. If you fail, try something else until something works out." That was her teaching that she never taught explicitly. Unfortunately, I was too young to learn her extremely sophisticated, silent, and somewhat harsh manipulation.

4

Drowning

11:45 am – Housekeeping of the Classroom

With their hands behind of their bodies, my students walk in the quiet line through the hallway out to recess. They are all happy for the free movement and their own social life in the small community called "Playground." As of my part, it is free from the instruction and supervision. And I get to go to the bathroom! I am not going to get the free movement or my own social life, but I can do housekeeping and preparation. As soon as I return to my classroom, I sharpen pencils, then straighten desks that kids pushed and pulled during the morning session. I grab a pile of homework from the blue tub and drop it onto my desktop. Now there is a pile of homework, notes from parents, a couple of worksheets for the afternoon session, and my teacher laptop all surrounding my lesson plan book. I don't notice the color of my desktop except from the coffee stains on my left side. I know my desktop is not the worst because I have witnessed other teachers' desktops over the years. Teachers' desktops easily can be the Olympic National Mountain Range. Mine is still a mild version, like the hill of our neighborhood loop. My daily goal during the students' recess is to clear the mountain range to the flat land, possibly to make it like a well-organized Wabi-Sabi Japanese garden that you could enjoy in Kyoto. Why? Because I want to dance with my students when they are in the classroom. Had any teachers invited me to dance with them when I was a student in junior high school? Perhaps dancing wouldn't be appropriate in the Wabi-Sabi environment.

* * *

13-15 Years Old – Unvoiced Truth

Junior High Confusion

A junior high school was supposed to be exciting. In fact, I jump-started the radio English course at home during the spring break prior to the first English class. English was a new subject for seventh graders. Although we had already learned the alphabet when Roma-ji was introduced at fourth grade, the English teacher, Mr. Excellent Field must go through it again. That wasn't as exciting as I expected. I didn't know anything about English, so I repeated after him without any doubts when he asked us to.

In the meantime, I continued to get up at 6 am every morning and listen to the radio English lesson for 20 minutes. The instructors, one Japanese and one American, were so fluent that I had a hard time following everything they were speaking even with a textbook. It was an entirely brand-new foreign language. That gave me encouraging hope! If I would master this new difficult language, I would be able to survive somewhere I was supposed to belong.

Our English teacher introduced himself as a home-economy technology teacher. He didn't mention his English degree. Now I got it. A reason why he closed his eyes when he demonstrated the pronunciation... He didn't have an English degree. He didn't know how to pronounce each word. He said, "Repeat after me, 'Le-ji-o.'" We all said, "Le-ji-o." Every morning when I turned on my radio, the instructor greeted, "Good morning. Welcome to the Radio English Course for Beginners!" A word looked and sounded R-a-d-i-o. I was confused. Then I realized why Mr. Excellent Field said "Lejio" instead of "radio."

Japanese "radio" was sounded and spelled as "ra-gi-o" in one of the Japanese characters, Katakana. *R* sounded like between *R* and *L*. Each of the five Japanese vowels had only one sound. The *A* in *radio* was a long vowel, but if you wanted to make a long vowel sound in Japanese language, you had to combine two short vowels like "e-i." As a result, Mr. Excellent Field and Mr. Radio English instructor had completely different languages.

The Q&A in the Radio English gave me some tips in the textbook.

Q: Why did my teacher have a different accent than the radio program?

A: There are several reasons. But you must respect whichever teacher who teaches you English in the classroom.

Thus, I didn't argue with Mr. School English teacher about his pronunciation. However, I increased more skepticism about this new language that Mr. Excellent Field spoke. It was quite obvious that the Radio English teachers were too authentic and advanced, hence Mr.

Excellent Field provided English instruction that was far away from authentic.

Similarly, Mr. Music taught Social Studies in my class. He played trumpet and piano so beautifully. He also told us that he had offered some of his original songs to famous popular singers. His musical knowledge and technique inspired me. However, in Social Studies, he was different. His eyes were glued to the textbook almost the whole time. He copied important information on the blackboard from the textbook, which I didn't think he understood well. Mr. Music seemed sick all the time in the Social Studies' class. He blew his nose into his handkerchief at least a dozen times in one lesson. Nobody seemed to care about their teacher's quality except me. Was I too picky? Other kids were quiet and obedient. I should do the same. So, I, too, became quiet and obedient.

The first year in junior high turned out not so exciting, except when I found my kindergarten marching band pal, Kazu. He had grown way bigger than he was supposed to, but his face hadn't changed much. I asked him, "Hey, are you Kazu in Ms. Aoki's class?" He replied, "You found me, my friend! It's been long six years. Do you know Nori is in this school, too?"

According to Kazu, Nori had been rebellious to every authority in the elementary school where they went. Nori would do the same in junior high, but at least I said hi to Nori a few days after I found Kazu. Even this dramatic reunion really didn't help pull me out of my withdrawal attitude in my junior high school life.

Turtle Mountain

Mr. Turtle Mountain came into my second year of junior high school as my homeroom teacher. He had a science degree and taught science only. He was a scarier version of my third-grade teacher, Mr. Lucky Sun. Mr. Turtle Mountain's homework was to copy every single word, picture, and diagram on three pages of the science textbook prior to the science class. I walked up to him and said, "Mr. Turtle Mountain, I did two pages, but I was too tired to finish the last page last night." He grabbed a broom at the corner of the classroom and spanked my bottom. Luckily, I was not the only one. At least three more students got a broom punishment on that day. Mr. Turtle Mountain was not like the science teacher, Mr. New Well, from my elementary school.

Mr. New Well always encouraged me to explore different things and reasons about my result and hypothesis. Even if my theory was totally wrong, he listened to my logic and reasons carefully instead of interrupting. For example, there was the comparison experiment. Which candle would go off first, covered by a jar, or uncovered? I predicted the covered one would survive longer than uncovered, which was totally wrong in common sense; however, Mr. New Well patiently listened to me and revealed the answer with a logical explanation and a demonstration.

He valued my organized notebook the same as my wrong prediction. Sometimes Mr. New Well stopped the class and asked students to observe my group and my notebook. He praised how well our group was working together and how we had notebooks that included all the results with detailed illustrations.

Mr. Turtle Mountain's approach was far more radical than Mr. New Well's. Mr. Turtle Mountain said, "I need a volunteer to measure the rock's hardness." A brave volunteer went up before him. "Show me your hand," he proceeded. As soon as this boy's hand was offered, Mr. Turtle Mountain grabbed it and made a scratch on his hand with this sharp rock. We witnessed blood on his hand. We gulped the air. "As you can see, this rock can cut your skin. The other one doesn't. If you lick it, it will heal in no time. So, who is the next volunteer?"

All frightened, the ending bell echoed in the classroom. We were so relieved that we didn't have to be the next volunteer.

As our homeroom teacher, he scared us by talking a lot about horror stories so we couldn't disobey him. One example was a story about his son. His son's left ear hadn't been working since Mr. Turtle Mountain beat him so hard. His own child! His military experience taught him three important things: "Sleep fast, eat fast, and poop fast." According to him, taking too much time on sleeping, eating, and pooping would make you vulnerable to the enemy and waste your study time. He said his military survival would apply to the "Examination Hell." The wartime intensity was as similar as an extremely long and persevered study period during junior high and high school. You didn't know when your enemy would attack you, so you could not relax. The enemy of junior high school sounded like time that we sleep, eat, or poop, according to him. If we didn't maximize our study time, we couldn't succeed competitive high school entering examinations. We had to study like hell.

One day after the midterm exam, he called me to his office. He opened my academic record book and asked me, "You don't like me, do you?" "Why?" I timidly asked back. "Well, I just don't understand your scores. Language Arts 85%, Math 80%, Social Studies 82%, English 89%, and," he continued, "your Science score is 52%." He pointed his finger at the Science grade. "How did it happen? You don't like science or you don't like me personally. You cannot pass any prestigious public high school if you continue this grade in science. You must have over 80% for all subjects." To tell you the truth, I didn't dislike science. But I didn't like science either. Science was a subject that gave me a headache from time to time. Science formulas didn't light my lightbulb instantly.

In fact, I rather enjoyed other things Mr. Turtle Mountain did in his homeroom. Students were required to turn in a daily journal to the homeroom teacher. Unlike other teachers, Mr. Turtle Mountain read his students' journals every day and made comments. When he could not respond, he apologized about how hectic his day was. His daily response was somewhat encouraging, a little bit poetic, and nothing negative. He called me at home and asked me to write about a certain type of essay because he liked my points of view from my journal entries. I enjoyed being recognized. Every day before school was out, Mr. Turtle Mountain spent a few minutes to read aloud books with intriguing titles. I looked forward to his read aloud every day. Reading aloud books other than textbooks was unusual in junior high schools. Even more, reading aloud to eighth graders was also unusual. I was one of his unusual and lucky eighth graders.

Anger Management

An English teacher, Mr. Rice Field, became the next homeroom teacher in the third year of junior high. We were so annoyed by his yelling voice. I suspected he had a hearing problem. In contrast, when he taught an important concept in class, what we heard was just his mumbling. We had no clue what he was talking about. These extremes were such a pain for us ninth-grade students.

One day, one of our classmates Take was in trouble. He stood up by his desk far away from the front podium. Mr. Rice Field was as red as a boiled octopus. "Do you care about what you have done?" Take replied with a sarcastically soft voice, "Why don't I?" "I can't hear you! Speak up!" Mr. Rice Field scolded again. Take rudely murmurs, "Are you deaf?" "Speak Up! I can't hear!" Mr. Rice Field outrageously continued.

Everybody in the class looked at each other with puzzling facial expressions. Now Mr. Rice Field was out of control. He picked up his guitar, started banging it, and yelled something that didn't make sense. "This is a guitar! IS this a guitar? Yes, this is a guitar!" All of our classmates were frightened by his insane performance. It continued until he realized he destroyed his guitar into many small pieces.

Another time, my friend, Yasue, and I were putting our heads down and laughing about something in the very back row. We didn't know Mr. Rice Field was approaching us. As soon as his arms were reachable to us, he smacked our heads really hard without any warning, and yelled, "What are you laughing about?"

"Nothing," we replied with millions of stars circling around our heads. Even with that episode, we could say Mr. Turtle Mountain and Mr. Rice Field were way gentler than Mr. Math.

Whenever Mr. Math walked in the classroom, the classroom froze. We were so scared of his unpredictable explosions. He asked the class to prepare our homework answers. After all the homework answers were revealed, the next person in the line started answering problems that were not homework. The next person did the same. No one ever mentioned, "Teacher, they are not homework." We were all frightened to death to speak up.

The next boy didn't answer. He murmured, "I don't have an answer for the next problem." Mr. Math marched over his desk, "What did you say?" Mr. Math started kicking the boy's desk. This boy collapsed from his chair onto the floor. We all witnessed Mr. Math's severe violence against this student.

While Mr. Math was thinking about his next physical action, the next students after this boy finally stood up and said, "Teacher, the last three problems were not homework." Mr. Math paused for one second. His embarrassment couldn't go anywhere.

He said, "Sorry, but you should've told me it was not homework." I was very sorry for what happened to this boy, but I felt huge relief that I was not this teacher's target at this time. What a pathetic and unfair world junior high school was?

Time to Speak Up

Even though I was frustrated about inequality in the places where I belonged, I had never spoken up. I had nothing to do in school or home except one essay I had written as my protest. In eighth grade, a whole city celebrated the Japanese traditional Ceremony of Attaining Manhood. Our school was planning to have a school assembly for eighth graders. This assembly includes students' essays about what kind of young citizen you want to be. I dreamt about speaking into the microphone at the lecture podium in the large gymnasium in the whole school ceremony. If my essay was selected, I would have an opportunity to speak up to the audience. The essay title I chose was *My Mother's Vacation*.

I wanted to speak up for her. Our society was not fair. People were treated and expected differently based on gender. Mother was working all day long with oily and sweaty machinery plus doing all the house chores without complaints. I had never seen my mother sitting and relaxing. When she was sitting, her hands were busily knitting our family's sweaters or mending pants. She constantly worked. I didn't plan to accuse male figures. I wondered if she ever had a vacation. How could I help her go on vacation? She would say, "Vacation? It's too good to deserve."

Miserably, my essay was not selected for the keynote speech in the ceremony. I thought it was because my topic was too controversial. But it was published in the school newspaper, in which no one in my family would acknowledge.

Advanced Friend in England

My head-smacked-friend, Yasue, told me about her pen pal in England. She introduced Michelle as my pen pal through hers. Michelle was a new window for me to peek through into another world other than my small, fenced world. Our correspondence was as frequent as once every two weeks. There were so many things I had never known in her letters. She was writing about her boyfriend and asked me if I had any boyfriend.

Mr. Turtle Mountain prohibited talk about girlfriends and boyfriends, because those topics were a huge distraction from precious study time. For my innocent mind, establishing the boyfriend-girlfriend relationship seemed impossible in junior high school. One of Michelle's boyfriends was a butcher. I wondered, "How would a fourteen-year-old girl meet guys other than students?"

I enjoyed reading her gossip from Yorkshire, England. The most shocking item enclosed were the pictures of her and her boyfriend kissing. I was little too shy on that scene. I brought them to school and shared them with my friends. We put our heads together and agreed, "People in England are too advanced."

Our discussion continued, "But girls in Japan, too, are courageous on Valentine's Day." Valentine's Day was the only time in a year when girls became proactive about their favorite boys. A big confession day from girls. Sending a chocolate gift to a specific boy would mean, "I like you. Would you consider me as your girlfriend?"

If the boy agreed, he would send some candy gifts back to the girl in the next month. The message would be, "I like you, too. I would love to have you as my girlfriend," on March 14th, which was called "White Day," the opposite color of chocolate. Completely hyper girls and completely blue girls could be seen as some kind of "Japanese" tradition on March 14th. You would enjoy "dramas" among Japanese teenagers on these two days.

When I found a Valentine's card in the envelope from Michelle, I didn't know what to think. From a girl to another girl? I did not even consider whether the Western countries celebrated Valentine's Day differently.

Mizu asked me if I could help with her Valentine confession. "I want you to give this chocolate to Taku since he is your neighbor." Was I going to be a cupid between Mizu and Taku? Absolutely. On February 14th, I stalked Taku to find a chance to give him a box of chocolate from Mizu. Finally, I pushed a beautifully wrapped box into his hands and threatened. I looked at him with a scary face and said, "This is from Mizu. You have to respond properly on the White Day. You know that, don't you?"

Unfortunately, Taku was not interested in the "girly" tradition. I felt so bad for Mizu, but I didn't know what else I could do for her. One thing I could tell was that it was extremely difficult to get a boyfriend in my school as Michelle did in Yorkshire, England. Taku shared some of his chocolates with me on the way home. He sure was a good friend of mine. Although I tried to help my friend match up with the boy, the Japanese Valentine's Day tradition didn't ring a bell in my brain. I wrote something in my diary like, "Boys should give girls candies first. Or could both boys and girls exchange things at a same time?"

Teenage Blues

Soon, I moved up to ninth grade. One day in my ninth-grade year, I sighed. Where is my energy? I had no more energy left over at the end of junior high. I randomly flipped my diary pages back. In the last couple months, I noted, "I don't like everything in junior high school," with sloppy handwriting. Another day I jotted, "Why is it happening to me?" My thoughts were so scattered, unfocused, and incomprehensive in my diary. But after only three years, junior high school was almost over. Perhaps I was a typical victim of "Examination Hell."

I didn't want to admit that "Examination Hell" was happening to me for a long time. And at the end of this hell, I really got into the hell. I failed in the important test. I became a pure loser. I didn't pass the high school entrance examination. While other kids visited the junior high teachers to announce their accomplishments, I had to go the alternative high school orientation. The public high schools were the high stakes in our city.

I was the first one in the family who failed the public high school exam. All of Grandma Fumi's sixteen siblings had attended public high schools. My parents had been in the public technical high schools. Aunties and uncles were all prestigious-level public high school grads. Even Brother was going to the same industrial high school where Father attended. Public high schools placed so highly in our family because no one had yet entered or graduated from college. At this point, it didn't matter if I was proceeding to college after high school. My high school was the losers' high school just because it was not the public high school. What a shame! That was the silent message I receive everywhere I went.

All of the relatives projected me as a kind of "smart" kid, so they wondered why I didn't pass. "She might not have been so smart after all," they would've talked about me behind my back. If you asked me right now what color described myself, I would answer "blue" without hesitation.

On the contrary, I had sensed that I wouldn't pass. I couldn't memorize anything during my test preparation, especially after dinner. I had been so sleepy and exhausted in my daily routine. I couldn't open my eyes during homework. I turned on the radio to keep me company, but instead I fell asleep or just focused on a radio show without studying. Someone gave me a tip to apply menthol ointment under my eyes. Another friend reported right the next day that it just made her eyes severely stingy and teary. As soon as the menthol evaporated, the stingy sensation was over.

In the middle of the night, I woke up in a panic. A geography's textbook was over the top of a math book. There were highlighters, pencils, rulers, and a compass scattered around on the desk. "Oh, brother. How can I catch up on all these materials by tomorrow?" Overwhelmed, but withdrawn, I said, "Forget it," and went to bed. There were quite a few nights like that. When I saw the exam paper in the testing center, my brain was blank. I even didn't recall whether if I had seen these items before. I was nauseous. I totally blew it. Yet the supervising teacher from my junior high told me, "You should be fine. Don't worry."

Well, he could say, "You should be fine," because he didn't know what I did. He didn't care. What would he say when he learned I didn't pass? I was just furious about his irresponsibly pitiful propitiation. Now I received the failing notification. I had a cranky and obnoxious attitude. "Well, I didn't want to go that high school anyway. If you didn't choose me, you ARE the loser." Then, in the next few minutes, "I am so stupid. I deserve this disappointment because I have to face my consequence. I am not as smart as I used to be (sob...)." I was a total wreck. My emotional wreck had continued for several days, but it ended eventually. At a certain point, I realized that I couldn't control what had already happened. Good news was that I didn't have to go to dreaded junior high school anymore where I had gotten so many headaches. On that day in my diary, I pathetically wrote, "There will be a lot of losers just like me in my new school. I should be okay among these losers." I told myself, "Face it. I'll find the way to survive just like I did before."

* * *

2:45 pm – Recess

When I come back to the classroom after releasing the kids to the 15-minute afternoon recess, my para-educator smiles at me. This para-educator's assignment is to support four students with special needs. Depending on their uniqueness, she approaches each student in different ways which works very well in the inclusion model. She stays in my classroom most of the day so we get to know each other pretty well, even though we don't have much time for private talk. Recess is only 15 minutes, but when I take the kids to the playground, walk back through the long hallway, and stop at the bathroom, the remaining break would be only five minutes because I have to pick them up at the playground again before the whistle blows. This five-minute break would often become condensed chats about things kids have done or something interesting in the day. Even some gossip about her neighborhood could occasionally be helpful. In this recess, she commented, "I liked your 'chopping bangs' story in the Writer's

Workshop today." I smile back and tell her, "Isn't that funny? I hated my bangs being chopped, but this old story turned out to be a good teaching tool." The para-educator mentioned one of her students who began writing on his own after he heard my story. She complements me, "It was amazing. You are a great teacher!" I reply, "I actually appreciate your individual support with these kids who need help. Your part in our classroom is immense! Japanese teachers rarely get para-teachers in their classrooms like here." "Really?" she says, surprised. "How many kids are there in the classroom in Japan?" "Maybe 30, I guess? When I taught in Japan, their policy was up to 40. If I had 32, it was considered to be a small class," I answer. "Wow. That's a lot." I continue, "There were even more students when I was in grade school. No para-teachers. Students were expected to be 100% obedient. If not, they had to expect the 'serious' consequences or a teacher could go crazy. Then my eyes would become as round as dinner plates!"

* * *

10-11 Years Old – Little Dynamite

To experience the worst was actually not a terrible thing. It was rather mirthful because you could take simple moments of everyday life in a humble way. You could focus on ordinary elements surrounding you as celebration. Also, if you got in another difficult situation, you could use the defiance that had grown from the worst time. Your attitude would be like, "It is nothing compared to what I have been through." In summary, you would be way stronger after each difficult moment of your life. So instead of complaining, I determined to be positive this coming year. While contemplating, my new fifth-grade teacher marched in the classroom.

Ms. Takahashi was shorter than most of us. Her puckered lips with red lipstick and her short and almost too strong permanent hair were quite an impression of a typical middle aged woman. I looked really hard where her eyes are when she smiled. Soon I would learn that this was the first thing I should celebrate in my fifth-grade year; to look for Ms. Takahashi's eyes. When we didn't see them, she was happy. Let's celebrate! If we saw two tiny dots on her face, there would be some serious matters in our agenda. I had heard several rumors about Ms. Takahashi prior to a back-to-school day. Soon we learned all these rumors were correct. She gave us lots of homework, she was strict in many ways, she had injured her spine permanently from the accident, and she was older than other teachers.

But what we didn't hear in the rumor list was that she was a little dynamite. Her energy and physical mobility were supposed be limited because of her injury. She must wear a corset around her body all the time. Again, she was physically shorter than most of us. But it was evident that her physical attributes wouldn't interfere with anything to do with having fun in our class. A miracle happened because of Ms. Takahashi's invisible power inside of her. Oh, this was a reincarnation of the hyacinth bulb! She was the living hyacinth bulb or beyond—a dynamite. All of her students looked at her awaiting the next exciting projects. I opened my eyes as round and big as a dinner plates so I wouldn't miss any excitement in class. I regained my confidence in this enthusiastic atmosphere she created.

Dodge Ball and Beyond

Unlike other fifth-grade classes, our class tended to play as a group during recess. According to Children's Psychology textbook in Japan, after the "Gang Age Year," kids were supposed to prefer a smaller unit as one on one, "My Best Friend," especially girls. There were some girls who needed to go to the bathroom with a certain person all the time. As an extreme example, these girls often held hands wherever they went. They loved having the exact same stationary, matching canvas bags, and even similar handwriting styles. It was a strange sight, although the textbook said that it was the appropriate development. These pairs didn't bother me at all as long as they were cooperative and had common sense in the large group. I didn't mind playing with any of my classmates, short or tall, stinky or clean, radical or conservative, boy or girl, quiet or chatty, and bossy or modest.

At the lunch recess, usually one quick lunch-eater went outside before any other classes and claimed our class' spot in the playground. That person might be drawing the dodge ball court lines by dragging his foot on the dirt field. As other classmates went out, they followed the first student to drag their feet to make the lines darker. When the last lunch-eater came out, we were all ready to play dodge ball. We all knew our dodge ball ability somehow. Each person grabbed a similar level friend and play rock-paper-scissors. The winning ones gathered as one team and others gathered as another team. That was how we made two teams. It was simple, fair, no favorites, and no complaints.

I preferred to set my position outside of the court. The tallest kid from each team went up to the center line to toss a ball. I was not the smallest on the team, but too small to be tossing a ball. Settling myself outside was more comfortable in the beginning of the game. A ball went back and forth until it hit someone. If you got hit, you had to go outside of the court. Since I started being outside, I could go in anytime I wanted.

When our team had last one or two players in the square, I finally went in the main court to save our team. My teammates appreciated I was still alive in the game. I was the one of the final ones who stayed until no players were in on the other team. I felt good about being a final "survivor" in the game. I used this strategy often to be the last one in on our side. And I felt empowered as a last man (woman!) standing.

Another alternate leisure during recess was a long group jump rope. Two volunteers began swinging a big circle. I didn't mind to be a first volunteer because I knew nobody would cheat to avoid the swinging rope chore. As soon as someone's feet got tangled on the rope, you switched your swinging turn. Endlessly each person went in the rope, jumped once, and left swiftly. This wave-like movement was breathtaking. All of us counted from one up until someone's mistake. We were overjoyed when we passed one hundred. No one complained about the person who caused the tangled rope. Instead, you could hear, "It was so close," "Way to go," and "We will make another record next time." Ms. Takahashi's eyes were invisible while we were fighting over who was to report each day's jump rope record after recess. She was never physically involved, but we wanted to give her the credit.

Parenting by My Parents

Growing up with a single mother, lack of food, fear of bombing, and in poverty, both of my parents' expectations matched. They demanded their kids be frugal and conservative with everything just as they had grown up with. My parents met by a traditional matchmaking, arranged by Mr. and Mrs. Turtle. A young man and woman were told that they were the best match because of their similar background. My mother believed in what the matchmaker told her. She didn't even doubt that there were some things the matchmaker didn't tell her. Her goal was to make her own mother happy. My mother and her mother were too innocent to be skeptical about things and people around them.

Under the family pressure, my mother successfully delivered the first baby boy. The baby boy struggled with an umbilical cord wrapped around his neck. Doctors picked up his feet and put him upside down, spank his bottom cheeks three times. Finally, his wimpy voice echoed in the hospital. Everybody cheered. After delivering a healthy boy, it didn't matter if the next children were boys or girls. Two girls arrived to the family a few years apart. All three children have been under the roof, fed, and decently dressed so we should be happy. Children were strongly prohibited to complain or desire something else other than human's basic needs.

Brother, though, got everything his way by taking advantage of his hierarchy. Worse, he wanted more. When he came home from a playdate, he asked his parents if they could buy a big toy robot like his friend owned. Of course, the answer was negative. But he was drawn into irresistible temptation. Father quickly learned his son's sticky fingers and became angry like a fire. Next time my sister and I saw him, Brother was miserably tied with the ropes against the post at the corner of the room. His face clearly showed the sever evidence of being beaten up. My sister and I scurried away from the scene.

Unfortunately, physical violence was allowed in my family as long as it was done by any male figures. Girls needed to be quiet unless you expected to be beaten up.

Contest Life

Despite recently imported modernized events like birthday parties and Christmas, traditional Japanese families like ours were reluctant to implement the irrelevant new Western traditions. Celebrating the Western culture was a sign of recovery from the dark times in the whole nation. Numerous filthy clothed children swarmed around American soldiers' jeeps and cried, "Give me chocolate!" on the devastated field just a few decades ago. Holding American goods and culture represented the significant hope for my parents' generation. Yet there were some touchy issues among them. Like many other people, both of my parents' fathers died in the fight against America. Though some old folks in town still think Caucasians would suck up human blood, I still dreamt about the mysterious Christmas presents. Just for me.

One December night, my mother told us kids, "When you completely fall sleep tonight, Santa might come to our house." I knew Santa in the picture carried a huge sack full of presents for the good children all over the world. So if he offered me one of them, I would be so happy. I wrote a letter to Santa that said, "I will be happy whatever you choose to give me, but please choose something different than my sister's."

I woke up in the morning to find the same rectangular shaped box with the same wrapping paper by our pillows. My sister and I opened the presents; of course, they were identical Kiki and Lara's notebook binders. Kiki and Lara were new popular characters in the Hello Kitty Company, which reminded me of a spoiled brat, Nobu, whom I just tried to get out of my picture. How insensitive! It was evident that Santa didn't read my sincere letter. That was when I realized that I had to be my very own advocate. If I wanted something, I had to get it by myself. No one was interested in what I wanted. I schemed seriously and concluded my strategy.

I dug through the newspaper ads after Father finished reading them. I found some contests that I could win with only little effort. I noticed that there were more resources available on TV commercials and magazines although the chances were slimmer. I had nothing to lose. If I won something, it would be a jackpot no matter what I got. I determined to win something for myself. I ripped the entry postcard from the newspaper ad and marked the correct answer. My first target was the new bike as the first prize.

Shortly thereafter, a little bigger and fatter mail arrived to me. Sadly, it was not a new bike, but it was my very first prize that I won—a brand-new white and red bordered handkerchief. Some cows in the pasture were painted as a dairy product's promotion. Thanks to Santa not coming to my house, my anguish turned into strength. My contest life had just begun.

Little Brother I Long For

The monthly magazines, *Learning* and *Science,* had been delivered since first grade by the delivery woman. These magazines were things that my parents invested in their children, hoping they would pick up something from them. As you already imagined, their policy was to provide some educational publications, and it was done. Fortunately, I was very independent and mature since an early age. I had no desire to read books with my parents. Such desire had never grown in me at all.

I turned the page alone and found another contest. It was a writing contest. The first prize was a large sum of cash. My eyes became dollar signs. The assignment was about "the important lesson from one of your family members." I took a deep breath. Had I gotten any important lessons? Don't steal things from the store because you will be beaten up by Father? Be quiet and obedient because I am a girl? Don't forget your umbrella because you will be hit by a car? Save money for three days to purchase more expensive items?

Father and Mother often told us, "Be a kind child," but they had never shown any practical examples. I was panicked that I had no lessons from my family members to write about.

That night, I had a dream. I couldn't believe my luck. Literally, I met my younger brother who never existed in my real life. This younger brother, Hiroshi, was actively involved in my life of my dream. I teamed up with my sister to spoil him and protect him from any distractions, just like we did for our new puppies. What a beautiful sibling love that I had longed for! This was how I wanted to treat my little brother with my little sister. And this was how I wanted to be treated. I was totally inspired by my own dream.

Reluctantly I woke up next morning, and I started scratching my first draft of the writing contest as soon as I put my folded futon away into my closet. It sounded pathetic that the only imaginary family member would be the main character in my narrative. Was I dishonored because I couldn't find any writing topic among my family members? In fact, I was disappointed that I was not able to look at my parents from different angles. Oh well, this was what I had—my dream was a gift for my writing, so I just took it. My pencil went back running from top to bottom on my paper until I was called for breakfast.

Things Associated with Food

I cracked open an egg shell and dropped it into the small bowl along with two spoonfuls of sugar. My left hand cupped my egg bowl. My spoon scooped the egg white up and down. "Don't play around. You will be late for school," mom scolded me. Quickly, I beat my egg with a metal tea spoon and grabbed my toast. I carefully dipped the edge of my toast in the raw egg and brought up this slimy toast piece into my mouth. After the second bite, I sipped my black tea. It reminded me of my very first nightmare at age three.

I woke up in the morning, sobbing terribly sobbing. "The icicles! The icicles! The icicles are scaring me!" My brain synapses kept sending the terrifying icicle nightmare information back and forth through my nerves. It petrified my mind. "Have some black tea," my mother tilted my tea cup into my mouth.

Magically, one sip of sweetened black tea blew my horrific mind away. Tears stopped coming out of my eyes. On that day, I ate the same raw egg dipped toast. Grandma Fumi didn't toast her bread. Instead, she spread white sugar all over her square soft bread piece, folded it in half, and munched away. Eating plain white sugar (not just supplementing or diluting in the drink) seemed like an elder's privilege, I thought.

Soon I heard a door bell at the gate. It was time for the fish merchant's morning visit. Every morning, this guy in his late fifties or early sixties rode his bike to the fisherman's wharf where our miserable kittens were abandoned in the past. He looked for the best fish with the best deal from the local fishermen. All of his dark skin and wrinkles met every requirement of expertise and superior resume in the fishing industry. He cheerfully greeted, "Good morning, what kind of fish would you like today?" On his back wheel, there were four or five racks stuck up. He untied the black rubber ropes over the racks and displayed them all on the ground. Mother bent her back and looked closely at the swordfish. Yes, we would have my favorite grilled swordfish with grated horseradish tonight.

Writing Contest

While my mother went back to get her wallet, I told Uncle Peko, the fisherman, "If I had a little brother, his name would be Hiroshi. I had a dream last night. I would take all bones away from the grilled fish just for him."

In three days, I was ready for some advice from respected adults on my essay. Since I overheard my mother and other grownups gossiping about how Mr. Fukushima, Brother's former third-grade teacher, was good at teaching Language Arts, I had no hesitation visiting him with my paper. "I know you are not my teacher, but I also know you are good at writing. I want to enter the writing contest. Would you be willing to revise my paper?" I asked.

"Why not? Come back tomorrow at lunch recess," Mr. Fukushima immediately answered.

I felt like I had already earned the first cash prize. Mr. Fukushima returned my essay with the red ink the next day and encouraged me saying, "Good luck." I worked on the final draft and mailed it out. I was done for what I could do. It was not too bad of a process. It would open my door at least slightly. It was okay to be ambitious. I was capable of accomplishing something.

Unfortunately, the cash prize never came. When the magazine delivery lady visited us three months after my entry, I opened the current issue of the *Learning* magazine. Its cover page colorfully announced, "Congratulations, the Writing Contest Winners!" I eagerly flipped pages to get to the winning essay page. It was not about my dream brother Hiroshi. It was about somebody's grandmother. I skipped this fantastic first prize essay impatiently and reached the list of the winners. Big fat bold letters showed the first prize, *Grandmother's Treasure.* I already knew that. What's next? The second prize was not mine, either. The third? Not even close.

Finally, little tiny ant-sized print started listing the "Fine Works," a.k.a. "Participation," category. About a hundred names were listed in this category. It was a minimum acknowledgement of their works. But at least their names were published in the national magazine. My indent finger nervously traced down the list searching for my name. "I found it!" Literally, I was yelling to myself. I rushed down the stairs. "Mother, Father, look! It is my name! Here! Right here!" I pointed my indent finger under my name and let them see. "What tiny letters, they are," exclaimed Father. "Sure they are," my mother agreed. I boastfully redirected them back to the main topic. "My name is here, published in this magazine. I won the fine work prize."

My mother noted with a little smile, "Oh, yeah. It is your name. That's good." Father's eyes were already back on his newspaper. With the least enthusiasm, he commented, "Good work." These cold and very short responses were my parents' version of celebration. Perhaps if my name were printed in the large bold letters, they might have reacted differently. Who knew? I cheerlessly went back to upstairs and reviewed my name again. I had an ear to ear grin. In the meantime, I was ready to criticize the judges' mistakes for not choosing me for the first place.

My Grandmother's Treasure was a heartwarmingly crafted story about the author's beloved grandmother who recently passed away. This young author found her commemorated photograph and appreciated her grandmother's love and legacy. The good story needed to have strong emotion and tragedy. Grandma Fumi was a tough turkey, quite far from "loving," and she was still alive. In a way, that fact was emotional and tragic. I should've picked Grandma Fumi instead of my loving dream brother.

Grandma's Fume

One day Fumi got ferocious at my sister's mischief; she was ready to beat my sister. My sister and I managed to evacuate to our bedroom and lock the door. Fumi banged on the door, screaming, "Open the door, you are in trouble!" We charged the locked door as hard as we could, and protested. Fumi's frightening footsteps were pacing back and forth in the hall and up and down the stairs. Within a few minutes, Fumi became quiet. But we were too scared to come out. That's when Fumi changed her strategy.

She lighted some incense sticks in front of door to warn us for the worst punishment, Moxa cautery. Moxa cautery was the painful Eastern alternative medicinal burning (!) method. You put a little dust like Moxa on the troubled body parts like shoulders, backs, knees, etc. It was sometimes used for headaches. Then, you lit Moxa with an incense stick. The heat gradually grew its temperature on your bare skin from comfy warm to a burning hot sensation!

Right before Moxa was completely burned out, you had to take it away because you would be burnt until a keloid remained on your skin. These certain techniques required a professional medicine man to practice Moxa cautery at their clinic, but older folks like Fumi were not afraid of using it at home. Three of her children had experienced this unforgettable painful torture at least once. Now she was trying to pass it on to her grandchildren. The incense from the stick was swiftly coming through the door crack. It reminded us of the apprehensive trauma of Moxa. Fumi hoped the girls would give up easily this way.

A lesson I learned was to not make your grandmother mad. It was clear to stay strong for your own protection. Unfortunately, these lessons were not what the judges favored in the contest.

The winning story, *My Grandmother's Treasure*, told a story about one photograph that this young author accidentally found in the cabinet after her grandmother passed away. In my real life, the scent of burnt

Moxa would remind me of Grandma Fumi and haunt me forever as long as I live. It would be the award winning non-fictional narrative.

Sharing Victory

My conclusions of why I missed the first prize were two-fold. One, I didn't have an extremely dramatic episode like someone's death in my daily life—that was actually fortunate. And two, my character Hiroshi was a fantasy brother, not a real living sibling. I wondered if I should have picked my other family members. It didn't matter whoever I chose. The lessons I had to describe from my family members were most likely what I would not want to do in my real life. The writing contest was over. I put the magazine in my backpack to share with Mr. Fukushima, Ms. Takahashi, and Auntie Okura.

Auntie Okura was a long-time custodian and usher in our school. Since I was in the first grade, I had been her favorite. If someone unconditionally loved someone, Auntie Okura was the one who showed me how it was supposed to be done every day in school. I visited her at least once a day to greet her. She had a glass of ice cold tea just for me during the boiling and humid summer.

She was the only warmhearted adult who gave me a hug in public which was very unusual in Japan, although she was a genuinely traditional mighty Japanese woman. When I complained to her about whatever happened at home, she put her hands on my shoulders to share her wisdom. "I know, but you better not say anything bad about your parents." When I showed my name in the tiny print in the magazine, Auntie Okura was overjoyed. "Wow, I knew you would do something extraordinary like this. I am so proud of you!" She squeezed me so tight that I was about to faint.

Instead of fainting, I received a big envelope from the *Learning* magazine on that afternoon. An enclosed letter said:

Congratulations for the Fine Work Award. It was a difficult decision to make in this writing competition. We hope you continue finding a joy of writing in your life. Thank you for your participation.

Then I put my hand in the envelope. I touched something hard and cold. I pulled it out. It was a brand-new set of twelve colored pencils with a special eraser and a pencil sharpener in a fancy tin case. I won a prize!

Compassion, Cooperation, and Contribution

My surprise prize was revealed in my class in the morning meeting; that made my life totally change. Ms. Takahashi seemed like she was more intentionally making a big deal out of every little thing that was accomplished by her students. In P.E., vaulting box, iron rod, jump ropes, high jump, long jump, straddle backward roll, and track were only a few of the countless opportunities you would be praised for.

She taught P.E. like other classroom teachers. Well, not exactly. She talked a lot, but she didn't model the activities herself. Although Ms. Takahashi had miraculously recovered from the paralysis caused by the car accident, her mobility was still limited.

Her P.E. lesson model was conveniently selected among her proud students. Nishi was one of the fastest runners and the highest jumper in our class. Nishi looked at the bar and took a breath, then, slowly started running. He sped up on the curved line toward the bar. His left knee lifted up high by the pole and his arched back was about to go over the bar. His upper body was flexibly curved and falling beautifully to the soft mat as we expected. We were about to give him an applause, but at that second, his right toe slightly touched the bar. It brought the bar down on him. He rolled quickly from the mat, but his left arm had made severe contact with the bar and then the hard ground. It was evident that Nishi broke his left arm. His face was showing agonizing pain. Unlike any other injured kid would do, Nishi bravely held his right hand over his injured arm by himself.

Then this injured student turned to another superior athlete, Yoshida, and looked into his eyes as if he was sending a message: "Yoshida, can you take over this exact same performance?" Although Nishi didn't say anything, all of Ms. Takahashi's kids understood what Nishi was thinking about. While Yoshida went up and performed, an assistant student took Nishi to the nurse. The next morning, Nishi appeared with his arm casted. Our morning meeting was all about celebration. Nishi's bravery and Yoshida's immediate support happened naturally, in a way as if someone had already planned it. It was captured as symbols of compassion, cooperation, and individual contribution among the team. I was extremely honored to be in this classroom with Ms. Takahashi and my classmates.

Pied Piper of Class

In addition, I was so thrilled that there was no hassle or whining to choose the class relay team on the field day. I was very excited about being a selected runner without any distress. My fifty-meter dash record made me well qualified for that position. It sounded strange to celebrate for the common sense. But remember, common sense was not necessarily valued in the chaotic and disorganized community. If I was able to recognize and practice the existence of common sense in my daily life, I should feel fortunate to belong to the civilized community with happiness and fairness. I had learned in Social Studies that on the larger scale, there were so many people in the world that lived in the unreasonable physical and philosophical conditions, like my fourth-grade class.

In Ms. Takahashi's classroom, when you made mistakes against the common sense, you would be remorseful instead of blaming another party. Plus, you didn't think any of other options but how to improve yourselves from your own mistakes. Soon you could go back to the right track again.

Ms. Takahashi was our Pied Piper of Hameln. She never threatened or ordered things that she hoped us to accomplish in class. But my fellow classmates and I desired to be better in multiplication, history, Chinese characters, jump ropes, dodge ball matches, and more. If it was not enough, we wanted go forward together without anybody left behind. Ms. Takahashi's magical pipe lead us to the right direction where we could feel secure and successful. I envisioned the little purple flowers of the hyacinth which I admired a long time ago at the window in Ms. Aoki's room. I wondered when, where, and how Ms. Takahashi found her own magic pipe in her hyacinth bulb. Since she found it in her bulb, her little flowers have begun blooming. I was proudly witnessing her blossoms by my very own eyes and my very own heart. My time would come someday.

Graduation Wish

Elementary school's graduation was near, but Ms. Takahashi never slowed down her academic demands upon us. Even cooking and sewing classes in Home Economy were as valuable as core subjects. Since we learned six nutrition groups, such as carbohydrate, fat, mineral, protein, vitamin A, and vitamin C, our lunch time become the daily live lesson. Everybody must identify which food contains which certain nutrition before they dig in. For example, "Today, we have bread, which is carb, Vitamin A, carrots, mineral is seaweed, horseradish is vitamin C, and pudding is sugar, so it's carbohydrate. *Itadaki-masu.* (Thank you for food.)" Everybody in the group stared at each other to make sure all were correct. We were pretty excited to eat with Ms. Takahashi in our own group. Our food discussion was even more sophisticated than other groups.

Students liked to compete among themselves in math and language practice books. When our works were neat and fast, she gave us more work. If not, you had to redo. How funny it was! It was not because we could be free after all, but we wanted to finish our work because we wanted more! Whatever psychology or strategies Ms. Takahashi used, they made us want to learn more. We loved learning!

One of the days towards our graduation, Ms. Takahashi asked us to write a short statement about what you would want to do in the future.

While I started thinking about it seriously, one of my mother's friends visited her and recruited for the Kids Adventure in Hawaii. I was sitting at the same table listening excitedly. "I can go! I want to go!" I interrupted. "But you are too young to remember anything. So, it is going to be a waste of a big chunk of money," my mother said.

"I will write a journal every day, draw pictures, and even take some pictures!" I begged. The pamphlet I saw had a lot of beautiful beaches, cabins, and sea creatures. My heart was dancing for the dream trip. Mother finally said, "Let's ask Father." I froze immediately. That was not a good idea. He didn't like anybody else but him having special activities. I expected that he would say, "No. It is not necessary." And he did. That was the end of the Hawaiian dream.

I couldn't depend on my parents to accomplish my dreams. I must wait for the right moment and appropriate support. For Ms.

Takahashi's graduation assignment, I wrote, "I would like to travel around the world, perhaps France, and report on TV and write a book about it." The world would be too far away to reach. But my new world would soon start with just a 30-minute walk from my house—junior high school—in two weeks after the graduation.

* * *

3:40 pm – Gratitude Journal

One of the highlights of the day in my classroom is the Gratitude Journal. At the end of each day, my students stop everything and think about what they are grateful for from the day. It is a very important routine we could not miss. Each day from Monday to Thursday, they list three grateful things or people in the small space. Friday is the "mini-essay" day during the journal time. Students pick one thing, person, or event and describe more details. First, some kids struggled to even think about what they "should" be thankful for. I told them on the first day of the school, "You don't have to fill in all three. You may start with one thing. What did you feel thankful for? Was someone kind to you today? Did someone invite you to play at recess?" Soon all the little hands grabbed their pencils and sounded out the words they wanted to write in their journals. Now this routine became smoother. I noticed that prior to journal time, it seemed like many kids purposely looked for someone's compassionate action to write about. Or some students seemed to be obviously making kind efforts so that someone would mention their names in the journal and hopefully share their names in the class meeting. Hearing their own name as a "kind" person really empowers their self-esteem and creates the compassionate learning community. Kids feel safe and good about being in the classroom. Gradually, the grateful list expanded to self-recognition. One kid said, "I am grateful for my perseverance."

Before the two-week long winter break, we had a special "complement" meeting. Each student shared one accomplishment during the trimester, one friend gave a complement to that student, a para-educator in the class gave a complement, and then I gave a complement and the report card. It was a long process, but it was worth it! Most second graders sustained being respectful participants, with little wiggles, in the whole meeting of 24 students. Understanding themselves, noticing their strengths, and being acknowledged by other people, they all were great through their learning journey. I was very humbled to be a part of their learning process and practice Mindfulness with them. Right after we broke up this meeting circle, I noticed one girl sobbing very hard. I asked, "What's going on? Are you sick?" She sobbed even harder, "I cannot see you guys for the next two weeks. I will miss them so much. Waaaaaa......" I knew she was the extreme case. But then, I pondered how much I understood myself and my future possibilities when I was growing up. Did someone precisely acknowledge my strengths? Did I feel the strong connection in the larger community? I admit I was feisty, but I was obedient to adults. But did my obedient actions mean I truly trusted and respected all adults? I may have been just quiet. It's easy to say "build the relationship," but it really takes time, effort, and willingness, especially on my own life journey.

* * *

19-22 Years Old – Free Falling

Open the Spring Door

Countless cherry blossoms were orderly standing along the river. The occasional gentle wind blew their numerous pink petals away. People walking by the river bank looked especially fresh and ambitious of their future. I didn't recall so many cherry trees planted along side of the river bank the last time I was here in November.

Just like other freshmen, I was now in my brand-new suits that Grandma Fumi had tailored for me. Walking on the bridge made me proud and a little bit shy. The first day of the University! So many After School Clubs' solicitors were actively lining up towards the school gate just like in November, recruiting new students. But this time, it was more colorful, cheerful, loud, and exciting.

More recruiters flooded both sides of the narrow school road so that freshmen hardly could walk through to get to school. Senior students didn't show any hesitation of friendly welcome to freshmen. They talked to the new students just like their old friends or long time separated brothers or sisters. I hoped they would be all good people. The University was way larger than high school and the number of people was beyond my imagination. These were female AND male students! I would no longer have to be punished when I talked to the boys, although the sight of boys looked a little unnatural for me. These men and women were not wearing uniforms, and many of them were unidentifiable in their ages. It clearly appeared to me as the new world.

Finally, I pulled open the door to my freedom! At the Admission Ceremony, as important as the Graduation, the University President and some guests were supposed to give their endless speeches in the huge gym. It's okay, because everything was upbeat in my mind since I was finally allowed to leave home. Even my mother left yesterday after helping me set up in the dorm room. I was officially all by myself!

During the ceremony, I learned that even friendly people are not necessarily good people. The school officials warned us about the student sector of the cult. I was too busy and poor to afford any out-of-school activities besides my study and new life, especially the ones that were against the social norm. Sadly, many people who got involved in this cult would end up losing money and leaving school.

Violet House

My dorm room number was A202, the second room from the corner room upstairs. All girls' dorm buildings were inconveniently located four train stations away from the college stop, unlike the boys' only one station away. Boys' dorm residents didn't even commute by train. They could commute by bike for 10 minutes. It took 12 minutes to walk from my dorm to the train station. After a 10-minute train ride, it required another 15-minute walk to get to the college gate from the station.

Right below A201 and A202 was the old landlord couple's residence. If I accidentally dropped a heavy text book or a frying pan, the landlord couple could hear its noise and get dust from their ceiling. I had to be extra quiet. The small square space included entry where I could keep my shoes, a two-foot by one-and-a-half-foot cubic kitchen with a tiny sink and one gas stove. This was such a desperately tiny space that you could not even dream about a place for the microwave. I barely managed the toaster oven on the floor. I needed to eat bread to be smart every day.

Futon, blankets, and my other belongings were stuffed in the closet. The floor had four and a half tatami mats that were the only space available. Traditionally, one tatami size was six feet by three feet. Four and a half tatami mats were placed orderly like a puzzle in the square room. I usually studied on the low table that became a heater in the winter time. On the bright side, I could reach everything from where I sat... the food in the fridge and the dictionary on the book case.

Only thing I had to be careful of was the emergency buzzer on the bottom of the kitchen column. You might easily lean over or accidently trip. No matter whatever reasons you had, as soon as you touched the emergency buzzer, it would ring with the frightening high pitch buzzer noise and echo in the entire dorm buildings, both the A building and the B building. That was when you had to evacuate from the dorm building.

In most cases, it usually was an innocent false alarm. You would be so embarrassed with your innocent accident. There you saw everybody's head out from each room throughout the hall. You had to run across the buildings and yell without any eye contact with anybody, "I am sorry, it is an accident! I am sorry!" We had at least one false alarm every other week, especially during the first couple months of the school year, because there was not much space for us big girls. Also, the freshmen hadn't learned how to get around the tricky buzzer as skillfully as the seniors. The landlord suggested to cover that button with an empty plastic strawberry package. It worked for a while, but while you were sitting on the floor, your bottom could easily smash the clear plastic pack.

Another kind of buzzer was very important for the college students' social life. When someone called you on the phone, the landlord pushed the buzzer to your room to beckon you. You had to run like a hyena to pick up the phone over the landlord's window. If your boyfriend was calling you, either you ducked so low that you are not visible from the landlord's office window, or you tried to stretch the cord as long as you could to get outside of the sliding door so you could keep your privacy. Yet, you could own your own phone line in your individual room under the dorm contract.

When you visited someone's room, you had to indicate which room you would be in on the chalkboard so the landlord could call you to the room where you had been. Let's say, three girls were gathering in my room. I would get one buzzer, the A203 resident, two buzzers, the A205 resident, three buzzers, and the B201 resident, four buzzers. If you wanted to make a phone call from there, you had to use the public phone outside of the dorm building. The most of the time, it was endlessly occupied by the girls who were homesick for their families, friends, and lovers. If it passed 10 p.m., you had to spend an extra 10 cents to call the landlord to apologize and beg them to open the gate.

There was a short plastic-roofed bridge between the A building's and the B Building's upstairs. Under the bridge, residents' garbage and recycle bins and cleaning tools were orderly set.

The bathhouse was also located in the same area. The corner of the tiny changing area was occupied the laundry machine. A pile of laundry baskets was in another corner. Outside of the bathhouse door was a blackboard for laundry sign-up. The sign-up board was filled so quickly on the weekends; however, girls were well disciplined to knock on the next person's door as soon as they were done.

I passed my time by reading comic books since I didn't have TV. You didn't have to buy new books, magazines, or newspapers if you checked the paper recycle box often enough. In the paper recycle box outside the landlord's room, girls tossed their finished day-old newspapers and the most current magazines. Once in a while, I dug like a homeless person and picked something interesting. It seemed like other girls was doing the same thing as I was doing.

One day I found a new comic book in the recycle box as usual and picked it up. As I flipped through the pages, I shockingly dropped it right away with a feeling of strange nausea. This magazine had explicit pornographic descriptions! I was scared, but curious at same time. I picked it up again and decided to examine it in my room while waiting for my laundry. My eyes were widened like dinner plates as I turned each page. I just couldn't believe this book was even in my own hands. Feeling as guilty as a criminal, I quickly went downstairs to make sure nobody was around the recycle box. I literally threw it back into the recycle bin and scurried back to my room. When I brought my laundry back to my room, I peeked at the recycle box again. "It" was already gone! That evening, my dorm friend held a secret meeting with uncontrollable curiosity. Who in our dorm had purchased the X-rated material by herself in the bookstore and bravely recycled in the public recycle bin? There was no good lead, but eventually we concluded some possible suspects including the landlord's 70-year-old husband.

This wooden dorm building had been built before the college merged into the co-ed university. That was still 25 to 30 years ago. Despite the age of the building and the ugly looking exterior and interior, the dorm had a charming name: the "Violet House." Its sign was written in the traditional, old-fashioned, Japanese calligraphy and posted right in front of the building, which was also aged. The siding outside of my window was beat up pretty badly by the strong west sun. The landlord lady commented that I was lucky to have a west–facing room because you wouldn't wake up with the eastern sun.

During the summer months, I could sleep as long as I wanted until I would start sweating, which was about 7:30 am, whereas the east side residents' morning started around 5 am with the bright and sweating temperature. They had no chance to sleep in. All of the doors and windows were wide open throughout the building during summer. Girls looked for some cool breeze in the hallway. The air conditioner was not an option. Pathetically, the electric fan blew out such uncomfortable lukewarm wind. Even worse, our term papers flew around and textbook pages were constantly lost.

Unwelcomed Friends

However, the west side residents' morning sleep was also disturbed without the morning sun beaming down. The first time I heard somebody or something yelling for more than 20 minutes at 5 am, I tried to think it should be a dream. When the sound source was revealed, the peacock was no longer my favorite animal. The west side of the house had the bird cage for a couple of peacocks. They even didn't have the beautiful feathers that I had dreamed of. Why in the world did someone have to own peacocks in their own residence? Why didn't you keep these birds in the zoo? The peacocks' cranky noise was absolutely useless and even harmful in our neighborhood.

The peacocks' noise harassed all Violet House's west side sleeping beauties every morning. The west side residents, including me, finally started complaining to the landlord couple. "Please ask the peacock neighbor to do something about their pets!" Since the landlord couple had suffered from the irritable noises in the west side of the building, they determined to take some action.

Thanks to the courageous act done by the owner of the peacocks, which wasn't clearly revealed in as many details, but after all, the haunted peacock noise stopped one day. Some girls bravely spied on the bird cage. The cage was empty, according to them. We looked at each other and looked at the landlord's window. We didn't want to think further. We were purely happy without any interruption of our sleep. None of us was interested in the peacocks' next destination in detail that could have been unthinkable misery.

White Lilies and Camellias

Next to the Violet House, stood another dorm building, the "White Lily House." The White Lily landlord was not as strict as Violet's for the girls who came home after 10 pm. Violet girls were often jealous about White Lily girls, but I really didn't care because I usually went to bed before 10 pm anyway.

The bath house was also closed at 10 pm. It meant if I came home late, I had to go to bed with stinky feet. I didn't like that at all.

A few blocks down the street, there was another dorm building, the "Camellia House." Further passing several train stations and after changing a train, there was another girl's dorm nearby the traditional soy sauce factory. It smelled of soy sauce as soon as you got off the train. I didn't know about these dorms as much as I did about my own, Violet, or White Lily because of the distance. Although most girls began their campus life at the dorm, they tended to leave the dorm life after their freshman year, or at least the end of the sophomore year. Girls got tired of rules. These girls moved out to the apartments nearby school. Then they would start wandering around the college town at 2 am with the heavy liquor breath.

One of my friends invited us for her new apartment nearby school at our junior year. She boasted how new and clean it was. She prepared nice meals in her brand-new kitchen, too. But there was one problem. When I went to the super tiny bathroom, I panicked. The door didn't close! "How do you close the door?" I hollered. "I am sorry I forgot to tell you about it. It doesn't close unless you sit on the potty. I am not going to see you, so you pull your pants down and sit on. Then, close the door." It worked that way.

These girls told their parents how desperately they wanted to focus on their studies by living close to their school. These parents had no clue about their daughters' scheme and simply gave in. It was very easy. Their parents were willingly sending more money for their daughters' expense of new apartment's rent and the hidden party costs that would never be revealed to them.

Conversely, moving out from the dorm was not my priority. First, I really couldn't afford it. Second, I knew how to frugally live. Last, living away from my parents' house was "free" enough for me. I was one of three seniors who lived in Violet House after all. I was cunning enough to get around the rules—I learned to use some friends in White Lily House. When I came home after 10 pm, I would walk through the Lily gate, and knock on a door or two. It was a piece of cake.

Some girls did things that were too brave and courageous that I could never try. The one bravest action was a girl climbing up the Violet Gate like a Ninja! Amazingly, she was so quiet that nobody noticed her. After that, Miss Ninja knocked on someone's window and came through. Yes, she needed to move out from the dorm unless she was pursuing a Master's Degree in Ninja with a mini tight skirt and high heels. Her parents would be amazed at their daughter's incredible ancient Japanese hidden agility.

Water Business

After the final exam, the tension finally disappeared from my shoulders. I should've practiced more for piano. But it was still better than Kahori who announced to the professors, "This is how far I know," then left the room.

If mastering the whole music piece was a critical requirement, she would've failed.

I had more than five mistakes, and although I completed the whole piece, I still got lower mark than hers. I should've stopped and left like Kahori before I made my first mistake.

"Oh well. It's done anyway," we grouched together at the cafeteria. "Bravo for all, no matter what. How about 'Malin' tonight?" Our "After the Final Party" was held at our regular hung out, "Malin." Some of us marched and some biked to the karaoke bar.

Most of my friends were from my homeroom, the Elementary Music program. My university had the homeroom system like elementary schools due to the specificity of the study. The Elementary Music class had only girls, despite my wish. I didn't know until the first day of college life. Since I was tired of the girls' high school experience, I picked a co-ed school. I didn't realize that studying classical music was not really popular among boys. The Violet House prohibited boys' access, too. Obviously, it was too late to realize my plans didn't work out.

Fortunately, my karaoke friends shared similar expectations and disappointments about "Campus Love." What I learned from them was that some girls already had boyfriends from their high school. Not fair! Some found boys in their after-school activities. It was common to find someone at the parties with other schools, too. Looking around among my friends, I was terrified. "I am the only one who doesn't have any contact with boys! It must be the 'Counseling Room Curse'!"

Because I had been rebellious against my high school, my teachers, and my parents, a certain curse would be following after me wherever I went and trying to destroy my wishes and chase my opportunities away. Or else, it must be another session of ordeal. Despite the obstacles and my awkward social skills, I went to the parties anyway because I was still ridiculously hopeful and curious to find a prospective "male friend."

At the karaoke bar, just watching the young athletic waiter, Ayama, who was our fellow student of the Elementary Math Department, was worth attending the party. Girls often talked about Ayama, how handsome he was and how good his soccer technique was. My disappointment came really fast. Ayama was a hospitable, handsome waiter, but he was not friendlier than a waiter. There was no hope of getting to know each other after the party.

Instead of grouching, we found another group from the Elementary Physical Education "boys'" party. It turned out to be a larger party than the girls expected. People loved us singing songs because we were seriously good. Don't underestimate us. We were literally in the "music" major! Our hard practice was finally paying off—we were the stars of the party.

The middle-aged owner looked very content behind the counter. The party lasted until the closing time. The owner came out from the counter table and asked me, "Would you like to work here after school?"

My brain immediately shrunk up. "Are you okay working in the 'Water Business'?" I thought to myself. My parents and older generations were very cautious of their daughters working in the water business, which refers to "service" jobs. Water meant liquid over all for old folks. Liquid equals alcohol. Quite frankly, Geisha was a symbol of water business in the nation's history. These beautiful women entertained wealthy men with singing, playing instruments, dancing, and pouring sake liquor. Did my parents want their daughter serving sake to the men? Was she going to be in an escort service?

Luckily, I was miles away from my parents now. Whatever people thought about the water business, this karaoke bar was the place to have fun. I was supposed to bring drinks and food to the customers who were most likely fellow college students. In addition, I would just take song requests from the customers and play them for the performance. There was no "dirty" part in this business. No Geisha. No escort.

My right brain commanded, "Okay. You go for it."

Two days later, I opened the same door I left out of from the party. This job must be a "breakthrough" opportunity in my life because I will finally get to know this popular boy on campus, Ayama. My heart was beating extra fast. "Owner, what time does Ayama come?" I genuinely asked. His response was something beyond shocking.

"Ayama left this bar. You are his replacement." I was trapped! Buddha knew my "dirty" expectation. Oh well, I could focus on my work after all without any distraction. My work schedule was only twice a week after school. The owner always complemented my hard work and cheered for me. All in all, I had to admit, it was okay without Ayama.

A couple of weeks after I started working in the karaoke bar, the owner asked me, "Do you want to hang out with me [alone] this weekend?" "What? Are you asking me for a date? I am your employee. What about your family? I cannot believe it!" Was this his purpose in hiring me? I threw the rag into the sink, glared at him disgusted, stomped out, and slammed the door.

It was the ugly reality show of the "Water Business" after all.

Let Me Fall

I continued failing to keep my part-time jobs, one after another. The tour guide assistant with the elders sounded pretty easy when I heard about it from my friend. It was actually too easy. She told me to just sit in the front seat of the bus and chat with elders during the trip. What I did was to sit in the front seat. What I didn't do was chat with elders. I didn't even have any chances to chat with people my age, why did I have to make old folks happy? I totally forgot that it was part of my job that was supposed to make money in my pocket. I had a set of headphones in that blocked the conversation from the elders. When I didn't hear, I didn't have to talk. I was very quiet for the three-hour drive in the large tour bus.

At the hot spring resort, I took a famous public bath, ate the Japanese full-course meal same as the elder tourists. I poured some beer and chatted with some people. On the way home, I fell asleep with my headphones. I normally didn't talk with anyone when I slept. Duh. When the bus came back, I stood by the door and bowed to each person. "Thank you for coming on our tour." My boss was not, though, as happy as me.

Next time I visited the office, my job was gone. He said, "You are not good for this job." I concluded that I was not meant to survive in the service business. I didn't have courtesy or respect unless I would receive them from another party, and comprehended the true meaning of them. No one seemed to teach me these important life skills and human qualities. It seemed like I must learn life's important lessons by failing almost every attempt of trying to grow up. Oh, I remembered. I learned how to ride a bike when I got some scratches on my knees. It hurt so badly.

Fortunately, private tutoring seemed to fit with my character of being bossy, opinionated, demanding, and pushy. The occasional obnoxiousness was even accepted by my clients and their parents. Tutoring became my main part-time job after school.

Thanks to our teaching-specialized college, people in the community had a certain respect for the prestigious teaching-college students. It was the most reasonable way to find a tutor for their own children in our college. The ads were frequently posted on the bulletin board in the office. What you had to do was to tell your interest to the receptionist. She would give each applicant an appointment time for the interview with the school official staff. Our school wanted to keep a good reputation by sending only high quality students to the clients.

My students ranged from four years old for the basic number sense to 18 years old for the college prep. Most cases, dinners or snacks were included in my jobs, which was most helpful for a hungry college student's stomach. Some families offered me a gorgeous Japanese cuisine after each session, including dessert. I didn't even have to do dishes!

One parent handed me a wooden paddle and said, "Teacher, feel free to spank him as needed." The 17-year-old boy looked terrified. Quite often I became a teenager's counselor instead of an instructional tutor. Teenagers had so much to talk about: their teachers, friends, boys, girls, etc. Sometimes I listened to them for two full hours without any academic work getting done. Their parents seemed okay with it. Parents must have had a hard time dealing with their teenagers on a daily basis.

One family made their high school son give me a ride on his bike to the train station after the tutoring session was over at 9 pm. It would take 20 minutes if I walked. The five-minute bicycle taxi service on the back seat was not so comfortable but sure was helpful to catch a train home on time. Tutoring was the perfect side business for college kids; it brought in some extra money and provided teaching experience for career readiness.

But I didn't think my mediocre teaching ability would last in this business with my grumpy attitude, especially in public education. I had become a selfish, self-centered, and heartless young adult who I didn't wish to be.

My hyacinth bulb might have been rotten even before it started growing. I contemplated, "What am I going to do? I am uncertain about my future. Yet, I am not comfortable sharing my anxiety with anyone because that is not my character." I wished I could hibernate before winter break began.

Freezing Temperature

"Free Boarding and three free meals. $10.00/hour. Fun Ski Resort. Free Ski Lift pass. We will pick you up. Send your resume with your photo A.S.A.P."

That was the headline I found in the weekly job magazine.

If I couldn't hibernate this winter, at least I could hide somewhere no one would see me. I didn't care about skiing, but I could earn and save money at the same time in the quiet rural snow country. Growing up in the orange-producing southern area, I was always curious about such a different world of snow. Whenever I sang about snow, skiing, or ice-skating in the elementary music class, my heart danced around and my vision of winter wonderland preoccupied my whole brain. If I didn't like it, my duty would be just inside anyway. I wanted to see the huge amount of snow with my very own eyes. The winter break was no longer for my family obligations. I didn't care about Christmas. Nor the New Year.

A week after I sent my resume, I still didn't hear from them. I picked up the phone, "Hello, I am wondering if the position is still available." The other end of the line cheerfully replied, "Oh, what is your name? Hmmmm... Well, actually, the position is filled. Sorry, maybe next time." Disappointed, however, I was about to call someone else for the job. At that moment, my phone rang.

"Hello?"

"Are you still available?" the ski resort man asked.

"What do you mean?" I quizzically asked back.

"Well, actually, we would like to hire you," he announced to me.

I gasped. I was not sure what was going on, but it sounded like I got a job. Yes!

Stepping off from the bullet train, the extremely chilly air spread over my face. The cold temperature stubbed my brain through my nostrils. The exhalation appeared steam-like white from my mouth. This chilliness was a brand-new sensation that I had never experienced in my life. The snow days back in my hometown sounded like an amateur version of winter compare to this temperature.

"That's how this climate stores three feet of snow for about five months," I contemplated. The minivan was waiting for me outside of the Echigo Yuzawa station. I greeted the driver, although I didn't get the rest of what he was talking about. His dialect was too heavy to understand. People in the cold region tended to mumble due to its temperature. Their lips couldn't move smoothly in this coldness. It was amazing to realize the fact that the dialect surely had developed based on the region's geographical features and climate.

The van passed between snow walls three feet high. That was the same scenery that I had once admired in photos of the geography textbook. They seemed to have enough snow to build the snow cave. A couple of people on the photo were baking snack mochi (rice cakes) in the cave. It's so "real" and exciting with the properly chilled temperature!

My basic duty at this inn was a combination of hotel housekeeping and waitress. Starting at 5:00 am, we quickly walked through the freezing cold hallway to the chilly kitchen. The very first chore was to boil a lot of water in the large kettle so the guests could get hot green tea with their breakfast.

There was a "rice room" behind the main kitchen where the inn owner's wife, Mrs. Wife, would wash plain rice. The rice cooker was 40 centimeters deep, and its lid's diameter was one meter. "The rice will be delicious when you cook a lot at once," said Mrs. Wife with a traditional Japanese towel covering her head.

Everybody's accent was too heavy. Paying attention to the main idea was one of the most critical tasks for my foreign ears. Gradually, it became easier for my foreign ears to interpret what they wanted to say in the context of the sentence.

The worst part was when they said only one word I had never imagined from the context. I couldn't predict what it would be at all, without any clues before or after that particular word. That word in a dialect didn't appear in the dictionary.

While stripping the sheets out in the guest room, I secretly asked one of the senior maids.

"What does 'Dasuke' mean? I didn't think it was important because Mrs. Wife didn't look at anyone when she said it. But she says that quite often."

After a big laugh, she explained to me, "Dasuke" means a transitional word from one speech to another topic or cause and effect. It's like when people often say "so…" in the middle of their conversations.

My roommate Chika and I nodded and practiced "Dasuke" with the transitional expression. Ms. Senior Maid wouldn't give us a passing grade on our new language so easily. "You guys sound so unnatural and terrible. Practice more on the dialect!" All the sheets and futons were cleared while our fun dialogues kept us moving. We then had a lunch break until 2:00 pm.

My roommate Chika and I stayed in the basement room far from the main part of the building. It was dark and cold even in the summer time. Three meters of snow completely covered the only one hopeful window that was supposed to bring us natural light. It was not the "Fun Ski Resort" after all.

The "Free Lift Pass" was the leftover punch cards which the customers couldn't use up during their stay. I could've used them if I knew how to ski or had the time and energy to learn it during the break. What I wanted to do during the break was to rest instead of ski anyway. My throbbing muscles and early morning rise made my body miserably exhausted. I laid down in the dark room during my lunch break.

All of the sudden, Chika stood up and declared, "I must do it!" and left our room. After that, Chika disappeared during our nap time and didn't tell me where she was going or what she was doing. I was too tired to press any further.

Her secret project was finally revealed five days later.

Knocking sounds woke my drowsy brain during my nap. I looked around and noticed the slight light through the window that was supposed to be covered by the snow. I was totally puzzled. Then, through the other side of the window, I caught Chika's huge smile with bright sunlight. "I made it!" she exclaimed. Chika uncovered the snow until our window glass was clear to receive a full amount of sunlight. "Wow, you really did it! We will no longer be in the dungeon." I just realized how I appreciated the mesmerizing natural light. Thank you, Chika! Chika was the skinniest yet toughest lady I had ever known. In addition, she was very determined.

During one lunch break, Mrs. Wife mentioned, "My oldest son will take you to ski today." Mr. Oldest Son was the typical spoiled first son in the family, just like Father and Brother. Mr. Oldest Son was even worse. He expected everyone to follow his demands because he was going to take over his father's business. Disgustingly true, he had no compassion at all except for himself. Mr. Oldest Son didn't expect us to say no to his "kindest" offer.

Reluctantly, I mumbled to Mr. Oldest Son, "Well, if you teach me how to ski, I would go." Chika told me, "Don't be too shy, I am almost a beginner, too. Last time I skied was when I was four with my dad. We would be the same level." I was not necessarily convinced, but I was in the van to the snow hill.

Skiing in the heavy snow was the same as traveling to the moon in a rocket. I had no knowledge about either. Zero. Would my curiosity be able to overcome my fear?

Just as I anticipated, the first time I put the ski boots on, I became an uncontrollable robot. I couldn't walk to where I wanted to go.

Somehow I managed to get myself to the flat space where I could finally bind my boot on the ski.

I nervously asked, "Mr. Oldest Son, first, just teach me how to fall down. I don't need a fancy ski lesson, but at least I want to fall down safely." His response was as cold as the air on this mountain. "You will figure it out. Just follow me." He led us to the lift. With my raising anxiety, I begged, "I don't think I am ready for the lift yet. I haven't even skied on the bunny hills yet." Mr. Oldest Son and I were in the lift chair line waiting for the next double chair. "You'll be fine. Here you go, one, two, three!" He grabbed my arm, pulled, and squeezed me next to his left side.

My bottom was at the edge of the lift chair. I scooted back and looked at the view down there. "Oh, boy... Mr. Oldest Son, I don't think I can get off from the chair," my terrified voice barely came off of my mouth. "You will be fine," Mr. Oldest Son pleasantly replied. As he swiftly jumped off from the chair, I followed him. Well, at least, I tried. The lift assistant pulled me out from the seat before my chair rotated back down. "Thanks..." but before I could say it to him, my skis slid down from the little mound without my control. The natural force somehow automatically brought me to the starting line where colorfully dressed skiers were about to take their adventure.

The rest of my first ski experience was the history.

Mr. Oldest Son just wanted to ski himself. He needed some excuse to get away from his duty at work. He skied fantastically, however, I didn't envy him or adore him at all. I was facing my own misery. I was a terrified creature on the top of the mountain. I had just learned how to wear ski boots 30 minutes ago. Chika's childhood memories quickly came back and completely recovered. She was halfway down on the slope. I was about to cry. "Can I get on the lift and go down? " I asked the lift guard.

"I don't know," he said. Putting the front tips of my skis together, slowly, I started moving from left side to the right. My skis were so parallel to the horizontal ground line so that my whole ski started sliding down on the sides instead of pointing downhill. Petrified on the steep slope, I saw Mr. Oldest Son confidently skiing down for the third time. This time, he spotted me and said, "How are you doing? Isn't it fun?" and left with snow powder in my face before I answered his questions.

Finally, I reached the place where Chika had been waiting. She nervously asked, "Are you okay?" I replied, "I don't know. But I have to get down somehow. Otherwise I will miss my afternoon work. You don't have to wait for me. I will be okay." Without any certainty, I let her go. I inhaled a lot of freezing air and exhaled with determination. My skis were now pointing down to the bottom of the hill.

My skis started sliding on the hill like an Olympic ski jumper. No turning. No tricks. Just go straight down. "Ahhhhhhhhh.....," my screams echoed during the whole town. There was a group in a ski lesson right in front of me.

"PLEASE MOVE! I CAN'T STOP! MOOOOOOOOOOOOOOOOOVE!"

The ski lesson group broke up and scattered instantly. Somehow, I was managing my balance with full speed. The bottom of the hill looked closer and my skis kept the same speed. What am I going to do? Within a millisecond, my eyes recognized the pile of snow by the safety net by the lodge. "That's it!" My skies pointed straight into the snow pile with full speed. Thud! The human imprinted snow pile was made when I finally got out.

My very first slope experience just created a fantastic human art sculpture. I could have won in the Winter Olympics with my speed record.

In my diary on that day, I noted, *"There is no 'Fun' Ski Resort. I have never and WILL NEVER wish for any Free Lift Pass."*

Guide without a Guidance

One day of my senior year in the university, I became very serious about changing my career from teaching to broadcasting. I lost my confidence in becoming a teacher after I failed the Physical Education Theory class. The professor seemed to like me in class. His friendly smiles were actually fake after all.

Here I was, marching into the career counselor's office. "I would like to take some broadcasting companies' exams instead of teaching exams." His eyes looked somewhat confused. He asked, "Why are you, then, in our college? Our college is exclusively for the future teachers. You will not pass the broadcasting companies' exams, but you have a great chance to pass teaching exams."

Totally discouraged, I slipped into the temporally (hopefully), but serious (in my scale) depression. I picked up the phone, "Mother, I want to quit the college. I want to be an actress or a news caster." I strongly thought I had potential to be an actress because of my creatively moving arms in kindergarten. The announcer potential would have been revealed in high school if I had continued. But these facts didn't convince my mother. Therefore, the conversation with her didn't last long. My ideas couldn't even convey to her brain accurately.

"Don't be stupid. You are almost done with your degree. Finish it anyway." After all, I had no choice. My tuition had been paid the last two years, and my final year's tuition was going to be paid by the college scholarship. Was I going to give it up? If I became a public school teacher and serve for them for eight years, I wouldn't have to pay the government student loan I had loaned since ninth grade. In other words, if I did something else besides teach, I had to expect an enormous amount of financial burden. It didn't sound like a bright future with a huge debt which I could avoid.

I was torn between my career decision and the predictable financial problem. I hung up the black phone and sighed. Without a certain decision, I left through the landlords' little sliding door. It was almost like I was creating more problems.

Bright Path

When I settled in my room, someone knocked on my door. It was Shino, my neighbor at A203. Through her silver-framed glasses, her genuine respect was expressed to me, though I was only one year older than her. "I wonder if you have just a little extra money and time in eight weeks," she spilled out. "What do you mean?" "Well, I sort of won the auto company's contest." "What do you mean by 'sort of'?" I asked curiously.

According to Shino, the first prize was a trip to New York that was paid in full. The trickiest part was that she won the second prize. It was only a partially paid trip to New York.

She continued, "So I need to pay $300 for this trip if I go, which is not currently available in my bank. I also have classes I cannot miss during that week," she quietly went on. "I just don't want to waste my winning ticket. Would you like to take my place? You even can take someone with you."

Within one second, perhaps quicker than the speed of the light, I blurted out, "I will take it! I can catch up on my classes later. And $300 is literally nothing compared to the highly-priced tour. Wow, I will be in New York in two months!" The winning ticket now was in my hand.

To tell you the truth, the foreign country I wanted to visit was Yorkshire, England, where my pen pal since eighth grade lived, if not France. A few months ago, I wrote to her about my interest in going to Michelle's motherland. To my surprise, she coldly responded back to me, "I don't have time when you visit me."

Our eight long years of correspondence ended just like that.

As you could see, my pen pal's recent unfriendliness had been one cause of my depression and as effective as other facts. Optimistically and surprisingly, this prize ticket successfully flipped my blue mood from dark foggy England to the bright sunny America! It was the opportunity I couldn't miss.

I told my dorm friend Yoshiko about my luck. "Hey, I want to go to NY with you, of course!" She smiled and revealed, "Guess what? My mom told me I have an uncle in New York City studying in Columbia University." Her excitement continued, "I am going to write him a letter so he might help our NY trip!" "Does your uncle live in New York? Have you met him when you were young?" I asked. She said with full confidence, "No. I have never met him. But it's okay. My letter will do the job!" I really hoped so. My imagination began growing larger and larger. Her uncle must be rich to be in New York. He must be a handsome man who might fall in love with me in the foreign land. There was an enormous thinking bubble over my head. I couldn't stop smiling!

Within two weeks, he replied to her, "I look forward to seeing you two." She was right. Her letter did the job. Practically, news of this trip already saved me from my depression before it actually happened, at least that was what I hoped. The letter from Yoshiko's uncle was additional medicine to ease my mood.

One November day, Yoshiko and I opened our wings and flew out for our dreams and traveled to our first foreign country without telling anyone! Our airplane finally landed in Washington D.C., and then we transferred to New York. The Japanese tour bus guide told us, "If you smoke in the bus, you don't need an ashtray. You can drop it on the floor, step it on, and leave it, just as the real New Yorkers do." Wow, I was amazed how the real New Yorkers were pretty rude and didn't have a sense of public ethics at all if it was true. We noticed a couple of old Japanese men in our tour who wanted to be "real" New Yorkers. They did the same as the tour guide explained. It was pretty disgusting.

After getting off the bus, we excitedly walked into the hotel in downtown New York.

People around me in the elevator were a bunch of giants, just like in *Jack and the Beanstalk.* What did they eat to grow that big? Although, at this point, my weight gain was evident around my belly from the contribution of the high level of my depression and unhealthy snacking. Here in New York, my depression was nothing compared to these giants! I was way smaller and skinnier than Jack's Giants in the elevator. My self-confidence gradually regained, "I can still survive."

The next day, Yoshiko's uncle was supposed to meet us in the lobby. My eyes were as round as dinner plates, looking for the handsomest Asian guy stepping through the door. Each time we stood up with our big hopeful eyes, each handsome Asian guy passed by. Disappointedly, we sat back down. After the same routine was repeated several times, someone patted my shoulder. "Yoshiko?" I turned around and pushed Yoshiko's right arm. Yoshiko exclaimed, "Uncle! I am Yoshiko!" There was a middle-aged man with black-framed glasses without hair standing in front of us. Wasn't he a student at Columbia University? "I am glad you safely arrived in New York. Welcome," he greeted warmly. I heard the sound of glass breaking in my head. I screamed frantically in my head, "P-p-p-please don't fall in love with me!" I was not ready to date with the person who looked just like my high school English teacher, Mr. Seaweed.

Yoshiko's uncle, Mr. New York, was very kind and generous. He gave us a tour of the pier where we could see the Statue of Liberty. He said, "You might want to go to Staten Island, but I suggest not to. Remember, the view from the inside of her crown is not the bigger size of this lady, just a view of New York. It's just boring. If you want to see the city view, you should go to the Empire State Building." Yoshiko and I agreed. He also took us to places where we could observe the beautiful and strong-standing Twin Towers where I could have never imagine what would happen in 2001. Mr. New York graciously paid for our dinner bill.

The Empire State Building was like Tokyo Tower. We rode an elevator for a few minutes to access the restaurants, some businesses, and souvenir stores on the top of the tower, in addition to the observation area. It was crowded with people from all over the country. I tightened my hands on my shoulder bag. Going between people, I noticed a little cute boy who looked little bit unsanitary. I wondered, "How does this cute but dirty little boy get here? Where are his parents?" At that moment of my wondering, his hand reached to a three-inch-tall Empire State Building model and grabbed it. I was in panic. What did I really see? "Yoshiko, I think I just witnessed a pickpocket," I told her with my shaky voice. She turned her head around and said, "Where? Where?" The professional pickpocket was quick in stealing and running. I was stunned at the reality of the young-aged crime in the U.S.

Other than that, we enjoyed every moment of our trip. In fact, Yoshiko and I skipped around 5th Avenue. I loved New York! No one complained about how fat I was or how stupid my decisions were. Everybody said I was cute and tiny. A genuine Japanese part of me warned, "A dream-like life will not last for long. Get real." True, but as I looked at Yoshiko, her focus was on the dream shopping spree in the dream city, New York.

When we found the candy store, Yoshiko started picking items as soon as we stepped in. She pointed several times to a kind of chocolate in the showcase with the enthusiastic eye contact to the store clerk. She repeated, "This, this, and this," with her ferocious pointing finger. "How do you say '*hanbun*' in English?" She asked me. I answered, "I think it's 'half.'" She complained, "I don't hear you well. It's too noisy in this store. But it sounds pretty similar." Then, she turned around again and demanded to the store clerk, "I need *han* pound!" *Han* (*hanbun*) means half in Japanese. Luckily, it really sounded like *half* to this store clerk, so congratulations! Yoshiko successfully purchased half a pound of mint and nuts block chocolate. We looked at each other, "Wow, English is easier than we imagined!"

Unlike ordinary Japanese people, I didn't have the courtesy or money of buying souvenirs for my classmates. Instead, I planned to surprise several friends by writing postcards. It must be a frugal enough and yet memorable enough way for my friends to recognize me for what kind of person I was. I would be back in school when these postcards could arrive to their mailbox. My friends might ask me numerous questions like, "Where have you been?" "We are so worried!"

"What were you thinking?" It sounded like I was going to get a lot of attention after all.

I was ready to answer these questions with a denim mini skirt and jacket from Macy's. Not only the New York trip itself, but my friends' attention could heal my depression. Although I felt a little guilty for acting like a boy who cried wolf, I concluded, "Life is short, live it happily after all."

A tremendous power of positive anticipation began growing inside of me since this trip started. In the future, it's possible that I could truly feel relevant and happy about regardless of the situation. I was determined to focus on what to do about my future. Even though I just didn't know what exactly was right now, I promised myself to be proactive to find the right path where I could be myself. And enjoy myself.

At the D.C. airport, a little older-than-middle-aged Japanese-American ground hostess told me with a friendly smile, "Please come back again." I hissed sarcastically to Yoshiko's ear, "I wish." I had no idea how my "wish" became the magical dust, how much of it spread all over my head, and that it unknowingly seeped into my system. This magical dust sensation seemed to be forgotten shortly after the trip, but it never disappeared.

LESSON

5

Reflecting

3:50 pm – Dismissal Bell

"Breathe in, and hold, two, three, four, and breathe out," I announce in front of the classroom one minute before the dismissal bell. I am fully aware that the kids' bottoms are wiggling and hardly ever staying in their seats at this time of the day. Am I torturing them? Absolutely not. This is the only way that makes excited kids manage their body movements safely during the most exciting "Going Home" time. Also, this simple breathing helps them remember where they must go after school. Some kids might even forget their backpacks, otherwise. Some of their families occasionally and unexpectedly change their after-school plans at the last minute, which makes young students extra nervous. In that case, even the patient bus drivers get confused from it as much as students. Being aware of the present moment is very critical, especially in chaotic times. While "herding cats" is challenging, what if I teach my cats how to tame themselves? Should "herding 'mindful' cats" be the win-win for students and teachers? Absolutely! I high-five each child and say, "See you tomorrow." The kids scatter off to the buses and the pick-up loop. Some of them excitedly reunite with family members on campus. This last ritual is very important for a day's closure. As I see all students find their designated area or person, it's my turn to breathe in and out. I am thankful for the feeling of calmness and peace in my mind at the end of the day. I find myself looking forward to the next day when I am able to see my students again. I wish I had known this tranquil moment and feeling when I started teaching.

* * *

23 Years Old and Beyond – Lessons You Can't Miss

First Year Teaching Survival 101

After some formal and quite a few private parties and the graduation ceremony were all over, I still hadn't had any calls from perspective schools at all in March.

Technically, I could not stay in the dorm anymore, of course, because I officially graduated from the university and didn't belong to it. I called up the Red Truck Moving Company to transport my belongings to my new nest, Green Heights apartment room, in northern Tokyo. From the four-and-a-half-tatami-mat-sized room to a room as large as six full mats sounded like a huge upgrade to me.

And I didn't have to share the bathroom. In the Violet House, girls needed to walk to a restroom on the concrete hallway and change shoes to the toilet wooden slippers to do our business. I never enjoyed waking up, walking in my jammies, and greeting someone in the bathroom with a "good morning" in the early morning. I was the grumpiest creature in the early morning until my first cup of coffee. Also, I didn't like that someone could recognize my slippers by the bathroom entrance while I was in the middle of the serious business of number two. In my new apartment, I didn't have to go to the bathhouse, either. I had my own separate toilet and bathtub with a shower. I had a separate room for the kitchen, too! I didn't have to worry about accidentally pushing the emergency button. Kahori gave me her dish cabinet and dishes when she moved back to her own hometown shortly before her marriage. I didn't have to hear a community buzzer and run downstairs to pick up the phone. I had my own cream-colored phone with a message recording machine installed. I was more ecstatic about my new living space than nervous about not having a job offer yet.

Then, the phone rang. My first lucky call in my freedom apartment life was from the officer in a perspective school district.

He explained, "We are interested in hiring you in our school district. We have a junior high schools' music teacher position. You have the secondary music endorsement, don't you?"

I stuttered, "Yes, b-b-b-but I have taken and passed a test in the elementary school category."

"Well, it doesn't matter. If you decline it, you might not to have a job this year," he threatened me.

"Am I going back to elementary school after one year?" I asked hesitantly.

He plainly said, "Yes."

"Okay, then, I will take it."

This was the beginning of the nightmare as a freshman music teacher.

I was assigned to teach music to students from seventh grade to ninth grade plus Japanese calligraphy. Students were all in black and white uniforms. No expression, but ugly acne on their faces. If you are lucky, or unlucky, you could see their obnoxious Halloween-like scary teenage expression, posture, and gestures. These kids looked as if they were about to join the street gang under the prestigious Japanese yakuza. Day after day, I dragged my feet to the subway station.

They didn't hesitate to wear my cigarette smoke and/or alcohol smell tainted jacket to school. "You smell like cigarettes," one middle-aged male teacher said, confronting a ninth-grade male student. The student sneered at the teacher, "What is the evidence? Did you find a cigarette? Huh?"

Can you imagine if you had a student like this in your class? Even just one could easily ruin a whole lesson, especially music. Usually, the class dynamic was controlled by two or three unwilling learners and all other students were merely bystanders. They didn't like to be in my class as much as I didn't like them to be in my class. On a lucky day, I might meet one enthusiastic learner in one class, which was really odd. Most kids didn't want to speak up for their education, at least in music. These kids looked at me through the black part of their eyeballs located on the top of their eyes, really close to their eyebrows. "Can't you keep your eyeballs in the middle of your eyes? Your muscles around your eyes must be really tight and tense just by keeping that unnecessary threatening look," I would have said, but I just kept it to myself.

My first year of teaching was pure horror. Literally, there was no hope. I felt like going to the zombie house where terrible things for sure

245

would happen every day. Even before I entered, I knew some part of my body was going to be bitten by terrible monsters. New scars wouldn't wait for the previous ones to heal. What I did was just let myself go down to the bottom of the bottom.

Since day one of my first job, I started counting down school days of the year. Sadly, time didn't pass as quickly as I hoped. One teacher told me, "You are doing a great job teaching music in every class. You are at least teaching the content and rules about music, even in the chaos. You are not just playing the kids' favorite popular songs during the whole 50 minutes." I asked, "What do you mean?" "Well, one music teacher in another school plays one popular music record after another to entertain the class for the whole 50-minute period because her classes are totally out of control. The kids stay in their seats while their favorite music is on. There is no music education there," she lamented. If my music classes were better than some other teachers, they must be worse than horrific. Why didn't the administrator or homeroom teachers help new teachers? I couldn't see that my teaching skills were any better than others just because some teachers were not able to teach because of the students' attitude and lack of support. I became more pathetic and bitter.

Speaking of lack of support, some of the senior teachers were even mean to new teachers. One middle-aged male teacher somehow seemed to overpower the principal. He was grumpy and grouchy about every little thing in the staff meeting. One day, he groused about my pierced ears. "What do you think about poking holes through your own ears and wearing earrings every day?" I looked him in his eyes and thought to myself, "My ears and piercings are not your business at all!" How much did I want to tell him that? A new teacher had no word against a senior teacher. He didn't have to know that my pierced ears and earrings were my mother's friend's graduation gifts. He just didn't like pierced ears and earrings on a teacher in HIS school. My pierced ears didn't distract me from my job, but evidently they distracted him. Unfortunately, I didn't know the word "harassment" in my early teaching days.

This teacher made often rude comments at the "required" staff parties.

"Why do I have to satisfy the same amount of salary that you yellow chicks are getting? I don't think it's fair at all. Did you know I get higher salary than what you get just simply because I have taught longer years, not based on the quality of teaching? The base salaries are the same as you, new hired, inexperienced teachers. Do you think it's fair?"

Why did he whine about his dissatisfaction on the salary schedule to me? I was not the one who was responsible for the pay scale.

With some alcohol at the party, he escalated. But no one seemed to want to argue with him, including me. I was so intimidated by this dictator with a loud voice and scary facial wrinkles between his eyes. He looked like a ferocious crab! He would really pinch me! When I mentioned my favorite music band on TV at his home party, Mr. Crab announced that people who like that band were stupid. I was not allowed to argue or throw a tantrum against the older people, no matter how upset I was.

As the youngest female teacher, all housekeeping jobs in the grade level came to me and another new teacher. Technically, the other new teacher was two years older than me, so my caseload was slightly higher than hers. It included taking orders for fellow teachers' Saturday lunch. Every Saturday, I had to visit each teacher individually to take an order, collect money from each, call up the catering restaurant between my classes, and pay as the delivery arrived. In addition, I had to make exact change for each teacher after the delivery.

All accounting business for students, such as lunch money, field trip fees, supply fees, PTA fees, etc., piled up on my desktop. A couple of young female teachers who were hired a year before me were released from these chores. They no longer had to serve tea or coffee to each teacher's working desk or shop for teachers' meeting snacks after work. These girls looked like the birds flying out of a cage for the first time. They enjoyed freedom from captivity. Thus, I was so envious to see their joyous smiles from captivation freedom.

Their joyous energy ended up with one joyous marriage with another school staff member. Also, joyous infidelity with other school staff was also revealed. Infidelity, of course, was not welcomed, especially by the middle-aged science teacher, Mr. Matsu, who sat by me in the teacher's room. The betrayed young wife of the unfaithful teacher used to be Mr. Matsu's beloved student, like his own daughter. Also, the guy was Mr. Matsu's right hand in the Science Department in our school. Mr. Matsu was furious at these joyous unfaithful colleagues without common sense. I quickly learned that the soap opera was not only on TV. Mr. Matsu was a wonderful mentor teacher, but I got tired of listening to his gripes over this infidelity story for many hours.

Self-Investment

No matter how difficult the situation was, I had to survive two hundred more days. After two hundred plus days, I would be an Elementary School Teacher. Everything should be better.

The person who gave me ongoing encouragement was another new teacher, Mayu. She was two years older than me. Although she was a new hire in Tokyo, she taught in Chiba in previous years. She was practical, cut and dried, and yet very caring.

Mayu took me to new places after the monthly "New Teachers' Orientation" meetings. Places like gourmet restaurants, the hidden movie theaters, and her fiancé's art studio were the world I had never dreamed of exploring. She lectured me, "You have to invest in yourself. Eat good food, take new lessons, and appreciate sophisticated fine arts. Once you absorb them in yourself, they won't go away. They will stay in you forever." Her message rang a bell sharply in my brain and its echo sustained.

Invest in yourself.

I had been too busy managing my finances just for surviving life in college, but I had my own income now. I didn't have to limit my possibilities anymore. My school sucked badly, so I decided to do something meaningful in my life. It was long overdue since I was eight years old and supposed to become French. I was smart enough to know by now that I couldn't become French. But I might be able to find out another possibility as I invested in myself.

First, I walked up to the vice principal to apply for English lessons that the school district offered. I noticed that a couple of vertical wrinkles appeared between his eyebrows. "You don't teach English, though," he grumbled. Then his eyes dropped to my application. I mentioned, "I would like to become a 'global' educator through learning English conversation." He was happy about my answer.

Although the series of lessons were dominated by one teacher, it was my first step to the new world outside my new school. The only word I could say proudly was "Hello," to a native Australian lady, who seemed a little bit like my high school exchange student, Charlotte. The

Japanese teacher who organized this workshop seemed overly protective of our Australian teacher. She translated and explained every single word that the Australian spoke. It was helpful at first, but gradually, it became annoying. Because of this dominant lady, other teachers could not get their turns to practice with the Australian teacher. I told myself, "Oh well, it's free. Don't be so mad."

Shortly after the annoying English class, my self-investment life had officially begun to blossom. In addition to the district classes, I joined an English conversation group, a cooking class, tennis lessons, a flower arrangement class, and an art class after school hours. I could pay for all of them by myself. I was investing in myself! Soon my brain generated positive and hopeful messages from the new exciting experiences. I wondered if I could become a better communicator in English even while I was petrified in the group discussion. Could I become a good cook, though the carrots that I sliced were like floating logs in the river? Could I play a serious tennis match in the tournament with someone? But the outcomes from my adventures didn't really matter to me because I was happy to feel "joy" in my life.

Doing something new and meeting new people I had never imagined meeting stimulated my curiosity. I felt a rush of energy surging throughout my body. I gained confidence at each odd moment. Sometimes it was the cooking instructor's pre-made Chinese food before her class. Sometimes it was an English newspaper article I brought that the English teacher was excited about. Sometimes it was a bright yellow tennis ball bouncing right at the white corner that the coach could not reach.

Out of the Box

Traveling came quite naturally as the next agenda in my self-investment process. After all, I had been looking for the "right" place where I could fit in since I was four years old.

If the definition of "traveling" was going on a vacation to a resort, I wouldn't have chosen it as my next endeavor because I really didn't have any good experiences with family trips. I wished my memories of family trips were pleasurable, at least less traumatic. At the famous volcanic hot spring resort, I threw up from the "healthy" sulfur aroma. I was blamed for ruining the entire family vacation.

On the road trip, we children were too excited in the back seat of the family car. Singing songs, making chants, and chatting endlessly were not Father's favorite things to hear while driving. Irritably, he yelled, "Too noisy!" Immediately, our car U-turned and the trip never happened. My traumatic vacation memories disabled my pleasant childhood travel memories and disconnected to a hopeful brain function about vacations.

None of beautiful pictures of resorts in the travel magazine associated with my nature. For a long time, I had no confidence or interest to enjoy a luxurious resort. I was almost afraid to go somewhere far away from my apartment. I didn't want to waste my time on unhappy trips. Until one November day, this particular page caught my eye after a stomach-churning work day.

"Experience the True America, the Home Stay for Ten Days."

It was the exact same spark that I had back in my senior year in high school when I found the university advertisement. It was the most delightful plan during winter vacation to transform from my dreadful first year teaching to somewhat hopeful rest of the school year, or at least I could just simply rejuvenate.

I had no intention or obligation to see my family during Christmas and New Year. During my short stay at my parent's house not long ago, I suggested to them to switch some furniture for Mother's convenience. Father scolded me by saying, "Don't stir up and interrupt our lifestyle by your selfish independence when you come home." I was literally unfit in their house. I couldn't compromise myself and pretend to be happy in an unwelcomed home. Christmas and New Year should have meant a time for celebrating with family unity and happiness. If my own family unity equated to a terrible disaster, an ideal solution could be to find an ideal family unity. And I could afford to experience a real Christmas with an American family with my very own eyes!

"The oasis finally appeared ahead of me in the driest desert," I whispered to myself with the travel magazine on my lap. Yet, I still didn't know that this was going to be my life transition.

Initiation

At the Fisherman's' Warf in San Francisco, the Irish coffee knocked me down.

My cheeks and ears turned red due to the typical Asian's lack of enzymes. My eyes were unfocused. I was about to fall asleep and melt into the echo of the noise in the crowded restaurant. Empty glasses and plates contacted each other making chittering and chattering noises on the waiter's tray. Unidentified languages from every direction behind my seat continuously sang a lullaby into my head.

My host family didn't explain to me enough about it, or I just couldn't understand their explanation. No wonder "Irish" sounded suspicious to me in the first place. It allured newcomers to this country

252

with the tricky name and then it confused them. Or, it probably was just the initiation in order to experience the country of freedom. My interpretation of coffee was initially correct, but when coffee became "Irish" coffee, that was different. I just learned by making myself drowsy.

"Initiation to the country?" I asked myself in the half-conscious mind.

Between my blurred vision and unconscious state, I envisioned a giant lady statue with a torch in her hand several hundred miles away from the West Coast. She questioned me, "Are you really ready to survive in the new land?" There was no problem with me cooperating with her welcome interrogation. I was dizzy but happy at the same time.

All new experiences were just like the shocking Irish coffee to me. A supersized shopping cart was a symbol of a "Super" market. How did you store that much stuff at home? The answer was easy. Their refrigerator was three times larger than my miniature refrigerator in my tiny apartment. "Do you drink Coca-Cola for dinner?" I asked innocently. "If you do, you would be instantly shunned in my family." One of the breakfast choices was a dried dog-food-like food called cereal, yet not exactly like dog food because you got to pour some milk in the bowl. I was the one to eat it. A large pizza to me was way larger than a true large size should be.

The construction signs were taller, wider, and brighter than Japanese ones. I asked my host sister in the car, "What is the word that means more huge than huge?" The answer was "humongous." It sounded like a kind of dinosaur or a scary monster for my auditory to the new language. I couldn't even find this word in my thick English-

Japanese dictionary, so I jotted down a new vocabulary word in the notebook.

My new discoveries had changed my perspectives of "common sense"—a high school girl must wear makeup to school and wait for her boyfriend's car. The boyfriend's hair must be punk and/or cool like a dark black Mohawk yet the bangs must cover his eyes... You would be the best candidate to the counselor room in my high school! My host sisters couldn't survive in the regular classroom even for one day in Japan.

And yes, the Christmas tree was a "real" tree inside the house, not a Bonsai-size tree, way taller than adult height, almost reaching to the ceiling! My nose started itching from the tree. Soon I had a big sneeze by the historically amazing tree in my life. "Bless you," my host mother said. I hesitantly replied, "Thank you, but I am not a Christian."

I was not exactly sure why everybody was laughing so hard, but I did the same as monkeys do. Laughing and showing off my crooked teeth and gums was embarrassing, but I just could not stop laughing. The power of Irish coffee must be absorbed deep into my blood carried over my whole-body system. I liked myself laughing. I enjoyed being here. I didn't want to leave. The pure profit of this trip was the excitement that I hadn't felt for a long time.

Is this the right place for me to live? I was experiencing a strange sensation of a light bulb lightening and flickering on and off. It was a unique, sparkling, and unforgettable sense in my life's portfolio. This feeling would be deeply etched in my brain and stay forever, even though I was not sure of what to expect.

Blame Game

Three months after the sensational Irish crash, an elementary school job was finally offered by a district in downtown Tokyo. Seventeen was the dream class size number in Japan considering the average national classroom size was up to 40. Most public elementary schools had the "looping" system. A teacher would keep the same group of kids two years in a row, like first and second, third and fourth, and fifth and sixth. I felt some oddness when I learned I was going to teach six grade, but not fifth.

Within a mile from my new school, there were prestigious department stores, the latest fashion stores, the traditional Japanese Kabuki Theater, the famous Buddhist Temple, the International Hospital, hidden Sushi restaurants among the fisherman's market ward, the fancy French restaurant above the shoe store, and much more than you could imagine. The trendy city life and facilities became extremely suitable for my after-school recreation.

While contemplating and dreaming of the bright and colorful urban life, I learned my sixth-grade class was going to be another nightmare. Their fifth-grade teacher didn't want to loop them. And no other teachers volunteered to take this group. I heard the rumor a few days after I was hired. Unfortunately, I could not do anything about it but to wait and see.

The principal assigned me to this terrible class because I was the youngest teacher in this school. It sounded odd but it actually made sense. No matter who took this class, the kids would be terrible. Technically, the principal was a manipulative bully even before I knew it. She took advantage of my lack of experience with a situation like this mess. Besides, since I was new in the school, no one had any empathy for me. This school was desperate to find a reason why this particular horrific class was so terrible. The answer they proposed was to point their fingers at me and in unison say, "Because of her." Complaints against a new teacher were way easier to make than against a 25-year experienced teacher. Also, a senior teacher got seniority. If she wanted to move to a different grade, it would be hers. The 25 years of experience made her eligible enough to get away from the Japanese traditional elementary school looping for this terrible class. This unsuccessful "experienced" teacher was now happy to be with her brand-new first graders. I was going to be the reason for failure even before I knew this sixth-grade class. I was the easy answer for them.

Quite evidently, these sixth graders were BAD from Day One! The female principal couldn't solve any problems by herself prior to my arrival. Other "old" and "experienced" teachers could not control this class anyway, so they started scapegoating to justify themselves. Falsely. No other teachers wanted to volunteer, either.

Sadly, it was a fact that no one wanted to be involved in this sixth-grade class. The female principal, who was planning to retire, ordered the male assistant principal, "You, as a 'man,' go to her room and show how to discipline the kids." Now the problem was my gender. The principal forgot that the previous teacher was female, too.

Did you blame her unsuccessful management just because she was female? Was the problem supposed to be my young age or gender or both?

Unfortunately, all of their fingers were pointing at ME as they initially planned.

I was a female matador in the large coliseum of Spain. With a bright scarlet cloth, I was standing alone in the middle of the field and waiting for a ferocious bull to come charging out. I didn't know where the fearless bull would come from. I didn't know how to flip the red cloth when the bull darted toward me. It turned out that one bull was not enough for the audience. One after another, bulls appeared without warning from four directions in the coliseum. The audience just watched me and cheered with a yellow voice when I fell to the ground. What kind of entertainment was that?

There was no adequate support or training provided for an "unexperienced" teacher. Hidden bullies in the class were even more severe than last year, according to the parents. One girl didn't come to school. An overweight boy was pushed by another student by "accident." His bottom got stuck in a big hole in the hallway's soft drywall in the portable building. PTA parents shut the classroom door in front of my face because they wanted to decide something important without me (their teacher!). All of these unthinkable events happened during this school year, among only 17 students in central Tokyo.

Unlike predictable Japanese culture, there was no respect. Though I was still thankful because I had places to have fun after school. Within ten minutes after school, I was able to sip a glass of red wine with a ribeye steak. A handsome waiter paid his full respect to me and my friend... I was determined to survive. After wiping my mouth with a spunky white napkin, I exclaimed, "Bring it on," and lifted my glass up high to toast with my date.

My distractive behavior continued. While being a hamster in the spinning wheel at school, I attended several classes mostly unrelated to my profession, such as cooking, flower arrangement, English conversation, painting, tennis, swimming, etc., as if the real-life problems would disappear during the escape from my work at the school. I obnoxiously acted like a rebel in these classes, too, which obviously I, as a teacher, would not appreciate if I were my own student.

A cooking teacher demanded, "Tie your hair during cooking." I replied, "I don't have to." The same teacher stated, "Your carrot slices are floating logs in a river." Under my breath, I mumbled, "Who cares?"

The flower arrangement teacher lamented, "Why did you cut that flower so short? Did you pay attention to my demonstration earlier?" I obnoxiously responded, "It's too late." But escaping from my reality didn't become the ideal solution as I had hoped.

One year after being a miserable sixth-grade teacher, the new group of third graders helped me regain my confidence. The kids wanted to talk to my eyes from Day One. Finally, I felt I was assigned the most proper job that I deserved. I had waited for this class for two long years since I passed the teaching examination. The kids were all happy coming to school, smiling friendlily to me every day. Feeling loved and respected by these little people was such a privilege in my life, I contemplated. The relationships with their parents were amazing, too. All of the activities including the annual home visits, trimester open houses, and conferences had been great opportunities to build home-school connections. Families, mostly moms, cared about me like their own little sister, yet were highly respectful for what I was doing in school for their children. The unexplainable blame game was finally over.

My students did the best they could do with the multi-digit multiplication, division, jump ropes, calligraphy, and endless amount of homework. They wanted to accomplish more sophisticated skills even after school. Their desire to learn was unstoppable! At only eight or nine years of age, children sincerely cared for each other. I loved watching their interactions, like, "Good morning," "Wow, you are doing great," and, of course, simple thank-yous and goodbyes. The classroom meetings were regularly run by students themselves. The youngsters enjoyed organizing fun parties like a card game day. Unlike American classrooms, Japanese kids were totally happy with games and parties without food! It was an interesting view of 23 students in a circle in the middle of an empty multi-purpose classroom. The 23 students sat, handed out cards to each kid, and played Old Maid! It seemed a little ridiculous, but they seriously enjoyed themselves and the moments they shared. Yet, I hadn't seen any bossy students like me, which was exceptionally fortunate.

Changing administration this new school year made a significant difference in the culture of the working community as well. Other teachers, including me looked happier and relaxed. The whole school actively engaged in all events and learning opportunities. "Collaboration" was the best word to describe my experiences that year. My energy level was maximized in my classroom every day. I became exhausted with joy and accomplishment by the end of each day. I didn't have to evacuate anywhere anymore. I purely enjoyed my time during and after school this year.

Libra

Ironically, around at the same time, I noticed the Irish coffee had secretly kept bubbling in my system for the past two years. That was why I was sitting on the leather couch in the principal's office alone with him one morning.

"So, Mr. Principal, I am proposing a one-year sabbatical."

I loved my students so much. I began to understand the joy of teaching. Besides, I passed the extremely hard teaching exams to enter into this career. I had no reason to walk away empty handed.

"I have an opportunity to teach Japanese culture and language in America for one school year. In exchange, I will learn and bring back American culture and education strategies into our school." Mr. Principal kindly replied, "It sounds very interesting. I will inquire with the district office." Despite the principal's support, the answer he brought back to me was "No." The district only allowed teachers who had more than five years of experiences to take a sabbatical. This was only my third year.

"I don't think I can wait another two years. I will be an old maid before the peak of my life," I told my reflection in the mirror. I collected the application materials for the teaching exchange program, took an exam, and passed based on my teaching and communication abilities in English. That process itself was my accomplishment. I could not walk away from this opportunity.

On one side of the balance scale, there is "continue to teach in Japan." On the other side sat "explore an American education." My balance scale moved back and forth for a long time, sorting out the pros and cons. When one side showed slightly heavier than the other side and stopped on the scale, that was going to be my final answer.

Libra, coincidentally, is my horoscope sign. I was astonished by how I determined my fate. Even more, I had been unknowingly training myself to be a most reliable Libra.

I remembered when I was with my college friends at the café. "What would you like to eat?" asked someone. "What are you going to have?" I asked back. "I don't know," she replied. Another girl said, "I'll take a piece of pizza." Then I said confidently, "I'll take the same." I fell into self-hatred every time I was not able to make my own simple choice. If I could not make easy decisions in regular life, I would never make any significant decisions either. I had to develop some discipline in me.

To start with, I practiced making my order within three minutes after I got a menu. My rule was not to regret my choice even if the food was not what I expected. I made a decision, so I needed to face the consequences. Because I was born under the sign of Libra, the simple and accurate instinct should be somewhere inside of me. If it could not be seen anywhere within me, I had to forcefully find and pull it out from my system. Someday, I should be able to make satisfying choices without any remorse if I practiced consistently. Thus, I continued practicing, "Fish burger or cheeseburger," "Milk tea or lemon tea," etc., on a daily basis.

Numerous occasions of disappointments were a big part of these lessons. I tried to hide my envy when my friend's food looked better than mine. The bottom line was I had to choose "my" best. Carefully. My best choice did not necessarily match with other people's. I had to build my self-confidence and self-trust. I desperately wanted to hear my voice from deep inside.

"What do I want? What do I want to do?"

All of a sudden, I realized. Thinking back, my inner Libra voice had been already functioning since I was four. My internal voice was continuously questioning whether things were the right fit for my life. It made a four-year-old girl desire to find the place where she could fully blossom. My origin is Libra—it always has been and always will be. My inner voice was as soft as the wind, yet its command was as sharp as a knife. "Go to America," my inner voice whispered, sending a chill down my spine with an inspirational sensation from the lifelong awaited excitement.

Transition

My high school World History teacher once said, "There are so many important transitions in history. But who really could tell they were in the transition of major historical events? You can only tell it's a transitional period in history because you are the one looking at the event as a past event."

I visited and asked my landlord couple, who were the same age as my parents, if they could keep my apartment room for ten months. Since I moved in, they had been more than landlords. Most of the time when I visited to pay my rent, they invited me in to join them for their very own dinner. Their daughter was close to my age and had studied piano in college. This couple, especially the husband, was curious and ambitious to learn new things. When they hosted an Australian teacher in one of their apartment properties, they threw several parties just because they wanted to learn English. I admired them. On these occasions, they always included me and let me help in the kitchen. Mr. Husband was a talented cook in addition to Mrs. Wife. He often went fishing in his spare time and then prepared the fish to serve for the parties.

This friendly, almost family-like landlord said, "No problem. We support your decision. We will open the windows once in a while to keep the air through in your room. Good luck on your journey. It must be a huge transition in your life."

Is it my life's transition?

I was not so sure about whether it was my life transition, but if so, I was sure the transition required a lot of financial investment. I refused to check the balance in my account and fearlessly flew to the potato farm land I had never dreamed of. I was about to step onto American soil again. For good. Ready or not, I was going. Several hours after I left Narita International Airport, I planted my feet on American ground.

The young principal assigned me the second-grade class with a veteran teacher who used to be a missionary in Japan. Less than a week later, I started teaching simple Japanese conversation, origami, and other arts and crafts from kindergartners to third graders in this primary school. The principal's son was in the third-grade class and his daughter was in the kindergarten class. It would be an impossible situation in Japan—I mean, the fact that the principal's children were in his same school was not heard of in Japan. Teachers' own children should not be in their school. It was quite awkward. Some of the third graders were as tall as me! If you want to talk about culture shock, this was it.

One evening the principal's wife called me, "Would you babysit our children tonight?" "Um... okay." She came to pick me up. She explained about their night out. This situation was impossible in my previous experience, too. Babysitting itself was not popular in Japan because people would label young parents as "lazy" and "negligent" if they would hire a baby sitter. The traditional Japanese principal could not be the model of a "failed" parent. I felt uncomfortable accepting this job because of the awkward situation and, boy, had I ever babysat before? I was full of curiosity, both good and bad. I remembered Ms. Queen's lecture in ninth-grade English class. She said, "Do as the Romans do." I accepted it.

The two older ones were pretty easy. I read some books and put them into bed. The two-year-old red-haired baby was a different story. His life purpose on this night was to stay up. Never sleep. I sang my favorite Shubert's soft lullaby and Japanese ones. Soon I exhausted the lullaby repertoire. His eyes were still wide open. Frustrated, I turned on the rock 'n roll radio station and hoisted him up. Dancing and singing around the room, the interactive American toddler finally decided to be sleepy. I concluded in my diary that night, "An American baby sleeps with rock 'n roll." The culture shock could be conquered by "Doing What the Americans Do."

After Christmas, the principal approached me and calmly asked, "Our music teacher is leaving. Would you be interested in teaching music the rest of this school year although we can't pay you?"

I was going to teach American students regular music classes!

Before I knew it, my ideas and creativity began pouring into my lesson plan book. I enjoyed creating, teaching, and sharing musical theory, songs, music appreciation, and instrumental music through lessons. I drew cartoons of Peter and the Wolf's characters. Pictures of Peter, Grandpa, Wolf, Cat, Duck, and Bird were all laminated and introduced in the music appreciation lesson for second graders. The instrument cards were organized in an empty tissue box. I made some slits where each card fit into on the face of an empty box. Kindergarten kids could pick up the card and match the instrument independently. First graders loved to hop on the keyboard carpet made of large construction paper. With a physical movement, they could learn music notes and create their own music. The third graders' recorder concerts including traditional American folk songs and Japanese tunes, the kindergartners' ABC concert, and the second graders' president concerts were all collaboratively done with classroom teachers, and even teachers wanted to learn Japanese conversation after school. This was a small but strong church community that did not easily welcome change or outsiders (they even banned coffee from the stores!). But luckily and amazingly, the different culture I brought in was embraced. All teachers, male and female, blonde and brunette, green and blue eyes, were very friendly beyond school activities. "Hi, I am Cindy," one teacher greeted me. I laughed, "My host family's black cat's name is Cindy, too." Cindy smiled back to me, "It's actually cute. I have a friend whose pet cow's name is Cindy. It is quite offensive, isn't it?" Culture shock after culture shock, I could not believe someone actually had a PET cow! Poor Cindy. How do you pick up after pet cow Cindy?

Toward the end of the school year, though, I became a little nervous. Time flew too fast. I looked down and started worrying about going back to Japan without any job lined up yet and I had a nearly empty bank account. I could not illegally stay and work here forever. I knew I had to go home to work. Then I had to save more money again, if I even wanted to come back to the U.S. But once I go back to Japan, I might never return to this country. I mean, really, what was I going to do?

"How are you doing? Why don't you visit my office?" The principal invited me to his room with a wall full of students' and family pictures. One of them was my Japanese third-grade class picture that I had sent when I applied for the internship. He mentioned, "Do you remember it? It's been almost a year since you came to our school. How do you think about what you have done? Are you planning to teach these guys again?" he said as he glanced at the picture. "No, I cannot go back to the same school," I replied discouragingly. "Oh. I am sorry," he apologetically replied. I just vented for a couple of minutes about my grief in leaving my American students. He patiently listened to me.

When the conversation came to a moment of silence, I anxiously mumbled about my future, "I wish I could stay here to be a regular teacher." His response was more than a surprise to me. "You don't have to wish. You can." I stared at him.

If that was not the life transition, what was?

* * *

After 4 pm – General Reflection in Education

With almost no exception, I hear the same thing every year from one among my fellow veteran teachers. "Kids have changed." Each time we find out what school children are lacking socially and academically; teachers always frantically look for the immediate answers. There are always smart people establishing some creative teaching strategies and tools in the educational market. Math manipulatives, computer reading programs, behavior seminars, interactive field trips, teachers' online discussion spaces, and on and on... I have tried so many things under the name of "Professional Development." If most teachers have tried as hard as I have, I would say, "teachers have changed" as well because it did not used to be that way 20 years ago. Rather, every year is different. The "kids have changed" phenomenon has caused teachers to dance nonstop. This dance might look gorgeous, but it wouldn't go anywhere. The dancers beautifully show their high technique spins, two-steps, tangos, cha-chas, and sambas on the floor forever, not knowing when the music ends. Where is the audience? Who would appreciate your glamorous movements? Maybe we have to stop dancing for a moment. Look at one student as a partner. Hold her hands, look in her eyes, and begin steps as easy as just swinging your bodies. Regardless of the ages, people and their behavior change from time to time. Instead of panicking about the low achievement and trying the "new" intervention as a patchwork, stop for a second. Look at yourself and ask, "Am I ready to face this challenge today?" If your answer is yes, look at your student with a smile and invite them. Ask your student, "Would you like to dance with me today?" Kids could not change by themselves. Teachers could not force them to change. Both teachers and students should "share" their experiences while shifting the developmental stage or exploring the relationships. Don't dance by yourself. Kids are waiting for your invitation. They have been waiting for the relationships. That fact has never changed yet.

* * *

10 years old – Unfair and Misfit

Quite coincidentally, my fourth-grade year was going to be somewhat similar to some unfortunate events at home. I, though, was resiliently determined to go to school every day no matter what would happen. The bully among human children would not occur as obvious as chickens; however, it would hurt as terribly as a chicken—physically, and mostly, emotionally. When I realized that I was eating lunch all by myself, I was desperate. If something like this happened, it was most likely too late to fix a situation. No one would tell you why they treated you in this way because they really didn't know. Perhaps someone had started saying nasty things about you or campaigning "Do Not Talk to Her." But no one remembered when it began or why they did it. Kids could be so cruel and mean, especially when they were empowered in the larger group against one.

Ms. Wada just graduated her college a month before school started. She was young, charming, and enthusiastic, but she couldn't catch bullies in her fourth-grade class. In the Elementary Education Psychology textbooks in Japan, third and fourth graders were labeled as being in the "Gang Age." It meant that kids had a tendency to form groups. They preferred playing and sharing only within the certain groups that they created. Ms. Wada might have observed some gang-age children, a variety of groups, which she had learned in school a few months before her graduation.

And she would have thought, "Yes, I am witnessing 'real' gang-age children!" Hooray for Ms. Wada's hands-on discovery! What had she forgotten? Me! I was not a part of a gang. I wanted to play as myself. I didn't want to go to the bathroom with a bunch of girls together. I refused to be "one of them." The type of independence I had might be a little bit more mature than others, and, well, obviously obnoxious for them, which technically really bothered my female classmates. That was why they decided to exclude me.

Being excluded was not comfortable. Being refused was painful. This group of kids disagreed with everything I brought up no matter how good it was. It didn't make sense because it was a kids' world. I even attempted to cry like a cowardly, miserable, heartbroken little girl so they would've eventually felt sorry for me. I hoped that they would include me as a weakest link in the group. I failed this plan instantly. Tears didn't cooperate with my intention. My liquid was too stubborn to appear in my eyes. Therefore, I had no choice other than continue fighting, as a valued individual, against the "gang-age" group, although I knew the majority always would win.

In the fall, the school field day was near. The class relay runners were usually selected based on the fifty-meter dash results recorded in the P.E. class. I was qualified for the team because I was in the top four. The gang-age group circled around me and started arguing. "Well, Kim is the number five, but she is getting faster nowadays. So she should be qualified." I snapped, "That is not fair because I am number four. But if you insist, we should race. I will do it."

Here we were in the track field. Kim and I were going to compete by racing a lap. "Okay, whoever wins, that is the class relay runner," a leader-looking girl declared while dragging her feet to draw a starting line on the dirt field. "On your marks. Ready, set, go!" My strength was the instantaneous force at the start. If I had any concerns, the endurance towards the end would push me across the finish line. Since this was a short distance dash, I really didn't have to worry about the endurance. As I contemplated about this race, my right foot stepped across the finishing line before Kim. I had proved myself. That was the clear and visible fact. It meant I was going to be the relay runner. That was the deal.

Only, that was. It was not anymore. The group of girls circled around me for a second time and told me, "Kim's homestretch towards the end was amazing. She was only a couple of steps behind you. It means she has more potential than you." These girls simply didn't want me to run in the school relay as one of the class representatives. In fact, the other three were in the "gang-age" group. They couldn't accept anyone from outside of their group. It was severe treatment for children at any age. I was the victim of it. It didn't matter even if I submitted any visual evidence right in front of their eyes. They refused to approve anything I did or said just because I was an outsider.

Finally, I decided to just walk away from the unfortunate situation instead of continuing to seek their approval. This unreasonable ending haunted me for a while, but there was nothing I could do. Just let it go. I could only move forward. Not backward. I annoyingly showed up in the classroom every morning. I never missed any school days. Gangs didn't like not being able to get rid of me from their sight. So, they changed the target to someone else who appeared to be weak.

Unfortunately, I witnessed several of my classmates who were picked on because of their size, hygiene, parents' jobs, speech, intelligence, etc.

The gangs' bullying escalated. Surprisingly, Ms. Wada became the next target. And that was the wrong decision. "Who messed up my desk?" Ms. Wada asked as she furiously glared at each individual. The room was dead silent. No one raised hand. She banged her fist on her desk and stood up. "If you don't say who did, everybody is responsible for this incident. I am going to slap everyone's face as a punishment. Come right in front of me one by one," she fumed as if she was breathing fire with her words.

I was confused. I was sitting in my seat the whole time while someone messed up her desk. Was I going to get slapped? Was it everybody's fault because the suspect didn't confess? What an unfair world! After Ms. Wada successfully slapped my face, I turned and went back to my seat. My stubborn tears finally appeared in my eyes, filling water on the surface of my eyeballs. I held both of my still tingling cheeks with my hands on my desk and repeatedly lamented in my head, "I don't belong here." It echoed a little louder than when I was five.

Miracle Letters

If I didn't belong here, where was I supposed to belong to? My future destination was in the hazy fog. I flipped page after page of the Language Arts textbook while daydreaming. My eyes caught instantly an intriguing headline. It read, "Roma-Ji." My lightbulb was lit. I told myself, "I am going to be able to communicate with people in Rome. Isn't it cool?" I didn't have to talk in Roman or whatever language they spoke. I had used Chinese characters when I tried to communicate with Excellent Flower in third grade. It was very practical to understand each other because each Chinese character had its meaning. We had been very successful.

Now, this time, I could write Roma-ji (Japanese Roman letters) on paper to communicate with Romans. I was ready to go to Rome to make new friends with a pencil and a notebook pad. I just couldn't wait for the Roma-ji lessons. I felt like I was coming out of the haze. I kept my fingers crossed that Roma-ji lessons would be the answer for my ambitious anticipation.

Soon, Ms. Wada introduced Roma-ji in class. Roma-ji was the application of the alphabet to write the Japanese language. It was simple to manipulate Japanese Roman letters based on Japanese sounds. Each Japanese sound can be written with one consonant and one of five vowels of Roman letters. As lessons progressed, a reasonable doubt grew in my hopeful mind.

Was this the way to communicate with Romans? Really? I was slowly realizing that learning Roma-ji didn't teach you how to say "Hello" to Romans. How would Romans understand written Japanese in Roman letters, "Konnichiwa"? Let's say they would understand. Were Romans going to continue the conversation with me like, "Ogenkidesuka (how are you)?"

NO!!!!! No Roman or French ever understood what I wanted to say on paper because they were just original Japanese words written in alphabet letters. My hopeful soul was immediately shattered. Facing reality was pretty tough. A reasonable doubt now became unwanted disappointment, just like weeds in the green grass.

Imagine, millions of dandelions in your yard. Although the bright yellow color attracts my eyes, soon I realize that they are useless weeds. I have to get rid of them, even if their roots are too tough to pull from the ground. No matter how hard it is, I have to eliminate my unwanted fantasy in order to keep my garden sophisticated. Many disappointments and hard times are like countless weeding chores. One day, my garden would be a perfect patch of dirt because I had weeded so hard. Then I can plant my dream hyacinth bulbs in rows. My soil is ready for authentic plants to grow. The number of days of life learning experiences have enriched the soil. Finally, I would enjoy watching my dream grow.

Don't forget to water and weed for your dream to grow even on my bad days.

Math Labyrinth

What a tough year fourth grade was! Algebraic math problems began to challenge me. The question was simple enough to find out the number of bananas and apples, but my brain was not simple enough to bring the answer. My notebook pages were full of apples, bananas, numbers, circles, scratches, equations, but not the answer. Literally, I was going bananas! I asked Ms. Wada if she could teach me. I thought I understood from her help, but immediately after I started working on it independently, everything got confusing again. The second time asking Ms. Wada was still fine, but she was obviously reluctant to face me a third time. I felt bad for her just because I was the cause of her headache by being lost in the algebra labyrinth.

Every night, apples and bananas haunted me in my dreams. I desperately wanted to understand this math situation. So, again, I decided to bring Ms. Wada the same problem. She tiredly looked at me and said, "Well, you don't have to understand this problem. Just let go."

On the math test sheet, I noticed the same problem that I had never been able to solve, in which my teacher told me to let go. Needless to say, I had no clue what to do. Ms. Wada had said, "Let go." So, I did. But that was not all. Almost 90% of the problems were apples and bananas questions! I had nothing to do with these fruity problems but let go. How pathetic! One day later, Ms. Wada was ready to return the math tests to us.

As soon as my eyes met my teacher's red marks, I learned that I made my worst record in the test: 10% out of 100%. My eyes welled with tears. My pride couldn't let go of this. But Ms. Wada was the one who spit her words at my very own face. "Let go." I wished I could've hated her.

Beyond Limit

Not only math, but I also kept failing to please Ms. Wada. She didn't like my art projects. One project was the handkerchief design. I had a clear vision of my handkerchief with multiple soft colored marbles swirled all over the square shaped handkerchief. Each mixed colored paint brush line was overlapping each other. These lines were collaborating as if making audible harmony on the paper when I saw it. At least that was my vision.

My handkerchief design betrayed my vision. The water colors miserably smeared instead of collaborating. As I tried to fix the trouble, water kept diluting. It eventually made a rip on my paper. Ms. Wada walked by and commented, "Oh, my... You made a hole because you didn't follow the directions." Maybe I missed the directions. I was not going to complain to anyone anyway. But I simply wanted to design my handkerchief as I visualized. Everything had been easy and fun until fourth grade. All of my accomplishments at school had made my life fulfilling. Now, I felt like everything I did was mediocre or less. I might be an empty hyacinth bulb that would never grow, or else, it would grow pitiful looking flowers with ugly diluted, mixed water color from it.

When I came home, I ran upstairs to my room. I dropped my backpack down. I heard someone was visiting downstairs. They might not even know I was home. I had tried to be perfect because I was supposed to, but I was kind of tired of this expectation. The episode of the TV cartoon, "The Limit," reminded me of my recent experiences and thoughts.

Limit is a girl who is killed by a car accident, but her surgeon dad operates on her and transforms her into the human-like cyborg. That is the only way their beloved daughter would survive... Limit comes alive again, after all. Nobody knows about her secret but her mom and dad. Limit does not make any mistakes because she is a robot. Everybody looks up to her because of her perfect behavior and grades. She is the fastest runner when she presses a button on her shirt. But she observes her friends' "human" errors as their gifts that she can never experience. She becomes frustrated in being perfect as the robot. She doesn't want to admit that she cannot act like a "real" human. So, she decides to make mistakes on purpose. Her first intentional mistake is to leave her homework at home...

This episode overlapped myself and Limit. Of course, I was not a robot, yet I could do anything like her. Her ability was natural as a robot, but my ability happened based on my human ego. Simply, I needed to please someone to get attention. I was totally tired of being a good kid and that I kept failing to meet adults' expectations. I determined to be Limit today starting right then. I would be imperfect in my own show. Here was my scenario for the special episode.

"How would my family respond if I disappeared?"

I quietly opened my closet's sliding door and sneaked in. Behind the dark closet door, I sat, bent my legs, and held my arms around my legs.

Only my hearing sense keenly concentrated on every noise outside of the closet. From downstairs, I caught my mother calling my name. "Where is she?" Someone's running feet were towards upstairs. "She is not here," my sister murmured in front of the closet. I covered my mouth with both hands, tried not to chuckle. "Did she go somewhere?" "I don't know." "Is she in the bathroom?" "No." I was a little bit empowered by knowing my family showed some interest in my existence.

Pretty soon, I got sleepy in the closet. All the conversation was gradually far away from my consciousness. I succeeded to be Limit although I was not the fastest runner or even approved as a fourth relay runner in my class. I was into a deep sleep in the closet. The dinner scent came upstairs through the crack of the closet door and woke me up. When I opened the sliding door, my room was already as dark as the inside of the closet. I saw the little leftover red sunset shadow reflection on the tatami floor. I might be in trouble when I go downstairs. Why?

If it was because I made them worry by disappearing, that was what I hoped to happen. If it was because I didn't help dinner preparation as the older girl, I would be disappointed. I went downstairs hoping they would punish me for the first reason. Unfortunately, yet predictably, the reason why I was in trouble was the second one. The new house, in which my own physical labor was forced to spent, didn't seem like my permanent place. I didn't know where I should be. I even had no place to hide here.

Supremes in Males and Riches

I had been wondering why people value males more than females in my neighborhood. Grandma Fumi once told me that it was because women were meant to be dirty due to their biological function. Women used to be prohibited to attend special worships at the purified shrine. The shrine was located as close as 0.3 miles. Every time we visited there, we counted 108 stairs to get to the top where people prayed.

Fumi also told me 108 is the number of sins that people had made during a passing year according to the old Buddhist's tale. One of 108 sins must be allowing girls in the shrine. I felt bad for the girls back in old days when they were not allowed to go such a fun local field trip. But, really, my time was not so different.

Girls could go to the shrines and temples, but girls couldn't carry or dance near the portable shrine in the harvest festivals. Public schools were even closed during the harvest festival in October. At 5 o'clock in the morning, large guys with white gowns and school-aged boys run up the 108 stairs to the main shrine to pray and give thanks for the harvest. The climax of the celebration was marching portable shrines around town. About twenty guys lifted up the portable shrine, stepped down, and marched on the sacred road which happened to be the street in front of our house.

Many villagers woke up in the early morning before sunrise. They would wait for the portable shrine caravan by the road side in the keenly chilly air. It is like the Asian version of a parade. Numerous portable shrines from different villages were carried up and down on men's shoulders. Bells were ringing as the men sang and moved their feet in a unique way. All men had practiced a couple of weeks prior to the ceremony so their steps and dances were all in unison. I had a hard time respecting this portable shrine ceremony. When the shrine didn't show respect for girls' participation, why did girls respect this ceremony that was conducted only by boys? So, every year, instead of standing by the road side, I opened my window and glanced at the marching spectators. My bedroom was on the second floor, like a balcony for the annual Harvest Parade. The view of villagers and colorful portable shrines moving forward with rhythmical music and steps on the sacred road was spectacular despite my opposition against the tradition. Girls could participate as spectators with a beautiful kimono outfit, but if any female villagers (besides the designated male shrine carriers) touched it, the whole village would face bad luck for an entire year.

For the same reason, I was not allowed to be in the "Pre-Building Ceremony" for our new house. When the house was still in a skeleton stage in this community, the new homeowner must offer the "Pre-Building Ceremony" to the community members. Family members, contractors, and carpenters would go up to the top of the house structure and throw out rice cakes from there. One- or two-day-old rice cakes were no longer sticky—they were rather hard.

A ceremony was announced by the community board prior to the scheduled ceremony. Every member in the community was technically invited to celebrate their new house by picking up rice cakes that would be thrown from the top of the house structure. The night before, women randomly put some money inside the rice cakes while they made them. This surprise generosity was a symbol of wealth of the new homeowner. The family wished and shared their good luck and health for their community members who picked up the lucky rice cakes.

I was so excited to climb up on the ladder to get up to the top of the new house. Not only that, it would be the very first time, and perhaps the last time, to throw rice cakes as one of the new homeowner's family members. It was going to be a once in a lifetime experience. I helped hard enough while female family members and villagers were making rice cakes. I should be qualified to participate in the ceremony because I was a daughter of this new house.

With my positive anticipation, I held the ladder with my hands. At the moment when my right foot stepped on the bottom ladder, someone's hand grabbed my shoulder.

"You are not going. You pick up rice cakes down here because this ceremony should be run by all men." I insisted, "But I helped Mother to make mochi last night. I want to throw rice cakes." "No. If a girl goes up, our luck will disappear."

Whatever "our luck" meant, it was obvious all of these superstitious ceremonial procedures and rudiments were unreasonably designed for men by men. If you got "our luck" by excluding a family member, why would I have to be interested in "our luck" anyway?

It was not my intention to sabotage my contribution for the family. But my contribution should be an active participation, not being out of the family circle just because of superstitious impurities in the female. All in all, that was how I was removed from the once in a lifetime experience that was evidentially available for only boys. There was no first time or last time for the girls. No opportunity for the girls.

Furniture Store's Daughter

I shared this unfairness with my classmate, Nobu. We should consider it to be a big problem in our society. But she didn't seem interested in the social injustice that I had agonized over. I shared my concern with her simply because I happened to be in her house for the partner project Ms. Wada assigned. I didn't even expect her to understand my agony. I thought my idea was too sophisticated and complicated.

To do our social studies' partner project, Nobu invited me to her home. I didn't think she was my close friend, but I decided to give it try. She might be the ultimate potential good friend beyond the gang-aged group. Her parents ran the furniture store business in our small town. Unlike my rice field neighborhood, her house attached to the furniture store was located on a busy downtown street.

Nobu looked so excited when I arrived at her house. Nobu took me to her room. It was a stunning sight of Hello Kitties! There was a clock, bed cover, calendar, chair, stuffed animals, backpack, and more, all labeled Hello Kitty. It was an ultimate Hello Kitty store. Yes, Hello Kitty was cute, but why did she need this many? I was totally petrified by her Hello Kitty collection. I would have had Hello Kitty nightmares if I slept in this room. Evidentially, this wealthy daughter was exclusively spoiled. How could you get so many Hello Kitty goods less than a year since its first sale? I just learned about Hello Kitty a week ago on TV. "Wow, Nobu, it is amazing. What a collection!" If I gave her almost too much lip service, we could start our homework right away, I thought. Instead, without saying thank you, Nobu continued showing off her over indulged possessions.

"Look! I have every issue of the Strawberry Newspaper, even the very first publication." A stack of colorful newspaper had more Hello Kitties and more characters like Hello Kitty. "Okay, okay." I told myself to take a big deep breath.

"Okay, Nobu, let's start the project," I suggested as I pulled out rolled up construction paper from my canvas bag. Nobu kept flipping the newest issue of the Strawberry Newspaper's pages and pointing her index finger to the next room. I saw a large rectangle table. "You can start working on it. I will be there as soon as I am done reading this." I mumbled, "What kind of friend are you?" "What did you say?" Nobu asked taking her eyes off from her newspaper for a moment. I quickly replied, "Nothing." It was not fair for me to work by myself on the group project, but I didn't want to get any worse grade on my school assignments besides in algebra. That actually turned out to be a good choice. By 4:45 pm, the project looked very good. I interrupted Nobu's quiet Strawberry reading. "Nobu. I did everything on this project, except coloring. You haven't done anything today so you ought to color it all." Nobu snorted, "I have a piano lesson at 5:30 today. So, you have to take it home and finish." She should have seen steam coming out of my head. Nobu used to be in the same Buddha school I attended. Didn't she learn any compassion? Well, she was not in Ms. Aoki's class. She was in Ms. Hori's class. Rumors about Ms. Hori that I had heard might have been correct. Her students were evil! My point was there was no hope or possibility to develop a decent friendship with Nobu even if she didn't belong to the gang-aged group.

While pedaling my bike back home, I felt the hopeful warm sunset behind my back. Let's move on. One day, I would find something, somebody, and somewhere I felt content. It might take longer than I would hope, like the bicycle's pedals might be heavier on your feet going uphill. But I had to keep pedaling until I found what I was looking for.

Breathing

Present Moment – Gift, Hope, and Future

The next several decades passed incredibly quickly like lightning.

Usually, there is a thunder warning before the lightening, but the reality is, things always happen all of a sudden, before you prepare for a frightening moment, whether or not you miss or ignore the warning signs. Its suddenness is not always pleasurable. It's rather shocking, isn't it? Although some life events develop gradually, the level of shock strikes someone's unprepared life, and it becomes intense agony. It is difficult to remind ourselves to be calm during these lightning moments. If you are lucky, you might be able to analyze each situation accurately even with your intense emotions. You also learn the fact that things have both sides; ups and downs, gains and losses, hopes and despairs, joys and disbelieves, accomplishments and disappointments, and sweet and sour in anyone's life. But after the big Tsunami is gone completely from the shore, people recognize only one side.

There is always the flip side of the coin that people have to deal with. I gradually acknowledged the other side of the coin while making mistakes or facing random desperate situations. Despite my best effort, choices I have made didn't necessarily turn out the way I expected. At least when I am in a bad mood, I try to lift myself up because the other end of bad must be good. But, boy, how hard it is for me to do so!

Sometimes it takes a long time to recognize the other side of the coin. Or my inner-self just refuses to see it because the specific life episode is too harsh to deal with. Even after so many years, an indescribable sadness still strikes me. I often wonder, "What is the other side of the coin?" The most painful experience of life can be the other end of the most precious gift of life. Its power could easily tear a person in half. Because overcoming tragedy is resilience—a gift from the desperate experience. Ironically, if this horrific event didn't happen, I didn't find *my gift*. Whenever I think of it, I shed my tears with a helpless moan.

The gift is in a treasure box full of beautiful and dramatic gems from each person's life stories. When the time comes, my "inner self" will whisper to me, *"This is the right time to share. Open it."* Then, even incredibly difficult episodes will spill out from the treasure box. The coping skill is one of the gifts I have as if the "pain" that I suffered is the cost of "gift."

In the meantime, *hope* and *future* are alongside "gift." They all have kept me going as strong as I should be. How could I survive without a hope? Can you imagine how hopeful you would be when you visualize your future? For instance, just watch a four-year-old's soccer game. Numbers of rambunctious bodies going back and forth, trying to follow and kick a ball. There is no doubt that all these kids are hoping to make a goal. They live their lives in full at the game in the neighborhood field surrounded by their families' roaring cheers. It is the typical example of joy. If it's not enough, it's a treasure. The treasure to visualize their future with unforgettable great memories with their families and friends. Being able to embrace and appreciate with your hope and future is your gift.

In the difficult days, loved ones' arms wrap around my shoulders to warm my heart. Their warmth does not only comfort me, but also strengthens my soul. My heart is full of love and resilience with my gift, hope, and future. I am privileged to appreciate them all in my life.

Surprisingly, *love* and *resilience* don't necessarily mean each other's ends, but they empower and strengthen each other. That is why and how I have survived my painfully difficult times. All in all, I couldn't have found, felt, or touched my precious gift in the country where I was born. It couldn't have offered me adequate support which I would've appreciated in order to survive. I couldn't have felt hope so strongly. I couldn't have envisioned my future so clearly. Moving to America was the choice I had to make after all. My inner self already knew the choice that I was going to make, when I was four. That was my fate.

I have never been regularly involved in any type of religious practices except my Buddhism pre-school and the Sunday schools at the Lutheran church. But somehow, I notice that the uniquely developed faith is living in me. Sometimes my fantasized thoughts wonder around in the unique scenario. "What if the people surrounding me are meant to be here for me even before they were born?" The stories might have come from Japanese folk tales that Grandma Fumi told me on her western bed. The story might have been from China that my mother told me. Itsy bitsy memory pieces somehow elaborate with each other and create some theories and visions in my brain.

The long red string is the one of these stories. The red strings connect to important people in my life randomly but purposely. Some parts of the string are too complicated to be untangled. If that relationship is important to you, you should be patient and put your hardest effort to untangle them. Otherwise, it will be forgotten. When you successfully untangle the knot, you can see the true relationship you have been longing for.

Some people randomly appear in front of me and try to give me some lessons, though they never teach me like I teach in school. "I" have to look for what some people are trying to teach me. Teaching is sometimes explicit, yet sometimes implicit.

Not only compassion and kindness, I am learning how to be humble in my reflective process. My angers, frustrations, and disappointments against day-to-day things and people have been all necessary grief in order for me to find important people, relationships, and the true meaning of life.

Teaching is not only offered by someone, but I have to cultivate it from others by myself. I have to interpret what a certain phenomenon is trying to teach me. What can I learn from it? What is my role in this world? I am meant to share and care for the *gift*, *hope*, and *future* of my life.

What Now?

A few years ago, my family took a camping trip to LaPush, Olympic Peninsula. The Pacific Ocean was unusually cold and stormy on one July day. It was somewhat normal Pacific Northwest weather, though, it's still hard to imagine this non-summer weather for a person like me who has experienced the extreme humidity and intense heat in summer. On the windy beach, we saw a little blonde girl running into the waves back and forth despite the harsh climate. Her beautiful smile and careless excitement truly reflected her name, Joy. Soon we learned her family was traveling from Switzerland. This Swiss family rented an RV and was exploring the area. The playful little girl and my kids began bonding without a common language. She showed us a Harry Potter book in German. Our family and Joy's family instantly became friends, our RVs parked side by side on the campsite. But as always, the last day came. We exchanged email addresses, and our new friends took off for more of their adventures on the road

Several months passed, and Joy's mom sent me a Christmas greeting and noted, "Joy is becoming fluent in French."

Suddenly and literally, lightning struck my spine.

It brought me back to my old obsession, "*I want to be French.*" My flashback produced agonizing memories that rushed through my red blood cells to my brain. It wasn't the sweetened black tea. It wasn't the sandwich lunch. It wasn't the Yamaha Music Academy. Why did I want to be French anyway? I still don't know the answer. Technically, I know by now I cannot be French. On the other hand, this little greeting card reminded me of the keen and nostalgic sensation in my system that I had never felt before. My fingertips felt so close to touch my endless dream. Maybe numerous lifelong obstacles have kept searching for the peace in me? Apparently, my resilience has wisely refused to allow my soul to fit in where I was not supposed to. I am living in a place surrounded by nature, fresh air, good books, exquisite arts, thoughtful community members, and loving human beings. And I am accepted in my living community as who I am, whether I am French or not.

Remarkably and harmoniously, rebellious thoughts... my inner voice... have been guiding me beyond my dream of being French. I am becoming "myself" every day by weaving and untangling thousands of threads of life events and people who I encounter in my life. Each day, I celebrate and appreciate the joy of being myself.

I squint with my eyes to see the bright halo over the vast and wildest waves of the Pacific Ocean. Then I take a deep breath.

Acknowledgments

I want to thank my editor Danielle Anderson for her professional and empathetic editing process, Sylvia Soholt for her mentorship and friendship, and CSTP (Center for Strengthening the Teaching Profession) for providing a Summer Writing Retreat. Also, I want to thank David Hovland for his guidance and support.

About the Author

Claire E. Hallinan, MAEd, was born in Japan and lives with her family in Washington. Claire has a passion for making sense of the world, building relationships, and inspiring others to find themselves in happiness. She is a writer, an entrepreneur, a mindfulness practitioner, and a National Board Certified Teacher. *Gift of Gratitude* is her first memoir.

Connect with Claire E. Hallinan:
claire.e.hallinan@gmail.com
https://claireehallinan.wordpress.com

Made in United States
Troutdale, OR
11/28/2024

25410789R00164